THE TAX EXILE REPORT

Citizenship, Second Passports and
Escaping Confiscatory Taxes

SIXTH EDITION
Revised for 1997-98

Marshall J. Langer

SCOPE
INTERNATIONAL
LIMITED

The Tax Exile Report

Scope International Ltd
Forestside House
Rowlands Castle
Hants PO9 6EE
England
UK

1st Edition 1992
2nd Edition 1993
3rd Edition 1994
4th Edition 1995
5th Edition 1996
6th Edition 1997
by Marshall J. Langer

British Library Cataloguing in Publication Data

A catalogue record for this book is available from the British Library

ISBN 0 906619 34 3

Typeset by Scope International Ltd
Printed by Hartnolls, Bodmin, Cornwall, England, UK

PART III. EXPLAINING THE US RULES

PART IV. A TAX EXILE LEAVES HOME

PART VI. SUITABLE COUNTRIES FOR RESIDENCE, DOMICILE, CITIZENSHIP AND PASSPORTS

REVISED PREFACE

My grandparents moved from Europe to America in the 1880s. About a hundred years later I moved back. My mother said I was crazy to leave the US; she may be right. Only time will tell. I think I must have some gypsy blood. I enjoy traveling and moving from one place to another. I also enjoy working on the problems of those who choose to migrate from one country to another, whether their motive is personal, political, economic or simply to escape confiscatory taxes.

Whether or not a particular country is a high-tax country depends on who is looking, what he earns, what he owns and what he plans to do if he goes there. Most high-tax countries charge their high taxes to their captive customers -- their own citizens or residents. They frequently offer generous incentives to attract wealthy outsiders who may hire local people and spend some of their money locally.

Britain is a perfect example. Taxes were confiscatory during the last Labour government. They are still high for the natives but not for outsiders who move in and live on a remittance basis, paying tax only on local income, if any, and remitted foreign income. Many people I know have lived in London for years on remitted capital (not income) and they have never had to pay a pound of British income taxes.

The UK Board of Inland Revenue published a green paper a few years ago that showed that parts of the present tax system date back to 1799. They proposed some changes but, following complaints by wealthy Greek shipowners who threatened to move large businesses out of the UK, the government and the opposition both agreed not to change the system. It remains to be seen whether a new Labour government will change the present rules when they begin to tax the "undeserving rich" to pay for ever increasing social benefits.

About fifteen years ago I chaired a program in New York sponsored by the Practising Law Institute. One of the speakers, Professor Harold Dubroff of Albany Law School, Albany, New York, discussed *Expatriation: The Ultimate Estate Plan*. His paper clearly demonstrated that the US government's original *anti-expatriation rules*, directed at those who abandoned US citizenship to escape taxes, were like a toothless paper tiger — all growl and no bite. This was confirmed by several later scholarly papers, one of which was prepared in 1991 by the Association of the Bar of the City of New York. It was further confirmed by testimony presented by government and private witnesses at three Congressional hearings held during 1995 and by a 500-page report issued in June 1995 by the staff of the US Congress' *Joint Committee on Taxation*.

Chapter 51 of this report discusses one wealthy family that could save as much as US $1 billion in US estate taxes by using the ultimate estate plan. You can become a tax exile. You can escape confiscatory taxes, but only if you carefully take all of the steps required to change your residence, your domicile and, if necessary, your citizenship. This report leads you through the entire process step by step. It tells you what to do and what not to do, where to go and where not to go. It focuses on the special problems of those who leave the US,

1

but it also covers the situation of those who would leave any other high tax country such as Britain, Canada, Germany or one of the Scandinavian countries.

While a reasonable effort has been made to ensure the accuracy of the information provided, neither the author nor the publisher will accept any responsibility for action taken in reliance on it. Appropriate individual legal and tax advice should be sought. Please also bear in mind that the laws and practical applications discussed in this report are constantly changing.

I am indebted to many of my colleagues for the vast amount of information and assistance they have given me on all aspects of the problem. I wish I could thank each of them individually but there are too many of them. I have, however, singled out some individuals whose input was especially helpful in the preparation of this report. My thanks go to Professor Harold Dubroff, of Albany Law School, who invented *The Ultimate Estate Plan*; Professor Harvey Dale, of New York University Law School, whose pentapus formed the inspiration for the *tax octopus* discussed in Chapter 3; my colleagues, Timothy Murphy, of Shutts & Bowen, Miami, Rosemarie Schadé, of Shutts & Bowen, Amsterdam, and Stephen Gray, of Shutts & Bowen, London, for helping me to brainstorm many of the ideas; Philip Baker, Joseph Field and Milton Grundy, of London, for their helpful suggestions; Joel Karp, Denis Kleinfeld and Michael Rosenberg, of Miami, Jay Hughes, of New York, and Bruce Zagaris, of Washington, for their insights into various legal aspects; Dr Harry Schultz of Monaco, Dr WG "Bill" Hill of *PT-Land*, and some clients who must remain nameless for their help with the practical aspects; Nicholas Pine, Richard Cawte and Sarah Hughes of Scope International; Andrew Langer, of Berkeley, California, and Jeffrey Langer, of Hollywood, Florida, for teaching me how to use my computer and word processing system to prepare this report; and my wife, Carole, for her inspiration and her patience while this report was being written and rewritten.

Marshall J Langer
London
31 March 1997

ABOUT THE AUTHOR

MARSHALL J LANGER, a member of The Florida Bar, practised law in Miami for more than 35 years. He has worked as an international tax adviser in Europe since 1985 and now lives in London, England. He was a partner in the law firm of Shutts & Bowen, Miami, and remains of counsel to that firm. He was also an Adjunct Professor of Law at the University of Miami for many years. In 1990, Mr Langer received The Florida Bar Tax Section's award as Outstanding Tax Attorney of the Year.

Mr Langer is a graduate of the Wharton School of Finance and Commerce of the University of Pennsylvania (BS in Economics) and the University of Miami School of Law (JD *summa cum laude*). He has lectured extensively at tax institutes and other seminars throughout the US and Europe, as well as in Japan, Hong Kong, Malaysia, Australia, Canada and the Caribbean. He has written numerous articles on international taxation and books on tax and other subjects. He is the author of *The Swiss Report*, published by Scope International. He is also the author of a leading book on tax havens and how to use them entitled *Practical International Tax Planning* (the third edition was published in 1985 and is updated each year). Finally, he is coauthor (with Rufus Rhoades of Los Angeles) of a six-volume treatise on taxes and tax treaties now called *Rhoades & Langer, U.S. International Taxation and Tax Treaties* (updated four times a year).

TO CAROLE

PART I

THE BASICS

1. WHO SHOULD BECOME A TAX EXILE?

Most people are not likely to become tax exiles. Most Americans and some British are insular; they tend not to invest abroad and wouldn't think of moving to another country. This report is intended for those few individuals who would consider obtaining a new citizenship and moving abroad. This chapter is unchanged from last year's edition.

NOT EVERYONE WANTS TO BE A TAX EXILE

A surprisingly large percentage of wealthy individuals seem to like the idea of being shorn like sheep. They live and work in high-tax countries and they allow their governments to take from them a substantial portion of everything they earn. They tolerate wealth taxes and transfer taxes that take away much of what they own, not only year-by-year but also when they try to transfer it to their loved ones by gift or inheritance. They sheepishly acquiesce as their governments use the power to tax to redistribute their wealth within the society. They tolerate an ever-increasing expansion of the Robin Hood theory of taxation under which governments take from the middle class and the rich and give to the bureaucrats and some of the poor. If you approve of and enjoy the present system, this report is not for you. This report is intended for the small minority of well-to-do individuals who are no longer willing to tolerate the present system and are prepared to vote with their feet. They are ready and willing to move somewhere else and to do whatever else may be legally necessary for them to escape the present system.

TAXES, TAXES AND MORE TAXES

People generally understand that they have to pay some taxes if they expect to receive any services from their government. Most of us accept that taxes are the price we pay for a civilized society.

The problem is that many of us now feel -- rightly I think -- that we are being gouged by taxes, taxes on taxes, and more taxes. We pay federal taxes, state or provincial taxes, and local taxes. We pay two levels of tax on corporate income -- first at the corporate level and again at the shareholder level when dividends are paid. Salaries are subject to both a gross income tax (called social security) and a net income tax on the same earnings. Investment income is subject to two different forms of taxes -- an income tax and inflation that strips away the value of the investment. Capital gains tax must often be paid not only on the real gain but also on the appreciation in value that is actually due to inflation.

MOST AMERICANS ARE INSULAR

I have represented non-American clients for more than three decades. Many of my clients were either Europeans or former Europeans who had fled to Latin America just before the second world war. These people had left nearly everything behind and had struggled to build a new life in a new land. Most went to Latin America only because they couldn't get into the US or Canada. Using their European know-how in third-world countries, some of them became immensely wealthy. One of their primary investment objectives was and still is *international diversification*. They keep perhaps one third of their money in their new homeland and they divide the rest of it between Europe (mostly through Swiss banks) and North America. More recently, some of them have begun investing a small part of their wealth in the booming Pacific Basin.

Contrast this picture with Americans who typically invest all of their funds in the US. Until very recently, most Americans hesitated to put even a small percentage of their assets in as foreign a place as Canada. Anything more foreign than that was unthinkable. Only during the past two or three years have some Americans begun to buy US-based mutual funds investing in the emerging markets of Asia and Latin America.

An article by Anatole Kaletsky in *The Times* of London discussed and tried to explain the insularity of Americans [*America overloaded with dollars*, 13 May 1991, page 23]. The article was based on a study by Philip Turner entitled *Capital Flows in the 1980s*, published by the Bank for International Settlements (BIS), Basel, Switzerland. The article asked:

> If Japanese, German and British investors have been diversifying their portfolios into dollars, why has this not been offset by American investors buying up assets in yen, marks and pounds? Financial analysts rarely stop to ask this obvious question. Perhaps it is because the answer, suggested in last week's BIS study, is too alarming, or simply too damaging to the financial markets' self-esteem.

> The fact is that despite the apparently sophisticated and overdeveloped financial industry operating on Wall Street, American investors are among the most primitive and insular in the world. In 1990 American pension funds and life insurers each held only 4 percent of their portfolios in foreign assets. Among individual investors, international diversification is almost unheard of.

> One reason for this is that, despite Washington's free-market rhetoric, America has some of the fiercest and most effective capital controls anywhere in the world. American banks make it almost impossible for individuals to hold foreign currencies, pension fund trustees frequently insist on "buy America" investment policies and marketing restrictions imposed by the Securities and Exchange Commission make it illegal for American citizens to invest in most offshore equities, bonds and investment funds.

And, he didn't even discuss the nasty tax problems that arise when Americans acquire foreign shares or mutual funds.

MOST AMERICANS WILL STAY AND PAY

The US Congress and the IRS both know that they have a captive market of taxpayers. Most Americans don't even think in terms of investing outside the US. They are incapable of moving abroad or becoming *perpetual tourists (PTs)*. They are horrified at the thought that anyone would give up American citizenship either to avoid taxes or for any other reason.

Congress could double present tax rates and most Americans would simply grumble. Most of them would not even consider leaving. They would stay and pay.

Many British are like that too. During the last Labour government investment income over about £20,000 a year was taxable at a whopping 98 percent. In the late 1970s I was asked to advise an elderly British woman how she could reduce her taxes. I suggested that she move to a tax haven such as Bermuda. Her response was: "Oh, but I wouldn't think of leaving London." She stayed and paid. She eventually got a reprieve in the form of lower taxes from Margaret Thatcher's Tory government.

2. YOUR TAXES ARE HIGHER THAN YOU THINK THEY ARE

Many different types of taxes are imposed in the US and other high-tax countries. Where income tax rates have been reduced, the tax base has been broadened so that most wealthy individuals now pay higher taxes than ever before. Americans pay taxes on their worldwide income and capital gains, social security taxes, state and local taxes, and up to 55 percent tax on their gifts during life and at death. This chapter is basically unchanged from last year's edition, but minor changes are reflected in the *1997 Update* at the end of the chapter.

Tax rates of 50 percent or more are now common in many major industrial nations. As a result of clever schemes called *tax reform* some high tax countries, led by the US, have diabolically reduced tax rates while simultaneously increasing the amount of taxes they actually collect.

A medical doctor living and working in America recently told me that he pays at least one-third of everything he earns as federal income taxes and that, when he dies, the federal government will take the other two-thirds of everything he expects to earn during the rest of his life. He added that he felt he was lucky that he lives in Florida which has no state income tax on individuals and, for practical purposes, no state tax at death. If he lived in California or New York, for example, his taxes would be even higher.

During the second world war, the highest US income tax rate on individuals was 91 percent. The maximum rate was brought down, first to 70 percent and then to 50 percent. In those days, most taxpayers paid a much lower rate on a substantial part of their income, and a much lower effective rate on their total income.

"LOW INCOME TAXES" ARE A MYTH

Presidents Reagan and Bush brought tax rates down. Until 1993, the highest US federal income tax rate on individuals was theoretically only 31 percent, but many deductions had been eliminated and virtually all tax shelters were gone. For most individuals with high earnings, the maximum tax rate became virtually a flat tax rate that applied to all of their taxable income. Some US accountants with sharp pencils told me that because of the way it was calculated the maximum 31 percent rate was actually nearly 34 percent for some taxpayers. State and city income taxes in many areas of the US raised the rate to more than 40 percent.

The most significant thing about the Reagan-Bush era was that although your tax rates came down your taxes did not. I don't know a single American with substantial income that didn't have to pay higher federal income taxes in 1992 than he did in 1980. A table published in USA Today in early 1993, based on IRS statistics, showed the following total individual income tax collected by Uncle Sam (in billions):

1970 ....$ 83.9
1975 ....$124.5
1980 ....$250.3
1985 ....$325.7
1990 ....$447.1

So much for reduced tax rates.

PRESIDENT CLINTON'S TAX INCREASES

In the first edition of this report, written in early 1992, I asked:

What will happen the next time America elects a Democrat as President? 1992? 1996? 2000? My guess is that the next Democrat elected as President with a Congress controlled by his party will quickly bring the maximum tax rate back to 50 percent or more. The elimination of most deductions and tax shelters will remain. The reduced tax rates almost certainly will not.

A year later, Bill Clinton had been elected President and his party controlled both Houses of Congress. Several tax increases were proposed by President Clinton and enacted during 1993 and 1994 by his Democratic-controlled Congress. Most of these changes took effect retroactively as of 1 January 1993:

- Two new income tax brackets were added, 36 percent and 39.6 percent. The maximum capital gains tax rate was left unchanged at 28 percent.
- If you are a married couple filing a joint return, you pay 36 percent tax on your taxable income between $140,000 and $250,000, and 39.6 percent on income exceeding $250,000. Yes, you pay President Clinton's "millionaires' surtax" on all of your income over $250,000.
- If you are single, you reach the 36 percent bracket on income over $115,000, but you pay the 39.6 percent rate only on income exceeding $250,000.
- If you are a married individual filing a separate return, you reach the 36 percent threshold at $70,000 and the 39.6 percent "millionaires' surtax" bracket at just $125,000.
- The alternative minimum tax (AMT) rate went up (from 24 percent) to 26 percent on some AMT income and 28 percent on higher amounts.
- Beginning in 1994, the wage ceiling was eliminated for the medicare portion of the social security tax.
- Also beginning in 1994, many taxpayers have had to pay income tax on 85 percent of

their social security benefits.
- The 55 percent maximum rates for the gift tax, the estate tax and the generation-skipping transfer tax were not reduced as they were supposed to be under prior law. Instead, these rates have been kept permanently so that you can contribute your share to deficit reduction.
- The federal corporate income tax rate was increased (from 34 percent) to 35 percent, but only on income exceeding $10 million.
- A corporation can no longer deduct executive compensation over $1 million unless it is linked to productivity.

THE GOVERNMENT HAS AWESOME REVENUE NEEDS

In 1993, I attended a roundtable discussion in London sponsored by ATI -- The American Tax Institute in Europe. The guest speaker was Fred T. Goldberg, Jr., of Washington, who had recently returned to private law practice after having served as both Commissioner of Internal Revenue and Assistant Secretary of the Treasury for Tax Policy in the Bush administration. Here is a summary of some of his comments on the tax changes that had been proposed by President Clinton, most of which were subsequently enacted:
- The revenue needs of the US government are awesome.
- Congress wants a boatload of money. The energy tax will raise big bucks. So will the income tax rate increase, even though it really only hits the top two percent of individual taxpayers.
- Tax rates are just rates. Many less obvious changes increase the amount of tax you really have to pay.
- An American making over $250,000 a year will pay between 25 and 30 percent more in federal income taxes under the Clinton proposals.
- The individual income tax is now over 80 years old. Prior to the second world war only about one-third of the people were subject to the income tax.
- The income tax is "broke" -- fatally. It doesn't work in a global economy. A VAT is the only way to pay for the huge appetite for money.
- The government is hopelessly bankrupt. The deficit will be up at $300 billion to $400 billion a year by the end of the decade.
- Asked whether he was enjoying his return to private law practice, Goldberg responded that as a result of the projected tax increases he felt that he was still working for the government for all practical purposes.

OUTLOOK FOR THE IMMEDIATE FUTURE

The Republicans' *"Contract with America"* calls for reduced taxes on capital gains and some tax relief in other areas. Most of the other tax relief is supposed to go to the *middle* class. No one has yet defined the middle class but I can tell you that it does not include you. Despite their best intentions, I do not foresee this Congress or any future Congress materially reducing your tax burden.

I personally like the idea of a flat tax, but I don't think we will see one anytime soon. The versions I have seen thus far don't meet the needs of most politicians. Today, a large percentage of the personal income tax is paid by a very small percentage of the population. If you reduce the amount of tax paid by these wealthy individuals and you insist on raising the same amount of revenue, then the middle class will have to pay more and the poor will have to give up their earned-income tax credit. That is not a politically acceptable solution. Another problem is the flat tax rate. Treasury says that 17 percent wouldn't work, even with no deductions. If sacred cows like the mortgage-interest deduction and the charitable deduction are to be maintained, the flat tax rate would probably have to be about 23 percent. And, that doesn't include social security tax or state and local income taxes.

THE NASTY ALTERNATIVE MINIMUM TAX

The US now has two distinct tax systems for individuals, one used by most taxpayers and a separate one that prevents many high-bracket individuals from escaping tax. You compute your regular income tax under the regular rules. You also compute your *alternative minimum tax (AMT)* on AMT income under the AMT rules. You pay whichever tax is higher.

In computing the AMT you lose some of your tax deductions and credits. You also have to take into account *tax preference* items that are not taxable under the regular rules. The AMT rate has crept up over recent years. It is now 26 percent on some of your AMT income and 28 percent on higher amounts.

THE *US* TAXES CORPORATE INCOME TWICE

The US is one of the few major industrial nations that still taxes most corporate earnings twice, first at the corporate level and then at the shareholder level. A corporation that earns $1 million pays about $400,000 in federal, state and city corporate income taxes. When the corporation distributes the remaining $600,000 as a dividend, its shareholders pay another 40 percent of that amount in federal, state and city taxes. About $640,000 of the $1 million earned by the corporation goes to the payment of income taxes. That is hardly a low tax rate. Nor is that all.

TAXES ON CAPITAL GAINS

Many countries do not impose any tax on capital gains. Some European countries levy a capital gains tax only on gains from the sale of real estate or gains from the disposition of shares by someone who has a substantial holding, like 25 percent or more of the shares of a company. The US taxes its citizens and residents on virtually all of their capital gains. It taxes foreigners only on gains from the sale of US real estate or real property holding companies.

In the past, the US generally taxed capital gains at a lower rate than ordinary income. Typically, it imposed a much lower rate on long-term capital gains such as those from selling capital assets held for more than six months or more than a year. For several years during the 1980s the highest federal income tax rate on capital gains was 20 percent. In order to reduce the rate on ordinary income to 28 percent, the Tax Reform Act of 1986 raised the capital gains tax rate to that same level. The rate on ordinary income has since increased as noted earlier in this chapter. After increasing to a maximum of 31 percent, the capital gains tax rate was again set at a maximum of 28 percent. The newly-elected Republican-controlled Congress promised to reduce the capital gains tax. A provision reducing the maximum capital gains tax rate to 19.8 percent was included in a 1995 budget bill passed by Congress but vetoed by President Clinton. This is one of the few areas where you may really get some tax relief.

The US continues to treat American taxpayers unfairly by taxing them at high rates on their capital gains but limiting their ability to deduct their capital losses. The only capital gains tax break available to most Americans is the right to postpone gain from the sale of a residence that is reinvested in a new home. An American over 55 years old can also eliminate some of the gain from selling his principal home once in his lifetime.

INFLATION IS ANOTHER FORM OF TAX

Your investments are also subject to another form of tax known as *inflation*. A good explanation of the problem appeared in a letter to the editor of *The New York Times* [28 July 1991] from Dwight W. Fawcett, of Winnetka, Illinois. The following is excerpted from his letter:

> "Interest Rates, the Real Ones" ...points out that the 6.3 percent return on one-year Treasury bills is actually a 1.8 percent rate after adjusting for inflation at the current rate of 4.5 percent. From this the article then concludes that these investments of savings are "winners" because they yield a net return after inflation.
>
> This calculation, however, does not tell the whole story, for it ignores the effect of income taxes, which are imposed on the entire 6.3 percent, even though most of the income is illusory, in reality representing merely a protection of principal.
>
> Thus, assuming a 28 percent income tax rate, the real rate of return is virtually zero: 1.8 percent after-inflation return and 1.764 percent for income taxes. Few people realize that the effect of taxing the inflationary segment of the nominal return dramatically increases the effective income tax rate. In the above example, income taxes consume almost 100 percent of the after-inflation return.

The true situation is even worse than Mr. Fawcett's letter suggests. First, as we have already seen, his assumed income tax rate of 28 percent is unrealistically low. Most wealthy Americans now pay from 40 to 50 percent in federal, state and local income taxes. Second, I always take the official government inflation rate with a grain of salt. I recall newsletter writer *Harry Schultz* saying some years ago that the official inflation rate is always about three percent below the real rate. I agree. The official inflation rate announced by the government is determined by comparing the cost of a basket of goods and services with that of the same items at an earlier date. I think the basket is rigged to include some items that typically do not increase in price as rapidly as those items that are actually bought by the average consumer.

The bottom line is that the combination of income taxes and inflation often takes more than 100 percent of the interest you receive on your investments. The result is typically even worse when the government taxes capital gains on assets that are not indexed for inflation.

SOCIAL SECURITY TAXES HAVE BEEN INCREASED

Social security is not insurance; it is a tax. It is an insidious tax because it is a second tax on the same income. That didn't matter much when the rate was one percent and the wage base on which it was paid was low. It matters now and it will matter even more in the future.

What Americans call the social security tax really refers to two separate taxes. One is paid for old age, survivor and disability insurance (OASDI) and the other for hospital insurance (HI, or more commonly medicare insurance). Neither is really insurance; both are taxes. These taxes are paid one-half each by employers and employees; if you are self-employed you pay both halves. Unlike real insurance, the more you earn and pay the harder it becomes to collect any benefits. If you continue to work after reaching retirement age you continue to pay these taxes and you generally don't receive benefits. If you continue to have a substantial income, up to 85 percent of any benefits you do receive may be taxable income.

During 1993, the most anyone could pay was $11,057.40. If that was all that was involved it wouldn't be worth discussing here. In the first edition of this report, written in early 1992, I predicted that within the next few years the wage ceiling on social security taxes would either be raised substantially or eliminated. I described this as too tempting a target for a money-hungry Congress to ignore. As indicated below, Congress has since eliminated the wage ceiling on part of the social security tax.

In 1993, the OASDI tax rate was 12.4 percent up to $57,600 for self-employed individuals. For those who were employed, the employer and the employee each paid 6.2 percent up to the same ceiling. In addition, the HI rate was 2.9 percent *up to $135,000* for self-employed persons (1.45 percent each for employers and employees). The increased ceiling for medicare insurance was itself relatively new. Until 1990, the lower ceiling had applied to both the OASDI and HI taxes. In the first edition of this report I said:

As I see it, this ceiling increase is the camel's nose under the tent. Before long the camel will have his entire body under the tent and there won't be any room for you.

American politicians know that some other countries have no wage ceiling for the employer or no ceiling at all. In Switzerland, for example, the total social security tax is only ten percent (five percent each for the employer and the employee) but there is no wage ceiling. In Britain, there is presently an upper earnings limit for the worker but none for the boss. The Labour party wants to remove the ceiling for the employee so that both the employer and the employee will pay National Insurance Contributions on all compensation, without limit.

Each day's newspaper carries stories of another American sports star signing a contract to receive a multi-million dollar salary. This creates a tempting target for Congress. If a baseball team paying a baseball star a $4 million salary had to pay combined OASDI and HI tax of 7.65 percent on the entire salary, it would pay $306,000 in social security taxes a year for him. If the player had to match this "contribution" the combined total social security tax would exceed $600,000 a year for that one player alone. The effect would be the same as a 15 percent increase in his income tax rate but it would only apply to those earning high salaries.

To prevent taxpayers from avoiding this tax by converting compensation into some other form of income, Congress would probably revert to a system it used in the 1970s. You may remember that in those pre-Reagan days the maximum federal income tax rate for individuals was 70 percent for unearned income but only 50 percent for earned income from personal services.

Part of what I predicted has already come true. At President Clinton's request, Congress eliminated the wage ceiling on the HI portion of the social security tax. It has retained the ceiling for the OASDI part. Since 1994, the baseball player making a $4 million salary pays $58,000 in HI tax and his team has to pay the same amount. Incidentally, the government has estimated that 1.2 million high-wage workers (those earning over $135,000 a year) are affected by this increase. I still predict that during the next few years the wage ceiling on the OASDI part of the social security tax will be increased or eliminated.

A VAT IS COMING

Almost every major country in the world has already enacted a *value-added tax (VAT)* or something equivalent to it. Canada and Australia call theirs a goods and services tax. Whatever it is called, it is a national sales tax. Its main attribute is that it is a money machine. It is usually brought in at a low rate of seven percent or so. Each percentage point of increase brings in billions of dollars of new revenue. It typically applies to everything you buy except food, medicine and a few other items that lobbyists have successfully made tax free.

Why doesn't the US have such a tax? There are several reasons. The states do have sales taxes and rely on them for substantial portions of their revenue. A federal VAT might inhibit the states from increasing their sales tax revenues. Many members of Congress are scared to even discuss a VAT because some of their colleagues who did so in the 1980s were defeated when they came up for reelection.

Most Democrats dislike a VAT because they consider it regressive. Most Republicans hate it because it is a hidden tax. Despite these and other problems, a VAT is coming. It is the only tax that is capable of meeting the revenue needs of a health care program like that still envisaged by the Clinton administration. Once in place, rates will be gradually increased and can even produce enough money to eliminate the present budget deficit. This, of course, assumes that Congress has the guts to enact it and that the people don't throw them all out at the next election.

DON'T FORGET STATE AND LOCAL TAXES

Some countries impose only one level of tax. Britain, for example, has a high national income tax, with a maximum rate at present of 40 percent. This is actually lower than the top rate paid by many residents of New York and California who have to pay two or three levels of income tax.

In the US, the federal income tax is the highest, but most states (about 43 out of 50) also impose state personal income taxes. Some counties and cities, including New York City, also have local income taxes. If you live in a place that has federal, state and local income taxes you compound your problems. Obviously, you pay higher income taxes. Less obvious, but perhaps more important, you substantially increase your chances of a costly tax audit. You may be audited by the city, the state or the IRS. Whichever of them audits you will pass on their findings to the others.

The few states that still do not have state or local personal income taxes are:

- Alaska
- Florida
- Nevada
- South Dakota
- Texas
- Washington (the state, not DC)
- Wyoming

Warning! The list of states without personal income taxes has been shrinking rapidly and some of those listed here may soon be forced to begin levying personal income taxes.

CONSIDER TAXES ON CAPITAL

Many European countries impose annual taxes on net wealth or capital. The US does not, at least not at the federal level, probably because it cannot do so without amending the US Constitution. The Constitution requires a direct tax to be apportioned among the states on the basis of population. If New York has twice as many people as Ohio such a tax is unconstitutional unless it collects exactly twice as much revenue from New York as it does from Ohio. To be constitutional, such a tax would have to be levied at a different rate on citizens residing in different states, a political impossibility. The income tax is a direct tax, but the Sixteenth Amendment to the Constitution, ratified in 1913, permits Congress to collect taxes on income without apportionment among the states. I believe that a federal tax on net wealth or capital would also be a direct tax and that it could not be levied without a new amendment.

If you now live, or plan to live, in a country that does levy a net wealth tax, please bear two things in mind. First, such a tax can eat up a substantial portion of your investment income. Even a one percent annual tax hurts. A three percent annual wealth tax, such as that imposed in Uruguay on local assets, will eat up your entire capital in about 30 years. Second, an annual net wealth tax imposed at even a low rate gives the government another way of checking on the accuracy of your income tax return. The tax authorities can compare your wealth tax return from one year to another to see if it is consistent with what is shown on your income tax return.

I suspect that the US Congress finds it easier to impose the estate and gift taxes discussed below than to worry about another constitutional amendment that would permit it to levy an annual wealth tax. The estate and gift taxes are not considered to be a direct tax on capital. According to the IRS and the US Supreme Court, they are an excise tax imposed on your transfer of capital from one person to another.

DEATH TAXES TAKE MOST OF WHAT IS LEFT

Most high-tax countries impose death taxes on the value of all property in your estate that passes on your death to your heirs or other beneficiaries if you are considered to be domiciled or living permanently within that country at the time of your death. In some countries, these taxes are *estate taxes* imposed on everything you leave, regardless of who the assets go to. In other countries, they are *inheritance* taxes on which the rate is much lower for assets left to close family members than for assets going to distant relatives and strangers. Generally, these death duties cover all your property no matter where in the world it is located.

Many high-tax countries also impose death taxes based on one or more other criteria, such as:
• The dead person's citizenship.
• The domicile, residence or citizenship of his heirs or beneficiaries.

•   The fact that either the person who died, or his heirs or beneficiaries, were at some prior time domiciled or resident in the high-tax country, or citizens of that country.

The US imposes a federal estate tax on the fair market value of the worldwide assets of its citizens and domiciliaries and on the US property of foreign domiciliaries who are not US citizens. There is a *marital deduction* for all property passing from one spouse to the other, *but only if the recipient is a US citizen or a non-US citizen who locks the assets into a special US trust called a QDOT*. The first $600,000 given by a US person during his lifetime or at death is effectively exempt. Everything above that is taxed at rates from 37 percent to 55 percent. The top rate was supposed to come down to 50 percent in 1993, but as requested by President Clinton, it has been permanently frozen at the 55 percent rate. Many US states also impose either estate taxes or inheritance taxes that are partially creditable against the federal estate tax.

Although the maximum possible federal estate tax is now 55 percent, there is a five percent extra tax (60 percent tax) on each dollar of fair market value between $10 million and about $21 million. *As a result, if your estate reaches $21 million you pay a flat tax of 55 percent on each and every dollar and the original $600,000 exemption disappears.*

The US collects about $8 billion a year in estate and gift taxes, only about one percent of its total tax receipts. As of 1986, less than one million Americans had net assets of $1 million or more. This is the group that is targeted by the federal estate tax. Anyone with less than that amount can generally avoid the tax with proper planning. Thus, only a tiny fraction of Americans are subject to the estate tax. An even smaller percentage of Americans are really clobbered by the estate tax. An estimated 80,000 Americans have a net estate of $5 million or more. These folks stand to lose half or more of their estates to federal and state taxes when they die. The IRS normally requires the estate tax to be paid in cash nine months after the date of death. Selling sufficient property to pay the tax during a declining market is a problem for those handling the estate, not for the government.

The worst part of the estate tax as it applies to wealthy individuals is that the taxpayer has the burden of proving the *fair market value* of the property subject to tax. It should not surprise you to learn that the IRS sometimes takes a rather aggressive view as to what real estate or the shares of a closely-held business is worth. If you have a large estate that is liquid with readily-valued assets, the federal and state taxes on the estate should not exceed about 60 percent of its real value. If you have assets that are hard to value, you may be assessed combined taxes that exceed 100 percent of the real worth.

A recent Tax Court case involved the *Estate of Samuel Newhouse*, a well-known newspaper and magazine publisher, who died in 1979. The IRS assessed a tax deficiency of over $600 million and it also sought another $300 million in penalties. The IRS lost after a seven-year battle [94 Tax Court No. 14 (1990)]. The arguments over valuation were mind-boggling. The family and its experts claimed that Newhouse's shares in the publishing company were worth about $178 million when he died. The IRS and its experts said they were worth more than $1.2 billion, nearly seven times as much. The estate paid about $46 million in taxes instead of the $914 million the IRS wanted. The scary thing about the case is that a less conscientious judge might have simply split the difference between the valuations set by the highly-qualified experts for the two sides. At today's 55 percent flat tax on large estates (over about $21 million) the effective tax rate would then have been several times the actual fair market value as eventually determined by the judge.

The family of *Malcolm Forbes* who died in 1990 is gearing up for a similar battle with the IRS. The late publisher's son and primary heir, Steve Forbes, is reported to have told a television interviewer that the IRS "...sort of wants to do to (the estate) what Saddam Hussein did to Kuwait" [*USA Today International Edition*, 17 October 1990].

GIFT TAXES BLOCK AVOIDANCE OF DEATH TAXES

To prevent you from easily avoiding death taxes, most high-tax countries also use similar criteria to impose gift taxes on lifetime gifts. They impose gift taxes on the value of all property located anywhere in the world that you give to anyone if you were domiciled or living permanently in the high-tax country at the time you made the gift.

Some countries cover all gifts made at any time during your life. Others cover only those gifts made within a few years before death, on the theory that these gifts were made in contemplation of death. Once again, some countries also impose their gift taxes based on one or more other criteria such as:
*   The citizenship of the donor.
*   The domicile, residence or citizenship of the persons receiving the gifts.
*   The fact that the donor or donee was, at some prior time, domiciled or resident in the high-tax country, or a citizen of that country.

Most high-tax countries also impose death duties and gift taxes on all gratuitous transfers of property located in that country without regard to the residence, domicile or citizenship of any of the persons involved. This is especially true in the case of real estate located in the high-tax country, but it may also cover other property.

The US federal gift tax is now unified with the federal estate tax. An American gets the equivalent of a $600,000 exemption on his total transfers. It covers those transfers made by gift while he is alive and anything left over can be used for transfers at death.

Some other countries -- even those with relatively high estate or inheritance taxes such as the UK -- do not impose any gift taxes or exclude lifetime gifts if you live a given number of years after making the gift. Several countries normally thought of as being high-tax countries, such as Australia, Canada, New Zealand and Israel, do not now have any estate, inheritance or gift taxes.

GENERATION-SKIPPING TRANSFERS ATTRACT A HUGE TAX

It used to be possible for very wealthy individuals to reduce the impact of high estate and gift tax rates by *skipping generations*. With proper planning, tax was payable only once every several generations. Great-grandfather (first generation) left his estate to grandfather (second generation) for life, with a further interest to son (third generation) for his life and the remainder interest to son's child or children (fourth generation). There was an estate tax payable on great-grandfather's death but none for the next two generations since there were only life estates.

The US now viciously attacks any such planning, although some of it remains *grandfathered* under irrevocable trusts created before the new law was adopted. The estate tax, the gift tax and the *generation-skipping transfer tax (GST tax)* are now integrated into a single system. There is an overall exemption of $1 million for all generation-skipping transfers by any one individual. After that, the GST tax is the highest possible estate or gift tax rate, now 55 percent. The combination of the regular gift or estate tax with the GST tax on a transfer that is a *direct skip* from a grandfather to his grandchild pays a combined estate tax and GST tax of nearly 80 percent if the intervening child is alive at the time of the transfer. The use of trusts may postpone the GST tax, but it does not eliminate it.

To add insult to injury, proposed regulations issued by the IRS in 1992 would have imposed the GST tax on a transfer of foreign property by a foreign individual (one who is neither a US citizen nor domiciled in the US) to a grandchild who is a US citizen or domiciled in the US if the intervening parent of the grandchild is also a US citizen or domiciled in the US. This proposed rule was sharply criticized by many tax practitioners as going far beyond the intent of Congress. The GST tax is supposed to supplement the estate tax and it would have been strange to have it apply to a transfer that was not itself covered by the estate tax.

Final regulations covering the GST tax were issued in December 1995. I am pleased to report that the rules in the proposed regulations applying the GST tax to transfers of property that were not subject to estate or gift tax have been eliminated. Under the final regulations, the application of the GST tax is limited to situations where an estate or gift tax is imposed on the property. Although no mention was made in the proposed regulations of former Americans who have given up their US citizenship, many such persons would have been affected by the rule since frequently it is the grandparents who leave the US while their children and grandchildren remain behind. The final regulations make careful estate planning more important than ever.

1997 UPDATE

The US continues to have a Democratic President and a Republican-controlled Congress. No major changes in US taxes are expected during 1997 or 1998.

Having seen the nature and extent of taxes imposed, let us now turn to the different criteria used by high-tax countries to impose their taxes. In Part II of this report, we will see the steps you will have to take to overcome the dreaded *tax octopus*.

PART II

OVERCOMING THE TAX OCTOPUS

3. EIGHT CRITERIA FOR IMPOSING TAXES

The *tax octopus* consists of eight different criteria used by the US and some other high-tax countries to impose taxes on you. The key criteria are your residence, your domicile and your citizenship, but five others are also significant. All eight criteria are introduced in this chapter and are discussed in greater depth in later chapters. Most of this chapter is unchanged from last year's edition, but the section on *Citizenship* has been revised and a *1997 Update* has been added at the end of the chapter.

The octopus is a sea monster with eight uncoordinated tentacles reaching out in different ways. If you are swimming in the ocean and *any* of its tentacles grabs hold, you are likely to have serious problems. If you have a knife and you succeed in cutting off all eight tentacles, you win.

Similarly, any of eight different criteria may subject you to tax liability on your income or your capital in your present homeland. Each of them is used by some countries. Most countries apply a few of them. At least one country, the US, uses all of them. To avoid these taxes legally, you must eliminate each of these tax tentacles, one by one. In this chapter, we will discuss the eight tentacles that comprise the *tax octopus*. They are:

*   Residence
*   Domicile
*   Citizenship
*   Marital Status
*   Source of Income
*   Location of Assets
*   Timing
*   Status of Beneficiaries

Let us take a preliminary look at each of them.

RESIDENCE

In many countries, you are resident for tax purposes if you are present in the country for more than 182 days in any tax year. The problem is that the converse is not necessarily true. You are not necessarily nonresident just because you spend less than half the year in that country.

The situation is like a traffic signal with red, amber and green lights. If you are in the red zone (more than 182 days) you are taxable. If you are in the amber zone you may be taxable depending on factors other than time. Some countries have a green zone (safe harbor) under which you cannot be taxed as a resident unless you are present in the country for at least some minimum number of days a year. Other countries have no green zone; in them you are always in either a red zone or an amber zone. In such countries, there is always a risk that the government will claim that you are resident.

Many countries impose income tax on worldwide income based upon the residence of the taxpayer. In some of these countries, mere residence is sufficient to tax an individual on both his domestic and foreign-source income. In others, taxation of worldwide income is imposed only on taxpayers who are permanently resident (or domiciled) in the country.

You may be able to escape your present country's taxes by changing your residence to a country that does not tax its residents on their worldwide income. You may even be able to escape residence anywhere by moving around from place to place as a *perpetual tourist (PT)*.

For further information, see Chapter 4, entitled *Change Your Residence*.

DOMICILE

The concept of domicile is particularly significant in the English-speaking world. Your domicile is not necessarily the same as your residence. Whereas your residence is usually redetermined each year, your domicile is generally more permanent.

Under British and American law everyone begins life with a *domicile of origin*. This can be changed to a *domicile of choice*, but not easily. Merely moving to a new place does not automatically change your domicile. The domicile concept made better sense 100 years ago than it does now. Picture a 20-year old Englishman in the days of Queen Victoria. He might take a job in India and live and work there for 40 years before returning to retire and die in England. While in India he was clearly resident there. He remained domiciled in England because he always intended to return there.

It is often difficult to determine an individual's domicile in today's jet-set era. One major problem is that the taxpayer always has the burden of proof. Each government is likely to claim that you are domiciled there if this results in you or your heirs having to pay them higher taxes. If you are an alien domiciled in the US, you are subject to US gift and estate taxes on your worldwide assets.

In the US, your place of domicile is determined by state law rather than federal law, so there are over 50 different sets of rules. Your domicile for federal tax purposes depends on the law of the state in which you are domiciled. There have been a number of cases in which more than one state has claimed to be a particular taxpayer's domicile. Similar rules apply in other countries. In the UK, for example, you are domiciled in some part of the UK such as England or Scotland.

Your domicile is very significant in determining your liability to various taxes in the UK. For example, if you are both resident and domiciled in the UK you are taxable on your worldwide income. If you are resident but not domiciled you do not pay UK income taxes on foreign-source income unless it is remitted to the UK.

In most civil-law countries, there is little or no difference between residence and fiscal domicile. For example, the day I moved to Neuchatel, Switzerland with a permit authorizing me to live and work there, I became both resident and domiciled there for Swiss tax purposes.

The scary thing about domicile is that the rules can be very erratic. A government may claim that you or your heirs owe taxes even though you thought you had abandoned that country many years earlier. Under US rules, for example, you can't abandon your old domicile without establishing a new one. If you try to live as a perpetual tourist (PT), you may find that you are still domiciled in some US state many years later. Under UK rules, if you abandon your domicile of choice without establishing a new one, your domicile will revert to that of your domicile of origin.

For a further discussion, see Chapter 5, called *Change Your Domicile.*

CITIZENSHIP

The US taxes its citizens on their worldwide income solely by reason of their citizenship. A US citizen cannot escape US income taxes merely by moving abroad. The US also imposes its gift and estate taxes on American citizens regardless of where they live or where they are domiciled. If you are an American citizen, you can get some income tax benefits by living and working abroad but these are of relatively little value to US taxpayers with substantial incomes. The US is the only major country in the world to impose income tax solely due to citizenship, but a few other countries impose death taxes based on citizenship.

If an American wants to become a tax exile, he must not only change his residence and domicile but he must also give up his US citizenship. Since he cannot afford to be stateless, he must have another nationality in a suitable country that does not impose taxes based on citizenship.

Some Americans are *dual nationals.* They already have one or more other nationalities. That does not help them taxwise since a dual national is still an American citizen for all US tax purposes.

If you are like most Americans, you probably do not have another nationality. The first step for you is to acquire another citizenship. The US State Department has now conceded that an American citizen may voluntarily acquire another citizenship (and another passport) without automatically losing his US citizenship.

The second step, a more traumatic one, is for you to give up your US citizenship. As an American who has relinquished US citizenship, you may be able to obtain a multiple entry visa permitting you to visit the US the same as any other foreigner. However, a provision enacted as part of the 1996 immigration law authorizes the US Attorney General to treat an individual who has renounced citizenship to avoid taxes as an excludable alien.

If you are treated as having relinquished your US citizenship *to avoid taxes,* you will remain subject to *anti-expatriation rules* for ten years. Until recently, these rules had more bark than bite. With proper planning, former Americans could avoid the impact of these rules until the ten years ran out. However, revised expatriation tax rules enacted in 1996 impose much tougher rules on citizens who have expatriated since February 1995. The revised rules are discussed in Chapter 21 below.

If you are a US citizen or your country imposes death taxes based on citizenship, you should read *Acquire Another Nationality in Chapter 6 and Relinquish Your Present Nationality* in Chapter 7. In addition, read *Avoid Your Country's Anti-Departure Rules* in Chapter 13. It introduces the US anti-expatriation rules and departure taxes imposed by Canada, Germany and other high-tax countries.

MARITAL STATUS

Your marital status may affect your tax liability. The significant factors include not just whether you are married but also where and how you were married and where you and your spouse have lived since your marriage.

Many countries have *community property* rules under which each spouse is entitled to a half interest in all property acquired by the other spouse during the marriage. These rules apply in virtually all civil-law countries. They also apply in some common-law jurisdictions, including nine states in the US. Places as diverse as California, Texas, Quebec, the Channel Islands, Italy and Argentina all apply community property rules. If you were married in, or had a marital home in, a community property jurisdiction you need special planning to become a tax exile. You may not be able to escape some taxes unless both you and your spouse take the same steps.

Your marital status may also be significant even if you have not lived in a community property country. If, for example, you are a married woman, your *domicile* may be the same as that of your husband whether or not you want it to be. UK reforms now permit a married woman to adopt a domicile separate from that of her husband. US rules are less clear; they permit a married woman to have a separate domicile for some purposes, such as filing an action for divorce. The states in the US do not always permit a married woman to establish a separate domicile for more mundane activities such as taxes.

I know of several cases where a wealthy woman once domiciled in the US now lives abroad. If her husband lives abroad with her but retains his domicile in some US state, such a woman may be incapable of establishing a foreign domicile for US gift and estate tax purposes. Problems relating to the domicile of a married woman are discussed in Chapter 5, entitled *Change Your Domicile*. Those relating to community property are covered in Chapter 8, entitled *Cope With Community Property Rules*.

SOURCE OF INCOME

Most countries apply a source test under which all income derived from sources within the country is subject to income tax whether the person earning the income resides in the country or not. Income paid to nonresidents is often subject to a withholding tax. The person paying the income to the nonresident must withhold the tax from the income and pay it directly to the government.   Withholding taxes are generally imposed at a flat rate on gross income derived by foreigners from domestic sources. The withholding tax rate is set by law but is often reduced by treaty. For example, the statutory US withholding tax rate on dividends paid to nonresidents is 30 percent, but portfolio dividends paid to a Canadian resident are subject to only 15 percent US withholding tax under the income tax treaty between the US and Canada.

Some countries impose taxes only on a territorial basis. Applying a source test, they tax all income derived from domestic sources. All foreign-source income is exempt from tax. The territorial principle applies in many Latin American countries. Residents of these countries pay income tax only on their earnings from sources within the country.

If you move from a high-tax country to one with lower taxes or none at all, you also need to derive as much of your income as possible from sources outside the high-tax country. In Chapter 9, we explore how to *Change the Sources of Your Income*.

LOCATION OF ASSETS

Most countries impose property taxes on real estate and other assets physically situated in the country. Many also seek to impose capital transfer taxes on the disposition of property by a lifetime gift or at death. These taxes may be assessed on your worldwide assets because you are resident or domiciled there or because you are a citizen. Even if you are not a citizen and are neither resident nor domiciled there, the country may impose such taxes simply because the property is located in that country.

A tax exile will try to remove as much of his taxable property as he can from the high-tax country to places that will not tax his assets merely because they are located there. Personal property can be moved from one country to another. Real property cannot be moved but it can be sold or mortgaged and the proceeds can be moved abroad. Read Chapter 10 entitled *Change the Location of Your Assets*.

TIMING

How income is taxed may depend on when it is considered to be earned. Timing can be very significant for anyone who moves from one country to another. Thus, for example, a tax exile will generally try to postpone receiving income until after he is no longer a taxpayer. Timing may also be important if one spouse is becoming a tax exile and the other is not. In the US, for example, large tax-free gifts can be made between spouses only if the recipient spouse is a US citizen when the gift is made.

It may be possible for a resident of a country to exchange domestic real estate for foreign real estate in a tax-free transaction while he is still resident. This possibility existed in the US until 1989. It may also be possible for a former resident to transfer domestic assets to a foreign corporation or to sell foreign assets without tax only after he has ceased to be resident. These and other similar planning ideas are explored in Chapter 11 entitled *Watch Your Timing*.

STATUS OF BENEFICIARIES

In my experience, not all members of a family become tax exiles. Frequently, one or both parents leave a country and their grown children and any grandchildren may remain behind. Knowing this, a high-tax country may seek to impose taxes, interest and even penalties when assets are eventually distributed to those who remained behind. Most of these problems can be resolved by careful planning at the outset. Obviously, the planning is much easier when the children leave with their parents. The situation is explored in Chapter 12, entitled *Plan for Beneficiaries who Remain Behind*.

THE *US* USES ALL OF THESE CRITERIA

The US uses all of the foregoing criteria to impose its federal taxes. Both US citizens and resident aliens are taxed on worldwide income because they are citizens or residents. Either is sufficient; domicile is not necessary.

Both US citizens and aliens domiciled in the US are subject to US gift and estate taxes on their worldwide assets merely because they are citizens or domiciliaries. Their residence is immaterial. In cases where spouses have been married in a community property jurisdiction and one spouse is a US citizen and the other is a nonresident alien, the US may apply community property rules to tax the citizen spouse on half of the income earned by the nonresident alien spouse.

The US taxes nonresident aliens on their US-source income. It taxes non-domiciled aliens when they give US-situs property by lifetime gifts or by transfers at death. Where all of its other attacks fail, the IRS may claim that the income was earned before the tax exile left the country. It may also seek to impose transferee liability on beneficiaries over whom it retains jurisdiction.

The answer to all of these attacks is very *careful planning*. If you plan to become a tax exile, do it right or don't do it.

THE IMPACT ON A HYPOTHETICAL FAMILY

In the remaining chapters of Part II of this report we will examine the impact of each tentacle of the tax octopus on an imaginary family consisting of *Larry Latour* and his wife, *Laura*. Both of them were born in the US and are US citizens by birth. They were married in California and have lived there since. They are both now domiciled in California. Each of them has grown children from a prior marriage. The Latours are quite wealthy; Laura Latour has net assets of about $25 million, most of which she inherited from her family. Larry Latour has about $1 million of assets in his own name.

The Latours have traveled extensively all over the world. Neither of them works on a day-to-day basis although they do take an active role in the management of their assets and both of them serve as directors of a large public company that is still controlled by Laura's family.

Larry and Laura may want to become tax exiles and hope that by moving abroad they can reduce their present income taxes and reduce or eliminate the estate tax that will someday have to be paid when Laura's assets are passed on to her children and grandchildren.

1997 UPDATE

As noted under *Citizenship* above, significant new legislation was enacted during 1996. Revised expatriation tax rules were enacted in August 1996, retroactive to February 1995. An immigration law amendment authorizes the US Attorney General to treat an individual who renounces citizenship to avoid taxes as excludable. These rules are discussed in Chapter 21 below.

4. CHANGE YOUR RESIDENCE

If you want to escape taxes in most high-tax countries, you must change your country of residence. You can avoid being a US resident if you avoid having a *green card* and spend on average less than four months each year in the US. The US residency rules are discussed in greater depth in Chapter 15 below. This chapter is unchanged from last year's edition.

If you are now resident in a high-tax country, you cannot escape the clutches of the tax octopus without abandoning your present residence. In countries such as Australia, Britain and Canada it may not be possible for you to terminate your present residence without establishing a new residence elsewhere. The new residence can even be in a tax haven such as Bermuda or Cayman that imposes no income taxes, but it must be a real residence. You must be able to show that you have permission to live there and that you are really there for a substantial part of the year. It cannot be an accommodation address in a place you have never been to or which you have only visited once. It helps considerably if you buy a home or condominium apartment and actually live in it. If that is not possible, you should lease a place for a term of at least a year, preferably longer.

TYPES OF RESIDENCY

The UK and some present and former British colonies have more than one type of residency. You can be *resident*; you can also be *ordinarily resident*, or habitually resident. The tax consequences may differ depending on which of these categories you are in.

ABANDONING YOUR PRIOR RESIDENCE

Most countries say you can be resident in more than one place. Thus, it is not enough to show that you have acquired a new place of residence. You must also show that you are no longer a resident of the country whose residence you are abandoning.

Since 1985, the US is one of the easiest countries from which to abandon residency if you are not a US citizen and you don't have a *green card* giving you the right to permanent residence. The US does not care whether an alien who terminates US residency establishes a new residence elsewhere. If he does not spend sufficient time in the US to meet the substantial presence test he is automatically a nonresident alien for income tax purposes. He can even be a *perpetual tourist (PT)* who does not spend sufficient time in any one place to be considered resident there.

Larry and Laura Latour can abandon their US residence (assuming they are no longer US citizens) by moving out of the US. During their first calendar year abroad they should spend 30 days or less in the US. In future years they should be able to visit their friends and family in the US for up to four months a year. They must also seek professional advice concerning abandonment of their residency in California for state income tax purposes. *US Residency Rules* are discussed in detail in Chapter 15 below. Part IV of this report (Chapters 24 to 30) discusses the problems of leaving each of several high-tax countries, including the US, Britain, Canada and Germany. Part VI (Chapters 36 to 64) discusses the pros and cons of moving to a number of different countries in various parts of the world.

5. CHANGE YOUR DOMICILE

If you want to escape estate or inheritance taxes in some high-tax countries, you must change your place of domicile. Under Anglo-American concepts, everyone has a domicile of origin. This can be changed to a new domicile of choice but you or your estate will have the burden of proving that you have done so. The US domicile rules are discussed in greater depth in Chapter 16 below. This chapter is unchanged from last year's edition.

The tax consequences of where you are domiciled may be very significant or totally irrelevant, depending on the country involved. You may be subject to income tax, capital gains tax and inheritance tax if you are domiciled in some part of the UK. Similar rules may apply in a number of present or former British colonies throughout the world. Your domicile may affect your liability to federal estate and gift taxes in the US, but only if you are an alien. If you are a US citizen you are liable for these taxes regardless of your domicile.

COMPARING RESIDENCE AND DOMICILE

In many continental European countries *residence* and *domicile* have virtually the same meaning. In those countries whose legal system is based on English common law, domicile has a different meaning from residence. In them, domicile denotes a more lasting connection with the country concerned. Where domicile is used as a basis for imposing tax, the term does not necessarily have the same meaning as it has in general law.

Many countries look to your residence rather than your domicile in determining your liability for income tax. They may look to domicile in seeing whether you are liable for estate or inheritance taxes. The theory is that you should be subject to these taxes only if you have a closer connection to the country than merely spending too much time there in a single year.

DOMICILE OF DEPENDENCY

Many countries still recognize a *domicile of dependency*. Typically, minor children (those under age 18 or 21) automatically have the domicile of their father. In some countries, a wife is deemed to have her husband's domicile unless they are estranged and living entirely apart.

DOMICILE OF ORIGIN

Some countries still give great weight to the *domicile of origin*, the domicile you acquired at birth and which you are assumed to retain for the rest of your life unless it can be shown that you have clearly abandoned it with no intention of reviving it again at a later date.

CHANGING TO A DOMICILE OF CHOICE

The UK generally follows the common law rules to establish where an individual is domiciled. Under these rules a baby takes his father's domicile when he is born and that becomes his domicile of origin. Growing up, the child's domicile changes with that of his father. When he is no longer a minor he is free to change from his *domicile of origin* to a *domicile of choice*, but he can generally do so only with clear evidence that he has intended to change his domicile. Under UK rules, if he abandons his domicile of choice, he reverts to his domicile of origin until such time as he clearly acquires a new domicile of choice. Under a proposed rule, he would never revert to his domicile of origin, Instead, he would retain his current domicile of choice until he acquired a new one. However, enactment of the proposed rule has been delayed indefinitely.

Upon marriage, the common law rule said that a woman automatically acquired her husband's domicile as a *domicile of dependency* even if she never actually set foot in that place. It is frightening to have major tax consequences depend on such peculiar rules. Britain has changed this quaint rule and permits a married woman to adopt her own domicile of choice.

Most present and former British colonies follow these rules, with or without the statutory change covering married women and other modifications. Fortunately, your domicile may no longer be material for tax purposes in some of these countries. This makes them good places to move to since you can safely establish a domicile there without any tax cost. Under the common law rule you can only have one domicile at a time. This has not stopped two or more states or countries from claiming that an individual was domiciled there at one particular time, such as when he died.

STATE LAW GOVERNS DOMICILE IN THE *US*

The question of domicile in the US is just as bad, perhaps even worse. Your domicile is a matter of state law rather than federal law. Thus, there may be differences from state to state. For most purposes, a married woman who is living with her husband probably still has her husband's domicile. The US rules do not follow the common law rule of reverting to a domicile of origin if you abandon a domicile of choice. The only way you can abandon a domicile for US purposes is to establish a new domicile of choice.

DOMICILE IS A PROBLEM FOR *PTs*

The domicile rules play havoc with anyone who leaves a high-tax country such as Britain or the US without clearly establishing a new domicile of choice. If, for example, you leave the US and become a *perpetual tourist (PT)* with no new permanent home that can be claimed as a domicile, you are still domiciled in the US. This means you are still liable for federal estate and gift taxes even if you are not a US citizen. Unless the UK changes its law, you may find that if you leave Britain, establish a new domicile in a safe place such as Jersey, and then leave Jersey to become a *PT*, you have reacquired your domicile of origin in Britain.

Larry and Laura Latour are now domiciled in California. Even if they change their residency and their citizenship they will remain liable to US federal gift and estate taxes unless they also change their domicile. If they leave California to become *perpetual tourists (PTs)* they will almost certainly remain domiciled in California, and they will still be liable for US estate and gift taxes. They must affirmatively establish a new permanent home in a suitable foreign country and take all steps necessary to claim that new home as their domicile.

If Laura tries to change her domicile without Larry changing his, the IRS may claim that her domicile remains the same as his, in California. The Latours understand that California currently has no state taxes on gifts or at death but they will double-check the current situation and continue to monitor any future changes there.

For an elaboration of the *US Domicile Rules*, see Chapter 16 below. For a discussion of the tax consequences of establishing a new domicile of choice in selected countries throughout the world, see Part VI (Chapters 36 to 64) below.

6. ACQUIRE ANOTHER NATIONALITY

Only a few countries impose taxes based on nationality. If you want to escape taxes in one of these countries, you may have to change your nationality. If you don't already have another nationality you must first acquire one. Then you can abandon your original nationality. The US nationality rules are discussed in greater depth in Chapters 17 and 18 below. This chapter is unchanged from last year's edition.

Unless your nationality is that of the US, the Philippines, Eritrea, Finland, Greece, the Netherlands or Sweden, retaining your present citizenship should not cause tax problems after you move. These seem to be the only countries that try to impose any tax burden based on citizenship. And, of all of these, the US is the only country to make a serious effort to collect taxes from its citizens that live abroad. Not only that, but the US also tries to collect taxes from some of its former citizens that it would not try to collect from persons who were not former Americans.

Details concerning the US rules are contained in several chapters in Part III of this report. Information concerning some of the other countries that tax based on citizenship is given in Chapters 29 and 30 below.

DUAL NATIONALITY IS THE FIRST STEP

An American can't become a tax exile if he remains an American citizen. If you think you might ever want to abandon your American citizenship, you will need to acquire another nationality as well as a passport on which to travel. The US State Department now concedes that an American citizen can have dual nationality and that he can acquire the other nationality voluntarily without automatically losing his American citizenship. These rules are discussed in detail in Chapter 18 below. The first step is to acquire another nationality. Do it now while it is clear that you can do so without problems.

There are many fine reasons for becoming a *dual national* if you can do so. For example, if you are fortunate enough to acquire citizenship in one of the 15 countries that is presently a member of the European Union (EU), you will have the right to live and work in any of the EU countries. You may be entitled to such a citizenship if your parents or any of your grandparents were born in an EU country. The rules are not uniform. They vary from one EU country to another.

EXPATRIATION IS REQUIRED TO ESCAPE *US* TAXES

Larry and Laura Latour cannot escape US taxes unless they obtain another nationality and abandon their US citizenship. They will review their respective family histories with their advisers to see whether they have any entitlement to a foreign nationality. If, for example, one of Laura's grandparents was born in Ireland she would be entitled to Irish citizenship. The Latours might think that since most of their income is derived from Laura's holdings and most of their assets are owned by her, it is sufficient for Laura alone to expatriate. Whether or not that makes good sense will depend on the extent to which their assets constitute community property (discussed in Chapter 8 below) and the way each of them plans to pass on his or her estate at death.

I have included some basic information about the possibility of acquiring citizenship and a passport in many of the countries discussed in Part VI. For additional information, read the latest edition of *The Passport Report*, published by Scope International.

7. RELINQUISH YOUR PRESENT NATIONALITY

If you abandon your present country's nationality, you should theoretically be treated by that country the same as it treats any other alien. However, legislation designed to discourage you from leaving may make things more difficult for you. This chapter has been revised from last year's edition to reflect new US legislation discussed in the *1997 Update* at the end of the chapter.

If you are a citizen of one of the countries mentioned in the preceding chapter, you may have to relinquish your present nationality in order to become a tax exile. I have had no experience with people abandoning citizenship in any of the countries listed other than the US. I suspect that few do so because they are able to find ways to circumvent the attempts by their governments to tax them based upon citizenship. The specific rules concerning abandonment of US citizenship and the impact of the US anti-expatriation rules are discussed in Chapters 20 to 23 below.

An individual who wants to become a tax exile is generally prepared to live overseas. In order for an American citizen to become a tax exile, however, he must also give up his US citizenship. I generally find that an American who has lived abroad for several years is more likely to consider relinquishing US citizenship than one still living in the US. For most Americans, giving up citizenship is a very traumatic act.

VISITS TO AMERICA BY EXPATRIATES

I am frequently asked whether an expatriate American can still travel to the US and whether he can ever recover his citizenship if he changes his mind. In my experience, an American such as Larry Latour who voluntarily relinquishes his US citizenship can obtain a multiple entry B-1/B-2 visa permitting him to visit the US for pleasure or for business. This is the typical visa held by many foreigners.

Some American consuls take away the individual's US passport at the time an oath of renunciation is signed. Others do not do so until the State Department approves the consul's action. This generally takes about six weeks, but I have seen cases where it has taken much longer.

At one time it was possible for an American relinquishing citizenship to acquire a US multiple entry visa the same day. This is generally no longer the case. American consuls now routinely delay issuance of a visa until after the State Department in Washington has approved the *Certificate of Loss of Nationality* prepared by the consul. The theory is that the individual relinquishing his citizenship remains an American citizen until the State Department approves the consul's action. Since he is still a US citizen, he is not entitled to receive a nonimmigrant visa. Once the State Department has approved the loss of nationality, it has been reasonably routine for the former citizen to be granted a ten-year multiple entry visa, the maximum that is now given to any foreign person.

RECOVERING YOUR CITIZENSHIP IS DIFFICULT

Recovering US citizenship is difficult and may be impossible. Some of those who lost their citizenship by committing acts of expatriation that are no longer treated as such may now be able to recover their citizenship. Those who lost their citizenship by obtaining another nationality or signing an oath of allegiance to a foreign country may be able to set aside the expatriation if the State Department's file does not clearly show that the American intended to lose his nationality at the time he committed the act of expatriation. Today, however, an American consul will not sign the papers unless there is either a voluntary renunciation or clear evidence that some other act of expatriation was committed with the intent to lose citizenship. With these records sitting in your permanent file at the State Department you are not likely to be able to overturn any expatriation carried out today.

REESTABLISHING YOUR RESIDENCY SHOULD BE EASIER

If you have a child over the age of 21 who remains a US citizen, that child can sponsor you for a green card. You could then enter the US as a resident alien and could become a naturalized US citizen after five years of residence in the US. Since Larry and Laura Latour both have adult children who will remain US citizens they should be able to obtain green cards if they ever decide they want to move back to America. After they have held green cards for five years, they could apply for US citizenship.

1997 UPDATE

Significant new US legislation was enacted during 1996. Revised expatriation tax rules were enacted in August 1996, retroactive to February 1995. An immigration law amendment authorizes the US Attorney General to treat an individual who renounces citizenship to avoid taxes as excludable. These rules are discussed in Chapter 21 below.

8. COPE WITH COMMUNITY PROPERTY RULES

Nine US states and many foreign countries have community property laws that may affect the assets and income of married persons. These laws may make it difficult for one spouse to benefit from a change in status if the other spouse does not make the same change, but they also present planning opportunities. This chapter is unchanged from last year's edition.

Your marital status can affect your tax position in several different ways. One of the most significant of these is the *community property* rules that affect persons who live or have lived in certain US states or in some foreign countries. The nine US states that recognize community property are:

- Arizona
- California
- Idaho
- Louisiana
- Nevada
- New Mexico
- Texas
- Washington
- Wisconsin

THE IMPACT OF COMMUNITY PROPERTY RULES

In a US court case discussed later in this report, William Dillin and his wife, Patrea, both moved from Texas, a community property state, to the Bahamas, which does not follow the community property system. William gave up his US citizenship; Patrea retained hers. William later received income that he had earned in an earlier year when they were still living in Texas. The court agreed with the taxpayers that the income was not taxable until it was received. The judge ruled, however, that under Texas community property law Patrea had a vested interest in that income from the time it was earned. She was taxable as a US citizen on her half of the income when it was received. See Chapter 22 below for a further discussion of the Dillin case.

Larry and Laura Latour may have similar problems since they are from California which is also a community property state. The easiest way for them to avoid future problems is for both of them to take the same action. If one of them gives up US citizenship, the other should do so too. If one of them changes domicile, the other should do the same. They should also determine at the outset whether the new country to which they plan to move follows the community property system, and they should find out the ongoing effects of their marriage in California under that state's community property rules.

Some community property jurisdictions, like Texas, permit a husband and wife to agree on a separation of some or all of their assets and income. Some of these places have a public policy that permits such an agreement only if it is signed before the marriage. A few places don't permit a separation of assets either before or after the marriage.

TAKING ADVANTAGE OF THE RULES

The community property rules can sometimes work to your advantage. Some US tax attributes of the community property rules seem strange. Take, for example, a situation involving *Paul and Polly Pommard*. They are US citizens, resident and domiciled in Texas, were married there, and all of their assets are community property. The Pommards have no children and the first of them to die plans to leave everything to the survivor. Their principal asset is a portfolio of stocks that has a $2 million cost basis and is now worth $20 million.

The Pommards want to become tax exiles but if they sell their stock portfolio they would have to pay 28 percent tax on the $18 million gain, a tax of more than $5 million. Instead, they obtain a second nationality and move abroad, but they keep their US citizenship and their Texas domicile. Paul dies. Since Polly is still a US citizen, there is an unlimited marital deduction and no US estate tax on Paul's estate. According to US tax law, when one spouse dies owning community property, the *entire* amount of community property owned by the couple is treated as property acquired from the one who died. The Pommards' entire $20 million stock portfolio (not just Paul's half) gets a new stepped-up basis equal to the fair market value of the stocks on the date Paul died. Polly promptly sells the entire portfolio without any US capital gains tax and acquires a portfolio of foreign securities. She then expatriates and abandons her Texas domicile so there won't be any estate tax on her death either. This is one example of the *ultimate estate plan*.

9. CHANGE THE SOURCES OF YOUR INCOME

Most countries impose income tax on income and gains derived from sources within the country even by nonresidents. With proper planning it may be possible to derive a greater portion of your income and gains from sources outside that country. This chapter has been revised from last year's edition to reflect new US legislation discussed in the *1997 Update* at the end of the chapter.

Most high-tax countries tax income derived from local sources no matter who earns it. Giving up residence, domicile and even citizenship does not eliminate your taxes if your income comes from sources in that country. Moreover, many high-tax countries take a fairly aggressive stance in determining whether income is from local sources. You and your advisers have to examine a country's source rules and make sure that most or all of the income you expect to receive will be treated as coming from sources outside the high-tax country. The goal of a tax exile is to convert income coming from a high-tax country to income that will come from a country that will not tax the income at its source.

SOURCE RULES ARE THE KEY

Let us take a brief look at the source of several different types of income under US rules and what Larry and Laura Latour can do to prevent US taxation of their income after they become tax exiles. The key is for them to have foreign-source income under US source rules. We assume that they have stocks (that produce dividends and capital gains) and some bank accounts and bonds (that produce interest). They also have some income-producing real estate (that generates rents and hopefully some capital gains). Larry Latour does some consulting (that produces income from personal services) and free-lance writing (that generates royalties). Finally, Larry Latour has a large pension that has been rolled over into an *individual retirement account (IRA)*.

LOOKING AT DIFFERENT TYPES OF INCOME

Each of these types of income presents a different problem:
*   *Dividends*. A dividend paid by a company incorporated in the US is from US sources and is taxable. A dividend paid by a company incorporated in a foreign country is usually from foreign sources and is not subject to US income tax when earned by a foreign person. The Latours may want to dispose of some of their US stocks and replace them with comparable foreign stocks from countries in which they will not be subject to high rates of withholding tax.
*   *Capital Gains From Securities*. A capital gain derived by a nonresident alien from selling stocks or bonds issued by a US corporation is normally tax-free unless the

corporation primarily owns US real estate. However, such gains may be taxable to tax-motivated expatriates. This provides another reason for the Latours to replace their US securities with comparable foreign ones.

- *Interest from Bank Accounts.* Many high-tax countries do not tax interest paid by banks to qualified nonresidents. The US has such a rule for interest paid by US banks to nonresident aliens, but the exemption may not extend to tax-motivated expatriates; they may be covered for ten years by the US anti-expatriation rules. Thus, the Latours should replace any US bank account with a comparable account in a foreign bank or with the foreign branch of a US bank.

- *Interest on Bonds.* Notes, bonds and other debt instruments issued by the US government and by US residents (including foreign corporations doing business in the US) produce interest from US sources. Those issued by foreign governments and by nonresidents produce interest from foreign sources that is not taxable when paid to foreign persons. The US and several other high-tax countries exempt *portfolio* interest on bonds and notes paid to foreign investors who are not also significant shareholders in the company paying the interest. The US exemption may not apply to the Latours if they are treated as tax-motivated expatriates, so they should switch to bonds and notes issued by foreign governments and foreign companies. They should also get rid of their US tax-free municipal bonds for reasons discussed in the next chapter.

- *Rents.* Income derived from renting real estate is likely to be taxable in most countries other than pure tax havens. The US would tax such rents whether they are paid to an American or a foreigner.

- *Capital Gains From Real Estate.* Gains from the sale of real estate are taxed by most countries whether the property is sold by residents or nonresidents. The US taxes all foreigners the same as Americans on their gains from selling US real estate.

- *Consulting Fees.* Income derived from performing personal services such as consulting is treated as income from US sources if the services are performed in the US. It is foreign-source income if the services are performed outside the US. The place where payment is made and the status of the payer are not material in the US although they may be in other countries. As a tax exile, Larry Latour should perform all of his consulting services outside the US, preferably in countries that will not highly tax such services.

- *Royalties.* Many countries tax all royalties paid by a resident to anyone anywhere. They impose a withholding tax on royalties paid to foreign persons, but tax treaties often reduce or eliminate the withholding tax on royalties paid to foreign persons. If the income derived by Larry Latour for his free-lance writing is really a "royalty," he may be able to reduce the tax by using a company based in a treaty country. If the copyrights on his publications are owned by the publisher rather than by Latour, he should be able to treat the income as *personal service income* rather than a royalty, making it non-taxable if he wrote the publications outside the US.

- *Pension Income.* Income derived from a qualified pension or profit sharing plan, or from an *individual retirement account (IRA)* into which the plan proceeds have been rolled over, may be subject to several types of tax when it is withdrawn. Most such income is ordinary income when it is taken out, either in a lump sum or in periodic payments. There may be a withholding tax when payments are made abroad to assure collection of the tax that is due. In addition to full regular tax, there may be an additional ten percent income tax for early withdrawal (before age 59 1/2) or a 15 percent penalty excise tax if benefits exceed $150,000 a year. If Larry Latour has to pay federal and California taxes, plus an additional ten or 15 percent tax, he will be paying over 60 percent tax on that income. Treaty relief may be possible, depending on his age and other factors. If so, it may dictate where he should become resident. He must review this situation carefully with his professional advisers.

In general, the Latours will find it advantageous to derive most of their income from foreign sources rather than from US sources. When they are no longer at risk under the anti-expatriation rules, they can reacquire US bank accounts and bonds that produce tax-exempt *portfolio interest*.

1997 UPDATE

Some US legislation enacted during 1996 has affected the rules discussed in this chapter. Revised expatriation tax rules were enacted in August 1996, retroactive to February 1995. These rules change some foreign-source income into taxable US-source income when derived by an expatriate. These rules also override conflicting tax treaties. Separate legislation has temporarily suspended the 15 percent excise tax on pension benefits exceeding $150,000 a year.

10. CHANGE THE LOCATION OF YOUR ASSETS

Many countries impose estate or inheritance taxes on property situated in the country even if owned by nonresidents. Although you cannot move real estate, you may be able to change the situs of personal property. This chapter is unchanged from last year's edition.

The location of your assets may determine whether they are subject to capital transfer taxes such as the estate and gift taxes. A US citizen or domiciliary is subject to these taxes on all transfers he makes no matter where the property is located. However, a non-domiciled alien is subject to these taxes only on property located in the US. With minor exceptions this rule extends to a tax-motivated expatriate.

SITUS RULES ARE THE KEY

Larry and Laura Latour will find that if they have made the changes in the source of their income suggested in the preceding chapter they have probably also changed the location of many of their assets to what they should be. For example, the stock of a foreign corporation that produces foreign-source dividends will normally be a foreign asset. However, a tax-motivated expatriate may be taxed on his share of the US assets owned by a foreign corporation if certain ownership tests are met. Foreign bonds and foreign bank accounts are foreign assets. Foreign real estate is also a foreign asset for transfer tax purposes.

TRY TO OWN ONLY FOREIGN ASSETS

In general, the Latours will find it advantageous to own only foreign assets. They should keep their gold, jewelry, antiques, art and other personal property outside the US. They should not keep large amounts of US dollars or foreign currency in the US. They should not keep their US tax-free municipal bonds because such bonds are tax-free only for income tax purposes, not for estate and gift tax purposes. They should not be partners in partnerships that own US property nor should they do business in the US. They should be able to retain their US life insurance policies. When they are no longer at risk under the anti-expatriation rules, they can reacquire some US bank accounts and bonds and own other US assets, such as stock and real estate, through a foreign corporation that will then shield them from the estate tax.

11. WATCH YOUR TIMING

Any time you plan to change your status as a taxpayer you and your professional advisers have to consider whether to do certain things before or after your change in status. This chapter has been revised from last year's edition to reflect new US legislation discussed under *Revised Rules Block Transfers After Leaving* and in the *1997 Update* at the end of the chapter.

When an asset is sold and when income is generated may determine whether or not it is taxed and how it is taxed. For example, if an individual receives income *before* he becomes a tax exile he will be fully taxed on that income. If, like most Americans, he reports his income on a cash basis he is not taxed on that income until he receives it even if he earned it in a prior year. If the income is from foreign sources and it is not received until after he is no longer a US taxpayer, the income will not be taxed. However, some items of income may be considered to be constructively received before they are actually received if the income is available without restriction at an earlier time. Here are some things that Larry and Laura Latour should do with respect to timing.

SELL PRINCIPAL HOME BEFORE LEAVING

The Latours should sell their principal residence in the US *before* they become tax exiles. Tax on the capital gain from selling their principal residence is postponed for up to four years if the sale is made by an American citizen who moves abroad. The gain is not taxed if the proceeds are reinvested within the four-year period in a new principal residence even if it is located abroad. If the home was sold after they were no longer Americans the gain would be fully taxed immediately. Similar rules have applied to a resident alien who sold his principal residence before moving abroad and giving up his green card.

REVISED RULES BLOCK TRANSFERS AFTER LEAVING

In prior editions of this report, I recommended that the Latours transfer their US securities (at least those on which there was a gain) to a foreign holding company in exchange for the shares of that foreign corporation *after* they were no longer Americans. If they did so before leaving, they would either be subject to an immediate capital gain or they would have had to pay a 35 percent penalty excise tax on the appreciated value of the securities. If they were considered tax-motivated expatriates they would be taxed on the sale of shares of the foreign holding company if they sold those shares within ten years. However, neither they nor the foreign holding company would be taxable on any gain when the foreign holding company subsequently sold the US securities it acquired from them. I used the following example to illustrate this:

Laura Latour owns 1,000 shares each of General Motors, IBM and Texaco, all US companies. *After expatriation*, when she is no longer either a US citizen or resident, she transfers this portfolio of stock to *Latour Limited*, a new Cayman Islands holding company, in exchange for the shares of the Cayman company. If she is still a US taxpayer, this transaction may require a notice to the IRS but it should have no unfavorable tax consequences if she has not already borrowed against the stock. She then owns Latour Limited which in turn owns the stock portfolio. Next, Latour Limited sells the GM, IBM and Texaco shares and uses the proceeds to buy foreign shares in companies such as Fiat, Siemens and Shell Oil. Even if Laura Latour is considered to be a tax-motivated expatriate, there is apparently no US tax on the gains or income derived by Latour Limited. However, Laura Latour would be taxable if she liquidated Latour Limited or sold her shares in that holding company within ten years following her expatriation.

The foregoing example worked for those who expatriated before 6 February 1995. It does not work for any citizen or long-term resident who expatriated on or after that date.

If the Latours have existing interests in foreign corporations which they control they should avoid selling their shares or liquidating any of these foreign corporations until *after* they are no longer Americans.

THE TIMING OF GIFTS IS CRITICAL

The timing of any gifts between Larry and Laura Latour or from either of them to their children is also critical. Gifts of US property between them are tax-free if made *before* expatriation but may be taxable if made later. If they plan to make large gifts of foreign property to their children this should be done *after* expatriation.

It should be apparent from the foregoing illustrations that careful timing is essential. All transactions should be reviewed on an item-by-item basis with your tax adviser. Due consideration should be given to the existing rules and to changes that may be made by new legislation.

If you compare the results of the *Kronenberg* and *Furstenberg* cases, both of which are discussed in Chapter 22 below, you will find that Max Kronenberg was treated as a *tax-motivated expatriate* because his timing was too perfect not to have been planned for tax-avoidance reasons. On the other hand, Princess von Furstenberg was not treated as a tax-motivated expatriate because her timing of certain transactions was considered too imperfect to have been planned for tax reasons. Both of them might have avoided the timing issue entirely if they had followed a different tax plan.

1997 UPDATE

Some US legislation enacted during 1996 has affected the rules discussed in this chapter. Revised expatriation tax rules were enacted in August 1996, retroactive to February 1995. As noted above, these revised rules have blocked the tax-free transfer by an expatriate of US securities into a foreign corporation. However, as noted in Chapter 21 below, there are new and different loopholes in the revised expatriation tax rules and these should be explored with your tax adviser.

12. PLAN FOR BENEFICIARIES
WHO REMAIN BEHIND

Special problems may arise if you become a tax exile and some or all of your beneficiaries remain in the country you have left. You must assume that the country you left will try to find some way of collecting taxes from your heirs and beneficiaries that you might otherwise have escaped. This chapter is basically unchanged from last year's edition, but one new item is discussed in the *1997 Update* at the end of the chapter.

It is unusual for all members of a family to become tax exiles. More typically, one or two people leave and the others remain behind. As already noted in Chapter 8 above, this can cause special difficulties in the case of a married couple if one spouse leaves and the other does not. In addition, however, the plan is likely to be closely examined by the tax authorities of the high-tax country when children and grandchildren who remain behind suddenly inherit great wealth from their parents.

THE REVENUE MAY MONITOR YOUR ACTIVITIES

If you are very wealthy, the revenue authorities of the high-tax country you are leaving may continue to follow your activities with great interest for the rest of your life. They may wait until you die to reassess the situation. Using hindsight, they can determine whether you really changed your residence or your domicile or whether you simply wandered around from place to place as a *perpetual tourist (PT)*. They may then go after your estate or they may seek to impose transferee liability on your children and others who have inherited from you.

Take the case of the late *Sir Charles Clore* who moved from Britain to Monaco in 1977 to escape confiscatory 98 percent income taxes then imposed in Britain. He visited Britain as often as he could and he also traveled extensively to other countries. He died abroad in 1979 and the UK Inland Revenue went after his estate, claiming that he had never really changed his domicile to Monaco. After years of litigation the UK government ended up with £67 million, over half of his estate.

TRANSFEREES MAY BECOME LIABLE FOR TAX

In some countries, including the US, the estate tax and the gift tax are imposed on those who make the transfer. The tax is assessed against the one who dies or the one who makes the gift. Under this system, the status of the individual receiving the inheritance or the gift is not material. However, even under this system, the one receiving the inheritance or the gift may be secondarily liable for the tax if it should have been paid by the transferor. If you are not careful the government may seek to impose such transferee liability on your heirs.

In other countries, such as Japan, the situation is reversed. There the tax is assessed against the one receiving the gift or inheritance. Planning under such circumstances must be done quite differently. A few countries combine the two systems, imposing the tax if either the transferor or the transferee is resident. That makes planning much more difficult.

A prominent US bar association committee has suggested to the US Treasury that one way to put some teeth into the anti-expatriation rules would be to enact a new law that would deny a step-up in basis for assets inherited by children from a parent who has expatriated. A proposal approved by the Senate in 1995, but rejected by a conference committee, would have treated gifts and inheritances received by a US citizen or resident alien from certain expatriates as taxable income. It would not shock me to see one of these recommendations implemented if Treasury ever felt that it was losing too much revenue to successful tax exiles.

Larry and Laura Latour should explore with their advisers what may happen when their children and grandchildren eventually inherit from them. Under present law, there is not much that the government can do if the Latours have carefully taken all of the steps necessary to change their residence, their domicile and their nationality. The Latours should make sure that their advisers and their children can prove that everything necessary was done properly. Otherwise, their descendants may someday face huge bills for estate tax and generation-skipping transfer tax, plus penalties and interest.

1997 UPDATE

New US legislation enacted during 1996 requires a US citizen or resident to report the receipt of any gifts or inheritances exceeding $10,000 a year from any nonresident alien. This will give the IRS an opportunity, for example, to determine whether the transferor was really a non-domiciled alien.

13. AVOID YOUR COUNTRY'S ANTI-DEPARTURE RULES

Some countries have special legislation designed to discourage their wealthy taxpayers from emigrating. If your country is one of them, you will have to take this legislation into account if you plan to expatriate. Despite all of the publicity concerning wealthy Americans who have expatriated, official figures show that fewer than 1,000 Americans give up their citizenship each year. This chapter has been revised from last year's edition to reflect the recent enactment of revised US expatriation tax rules.

Some countries have specific laws designed to inhibit taxpayers from leaving. Other countries simply apply their normal rules. Thus, for example, the fact that Britain had no specific anti-avoidance rules didn't stop Inland Revenue from assessing huge taxes against the estate of the late *Sir Charles Clore* on the theory that he had not really changed his residence and domicile sufficiently to escape UK taxes.

DIFFERENT KINDS OF RULES

Canada has a departure tax; the US has until now taken a different approach. The US seeks to impose some of its taxes for ten years against a former citizen who the IRS claims has expatriated to avoid taxes. There is a reason why the US chose this cumbersome approach instead of a simpler departure tax. Blame it on the former Soviet Union. During 1965 and 1966, the *Foreign Investors Tax Act* was working its way through the US Congress. Some Congressmen were afraid that its benefits for nonresident aliens would be so great that some Americans might choose to become nonresident aliens just to get those tax benefits. A departure tax was suggested under which an American would have had to pay a capital gains tax on all of his appreciated assets in order to escape. The problem was that the USSR imposed a departure tax on dissidents who sought to emigrate from the Soviet Union. The US criticized the USSR departure tax as a device to prevent Soviet citizens from emigrating. It was politically unacceptable for Congress to impose a "departure tax" on Americans while attacking the Soviet Union for imposing a similar tax. Someone dreamt up the anti-expatriation rules as another way of accomplishing the same goal without the political flak.

CANADA'S DEPARTURE TAX

Canada's departure tax is imposed on anyone who has been a resident of Canada for income tax purposes for 60 months out of the previous ten years. He is treated as having sold all of his non-Canadian assets just before he left and he pays a capital gains tax on the resulting gain. Having done so, he is free to leave and he is thereafter treated as a nonresident if he acts like one.

Canada has reduced the period of time required for a new resident to obtain Canadian citizenship from five to three years. It is therefore possible for a newcomer to become resident in Canada for more than three but less than five years during which he can become a Canadian citizen. He can then move to some exotic tax haven and never again have to worry about Canadian taxes.

Other countries with departure taxes include Denmark and Germany. The application of Germany's *Aussensteuergesetz (Foreign Tax Law)* is discussed briefly in Chapter 27 below. Denmark has a departure tax on some securities owned by Danish residents who leave. It also continues to tax for up to four years former Danish permanent residents who have moved to a country with less onerous taxes.

FEW AMERICANS ABANDON THEIR CITIZENSHIP

Some years ago Professor Harvey Dale obtained figures from the US State Department under the *Freedom of Information Act (FOIA)* which indicated that about 350 Americans terminated their US citizenship each year. My law firm filed a FOIA request for more current data in 1991. At that time, the State Department was unable to find the information. Much to my surprise, in July 1994, about three years after the original request was made, we received a response. It contained a table of *Naturalizations and Renunciations 1962-92* with some handwritten figures for 1993. This table is reproduced at the end of this chapter. There was no explanation of the table or its contents, so I have had to make certain assumptions. First, the number of naturalizations is far too small to be persons naturalized in the US; it must therefore be the number of individuals who lost their US citizenship by voluntary naturalization in a foreign country with the requisite intent to lose US nationality. Second, I suspect that the figures may cover government fiscal years which end on 30 September, rather than calendar years. Thus, the 306 individuals who reportedly renounced US citizenship in 1993 may not include those who did so during October through December of that year. This could be significant since most people who renounce tend to do so late in the year. If my supposition is correct, the real figures tend to run a year behind. In any event, here are some conclusions that I have drawn from the table:

- Over the entire 32-year period from 1962-93, an average of just under 1,000 individuals lost US citizenship each year. Over two-thirds of them did so by voluntary naturalization in another country; less than a third did so by formal renunciation.
- The numbers in both categories were significantly higher during the 20 years from 1962-81 than they were during more recent years. During the most recent 12-year period from 1982-93, the combined average of naturalizations and renunciations was down to about 313 per year (about 195 voluntary naturalizations and 118 renunciations a year).

Later information is now also available and it is generally consistent with the earlier data. The staff of the Joint Committee on Taxation issued a 500-page report to Congress in June 1995 entitled Issues Presented by Proposals to Modify the Tax Treatment of

Expatriation. An appendix to the report names all of the persons who received certificates of loss of nationality from the State Department during 1994 and the first few months of 1995.

US EXPATRIATION TAX RULES REVISED

Revised US expatriation tax rules were enacted in August 1996, retroactive to February 1995. For details, see Chapter 21 below.

TABLE OF NATURALIZATIONS AND RENUNCIATIONS

Set forth below is a table of *Naturalizations and Renunciations 1962-1992* with handwritten figures for 1993 that we obtained from the State Department under the Freedom of Information Act. The table was discussed earlier in this chapter.

Year	Naturalizations	Renunciations	Year	Naturalizations	Renunciations
1962	561	746	1978	1482	271
1963	611	649	1979	779	167
1964	755	615	1980	812	307
1965	586	675	1981	1100	346
1966	608	740	1982	50	0
1967	486	450	1983	82	3
1968	1241	466	1984	130	4
1969	573	431	1985	168	11
1970	1607	494	1986	233	165
1971	972	451	1987	296	126
1972	1036	474	1988	285	90
1973	846	331	1989	301	174
1974	1256	300	1990	206	140
1975	1308	204	1991	206	240
1976	1620	260	1992	114	157
1977	1267	237	1993	263	306

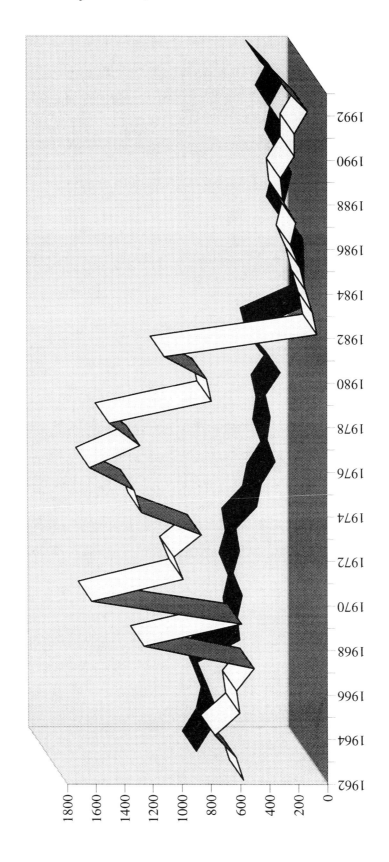

NATURALIZATIONS & RENUNCIATIONS, 1962 - 1993

compiled by Fred Smith

□ Naturalizations ■ Renunciations

60

14. CHOOSE BETWEEN BECOMING A *PT* OR MOVING TO A NEW COUNTRY

For reasons set forth throughout this report, I believe you would be much better off moving to another country than you would be trying to become a *perpetual tourist* (PT). This chapter is unchanged from last year's edition.

Some advisers suggest that the best way to escape from big brother's tax clutches is to become a low-profile *perpetual tourist (PT)*. I disagree. That may have worked well in the pre-computer days when people could simply disappear from the system never to surface again. Today, if you are a significant taxpayer in any high-tax country, the government's computers should quickly notice your absence. The tax authorities may simply monitor your situation on an ongoing basis, waiting for the right time to pounce. If you review some of the court cases discussed in various parts of this report, you will see several examples of former taxpayers whose absence was noticed and whose tax plans were subsequently attacked.

LOOK FOR A HOSPITABLE NEW COUNTRY

It is very difficult to become a true *PT* in today's computerized world. If you move from a high-tax country to a tax haven such as the Cayman Islands everyone will know exactly what you have done. If, on the other hand, you move from one high-tax country to another high-tax country you may not be watched nearly as closely. As you will see from a careful reading of Part VI of this report (Chapters 36 to 64), some high-tax countries treat newcomers rather well. I suggest that you consider establishing a new homeland in a hospitable high-tax country rather than moving to a notorious tax haven or wandering from place to place as a *PT*.

LOOKING AHEAD

Now that we have explored *The Basics in Part I and Overcoming the Tax Octopus* in this part, we will move on to explain the *US Rules* in Part III. After that we will examine the consequences of *Leaving* various high-tax countries (Part IV), discuss *Choosing New Home Countries* (Part V) and try to find *Suitable Countries for Your Residence, Domicile, Citizenship and Passports* (Part VI). Finally, in Part VII, we will try to answer your most important question: *Should You Become a Tax Exile?*

PART III

EXPLAINING THE *US* RULES

15. *US* RESIDENCY RULES

With limited exceptions, you become a US resident for income tax purposes if you have a *green card* or you spend an average of over four months a year in the US. This makes you fully subject to US income tax on your worldwide income. This chapter is basically unchanged from last year's edition, but the impact of the revised expatriation rules on long-term residents who abandon green cards is discussed in the *1997 Update* at the end of the chapter.

In later parts of this report, I will discuss the status of tax exiles leaving several high-tax countries and moving to a number of countries where they may find their situation more tolerable. The US rules concerning residency, domicile, citizenship and expatriation are considerably more complex than those of some other countries. In this part, I will try to give you a basic explanation of these US rules. If you are not interested in the US rules, you can skip ahead to Part IV, *A Tax Exile Leaves Home*.

DEFINITION OF RESIDENT ALIEN

Since 1985, US income tax law provides an objective definition of *resident alien*. As a result, there is now some certainty as to whether any individual is a resident alien or a nonresident alien for income tax purposes. If you are neither a US citizen nor a US resident under the new definition, you are a nonresident alien. The new definition of resident alien applies only to the income tax and does not affect whether you are a US domiciliary for estate and gift tax purposes. For income tax purposes, the residence status of each family member is determined separately. It is therefore possible for one spouse to be a resident alien and for the other to be a nonresident alien. Tax treaties may change these rules. For details, consult your tax adviser.

Two basic tests are applied to determine whether an alien individual is a US resident for any particular calendar year. They are called the *green card test* and the *substantial presence test*. Typically, only one of the two tests is material to any individual. An alien individual who is a *lawful permanent resident* under the immigration laws is automatically a resident alien under the green card test. An alien individual present under a non-immigrant visa (such as a B-1/B-2 visa) is subject to the substantial presence test, an objective test based on the time he spends in the US. It is a complex test with exceptions, and with exceptions to the exceptions.

LAWFUL PERMANENT RESIDENT DEFINED

An alien is a *lawful permanent resident* if he has been granted the privilege of residing permanently in the US as an immigrant under the immigration laws. Once obtained, that status continues indefinitely unless it is revoked or abandoned. Voluntary abandonment does not count unless there is an administrative or judicial determination of abandonment. A lawful permanent resident holds a *green card* and is subject to the *green card test* described below.

THE GREEN CARD TEST

The holder of a green card is automatically a resident alien for US income tax purposes, regardless of how few days a year he spends in the US. A green card is an alien registration receipt card (Immigration Form I-551) given to a lawful permanent resident of the US as a receipt for his immigrant visa. An alien individual who immigrates to the US enters the country on an immigrant visa issued by a US consul. Upon entry, the immigrant visa is taken from him and kept in his permanent file. In due course he is given a green card and uses it to prove that he is a lawful permanent resident. The green card used to be green. At present, mostly white and blue, it is still called a green card.

The holder of a green card is really supposed to live in the US. He can do almost everything a US citizen can do except vote. He can work without a permit and he can freely leave and reenter the country. If you had a green card before 1985 and you have continued to hold it, you are a resident alien for income tax purposes for all years since 1985, even if you did not live in the US or visit there.

IRS RULES FOR GREEN CARD APPLICANTS

A 1986 law and proposed IRS regulations require all persons filing applications for green cards after 1989 to answer certain questions relating to their tax liability. The Immigration and Naturalization Service (INS) must pass this information on to the IRS. In addition to routine identifying information, the immigration applicant must answer these questions *for each of his three most recent years*:
- Did he have any *US-source income*?
- Was he present in the US for *more than 182 days*?
- Was he *required to file* a federal income tax return?
- If so, *was it filed* and, if not, why not?

The new rules are intended to improve tax compliance by resident aliens. Similar questions will be asked of US citizens who file passport applications.

THE SUBSTANTIAL PRESENCE TEST

The substantial presence test applies to those alien individuals who are not lawful permanent residents, that is, who do not have green cards. It is a mathematical test. Although it refers to 183 days, it does not mean 183 days during any one calendar year. It is based on the number of days (other than excluded days) spent in the US during the most recent three-year period. The test is weighted quite heavily toward the latest year.

There are several circumstances under which you can exclude days so they will not count as days spent in the US. These may make it possible for you to avoid the impact of the substantial presence test notwithstanding the time you actually spend in the US. Thus:

- You don't count a day if you were unable to leave the US that day because of a *medical condition* that arose while you were present in the US. This exclusion is strictly construed by the IRS.

- You don't count a day if you were a qualified student, teacher, trainee or foreign government-related individual (such as a full-time diplomat or consul) for that day. As a result of a *"technical correction"* introduced in 1986 by then Senator (later Vice President) Dan Quayle, a professional athlete is also exempt on any day on which he is temporarily in the US to compete in a charitable sports event.

- If you live in either Canada or Mexico and regularly commute to work in the US, you don't count days on which you commute.

- If you are in *transit* between two foreign points, and you are physically present in the US for less than 24 hours, you don't count any day during such transit.

In counting days that are not excluded, you are treated as present in the US on a day if you are physically present in the US at any time during a calendar day. After eliminating excluded days, you count the remaining days you spend in the US during the current year, plus one-third of the days spent last year, and one-sixth of the days spent the year before. Here are two examples:

1. Robert Riesling spends exactly 120 days in the US in each of the years 1994, 1995 and 1996. In determining his status for the year 1996, he counts all 120 days spent in the US during 1996, plus one-third of the 120 days he spent in the US during 1995 (40 days), and one-sixth of the 120 days he spent in the US during 1994 (20 days). The total of 120+40+20 equals 180 days which is less than 183 days. Riesling does not meet the substantial presence test and he is a nonresident alien for 1996. He is in the green zone.

2. Riesling's wife, Rita, is present exactly 122 days in each of the years 1994, 1995 and 1996. She counts 122 days for the year 1996, one-third of 122 days in 1995 (40$\frac{2}{3}$ days), and one-sixth of 122 days for the year 1994 (20$\frac{1}{3}$ days). The total of 122+40 2/3+20$\frac{1}{3}$ equals 183 days. Since the number of days equals or exceeds 183 days, Rita Riesling meets the substantial presence test and she is a resident alien for income tax purposes for the year 1996 unless one of the exceptions discussed below applies. She is in the *amber zone*.

SUBSTANTIAL PRESENCE PRESUMES RESIDENCE

If you are an alien individual without a green card and you do not meet the substantial presence test for the current year, you are a nonresident alien for that year. If you are an alien individual with no green card but you do meet the substantial presence test for the current year, you are presumed to be a resident alien for that year. Whether you can rebut that presumption depends on these rules:

- If you are in the US for less than 31 days during the current year (after eliminating excluded days), you are exempt from the substantial presence test for that year even if the three-year total would otherwise meet the substantial presence test. That could happen if you were present in the US during most or all of the two preceding years. You are in the *green zone.*
- If you are actually in the US for more than 182 days during the current year (not counting excluded days), you are automatically a resident alien for income tax purposes for that year. You are in the *red zone.*
- If you are in the amber zone and you can't prove to the IRS that you have a *tax home* in a foreign country and a *closer connection* to that country than to the US, you are a resident for that year.
- If you are in the *amber zone* and you have an application pending with the Immigration Service for adjustment of status, or you have taken other steps to apply for status as a lawful permanent resident of the US, you are automatically resident for the current year once you meet the substantial presence test. You are precluded from trying to prove that you have a tax home in and a closer connection to a foreign country.
- If you are in the *amber zone* and you can prove that you have a tax home in a foreign country and a closer connection to that foreign country, you may escape being a resident alien even though you meet the substantial presence test. This does not work if you are actually present in the US for more than 182 days in the current year or you have an application pending for a green card.

DUAL-STATUS YEARS

There are special rules for the first and last years of residency. These rules make it possible for an alien individual to have dual-status years.

First Year. If you are a resident alien this year, but you were not a resident alien at any time last year, you are resident only for that part of this year which begins on the *residency starting date.* If you meet the substantial presence test, your residency starting date is generally the first day this year on which you were in the US. If you acquire a green card, and you do not meet the substantial presence test this year, your residency starting date is the first day this year on which you were in the US while a lawful permanent resident. Thus, if you acquire a green card and enter the US on October 1, 1996, you are a resident alien for the last three months of 1996 no matter how few days you spend in the US during that year.

Last Year. Similarly, if you are a resident alien this year, but you are not a resident alien at any time next year, you are resident only for that part of this year which ends on the last day on which you were a US resident. That is generally either the last day on which you were present in the US or the last day on which you still held a green card, whichever was later. To avoid US residency during the last part of the year, you must prove that you have a closer connection to a foreign country than to the US.

THE TAX HOME/CLOSER CONNECTION EXCEPTION

One way for you to avoid the substantial presence test is for you to prove that during the current year you had a tax home in a foreign country and a closer connection to that foreign country than to the US. Note that the term *tax home* has a peculiar meaning which is discussed below.

The exception from the substantial presence test then applies, but only if you are present in the US fewer than 183 days during the current year. The effect of this rule is that if you are present in the US for more than an average of 121 days per year but are present in the current calendar year for fewer than 183 days, you can exempt yourself from the substantial presence test by proving that you have a tax home in a foreign country and a closer connection to that foreign country. If you are present more than 182 days during the current year, the exception will not apply. You will be resident for that year even if you have a tax home in another country and a closer connection to that foreign country than the US.

TAX HOME DEFINED

Tax home is a confusing term that has nothing to do with where you pay taxes. There is nothing to prevent you from having your tax home in a tax haven such as the Bahamas that does not impose taxes. Your tax home is located at your regular place of business. If you have more than one, it is located at your principal place of business. If you have no regular or principal place of business, your tax home is at your *regular place of abode in a real and substantial sense*. Maintaining a vacation home or temporary abode in the US does not preclude you from having your tax home in a foreign country.

The tax home concept was originally designed to determine when a taxpayer is away from home so as to permit him to deduct business expenses. If he cannot prove that he has a tax home, he is considered to be an itinerant who has his home wherever he happens to be working. He is never away from home and never gets a travel expense deduction. Some foreign persons will have difficulty proving that they have a tax home in a foreign country. A *perpetual tourist (PT)*, for example, will almost never have a tax home.

CLOSER CONNECTION DEFINED

Regulations issued by the IRS list ten specific criteria that should be considered in determining whether you have a closer connection to a foreign country than to the US. The test is based on the facts and circumstances. The criteria to be considered include:
1.   Where is your *permanent home*?
2.   Where is your *family*?

3. Where are your *personal belongings* and those of your family, particularly automobiles, furniture, clothing and jewelry?
4. Where are your current social, political, cultural and religious *organizations*?
5. Where do you conduct your routine personal *banking activities*?
6. Where do you conduct *business activities* other than those that constitute your tax home?
7. Where do you hold a *driver's license*?
8. Where do you *vote*?
9. Which *country of residence* have you designated on forms and documents?
10. What have you stated on *official forms* and documents filed with the IRS?

IRS REPORTING FORMS ISSUED

The IRS issued two new reporting forms in 1994. IRS *Form 8840* must be filed by an alien who meets the substantial presence test but claims that he is a nonresident because he has a closer connection to a foreign country than to the US. IRS *Form 8843* must be filed by an alien who seeks to exclude days of presence in the US because he is a student, teacher or professional athlete, or is receiving medical treatment.

ANTI-AVOIDANCE RULE FOR ALIENS WHO LEAVE

Residence is not carried over from year to year. The objective test is reapplied each year without reference to your status during the preceding year. However, an anti-avoidance rule is designed to prevent a long-time resident alien from disposing of US property tax-free as a nonresident alien before resuming a new period of residence. The rule is patterned after the anti-expatriation rule applied to former US citizens who have abandoned citizenship to avoid taxes. If you are a resident alien for at least three consecutive years, you thereafter become a nonresident alien and once again become a resident alien during one of the next three years, you will be taxable for all intermediate years as though you were a tax-motivated expatriate. This rule was adopted to prevent a long-time resident alien from leaving the US for a short period, disposing of his assets free of US tax, and then resuming US residence. This rule covers only US assets and it would therefore not prevent you from disposing of your foreign assets free of US tax. However, a newer rule aimed at tax-motivated expatriates would prevent you from making a tax-free exchange of US property for foreign property and then selling the foreign property without tax.

UNINTENDED *US* RESIDENCE CAN REALLY HURT

Virtually all of the reported court cases to date dealing with whether a foreigner was a US resident for income tax purposes were decided under pre-1985 law. The rules were then much vaguer than they are today. I suspect, however, that future cases will reach similar results when they deal with foreigners who are in the *amber zone*, averaging between four and six months a year in the US.

A case decided in 1991 illustrates the nightmare you can face if the IRS decides that you are a resident and that you should have been filing US income tax returns. Acting on a tip by an informant who was claiming a reward, the IRS decided in 1988 that Victor Bigio had been a US resident for the years 1981 through 1984. The IRS claimed taxes for these four years totalling over $8 million and another $7 million of penalties, plus an undetermined amount of interest. Apparently fearing that Bigio would dispose of his US assets and leave the country, the IRS began its action by making a *jeopardy assessment* which placed a tax lien on all of his US assets. The case went to the Tax Court and the IRS won [*Victor Bigio v. Commissioner*, Tax Court Memorandum 1991-319 (1991)]. The decision was affirmed on appeal.

Let us look at some of the relevant facts. Bigio had never had an active business in the US but he did have some US investments in securities and commodities. Most of his income came from a very successful family-owned textile business in Colombia. This was foreign-source income but, if he was resident, he was taxable on his worldwide income.

Bigio had been born in England, had been naturalized as a US citizen while he was a child, and had formally renounced his US citizenship in 1965 when he was 45 years old. He thereafter traveled on a British passport and he entered and left the US frequently on a tourist visa. He never overstayed the time granted him by US immigration authorities when he entered and he never asked for an extension. Despite his extensive business operations in Colombia, Bigio was also a tourist there for Colombian immigration purposes. His holding company in Colombia paid income taxes but he did not pay any taxes there personally. Among other things this meant that he had paid no foreign taxes that he could credit against his US income tax liability.

Bigio's condominium apartment in Miami Beach, Florida and some other Florida real estate was nominally owned by a Panamanian corporation, but Judge Swift treated Bigio as the beneficial owner of the real estate. The Miami Beach apartment was available for Bigio's use whether he was there or not. It was not rented out or occupied by others when he was away. He didn't own a house in Colombia, and the one owned by his wife had been leased to tenants.

The Tax Court judge considered it significant that Bigio spent more time each year in the US than he did in other countries, and that his time outside the US was divided among several countries. He also found it important that Bigio did not maintain an abode in any other country.

If you think you might want to spend substantial time in the US as a *perpetual tourist (PT)*, reread this section a couple of times. If you still think it's a good idea, ask your tax adviser for a copy of the Bigio case and others like it that have previously been decided against taxpayers. Read them carefully and then do one of two things: either (1) make sure that you do not have a green card and that you can prove that you spend less than four months each year in the US or (2) spend as much time as you want to in the US, concede that you are probably resident, file US tax returns and pay US income tax.

1997 UPDATE

Revised US expatriation tax rules were enacted in August 1996, retroactive to February 1995. A long-term resident who gives up his green card after holding it for eight out of the most-recent 15 years is now covered by these expatriation tax rules. For details, see Chapter 21 below.

16. *US* DOMICILE RULES

You are fully subject to US federal estate, gift and generation-skipping transfer taxes on your worldwide assets if you are domiciled in the US. You or your estate must prove that your domicile is not in the US if the IRS claims that it is. Your domicile does not affect your status for US federal income tax purposes. This chapter is unchanged from last year's edition.

Domicile is significant in determining whether or not an alien is subject to US estate and gift taxes. The rules determining whether an alien is a nonresident for income tax purposes do not affect his residency for estate and gift tax purposes. Although the US tax law uses the phrase nonresident not a citizen in several sections dealing with estate and gift taxes, it is clear that for these purposes *"nonresident"* means an *individual not domiciled in the United States*. If an alien individual is not domiciled in the US at the time he makes a gift, he is nonresident for federal gift tax purposes. And, if he is domiciled outside the US at the time of his death, he is nonresident for federal estate tax purposes.

EVERYONE MUST HAVE A DOMICILE

US rules generally provide that every individual must have a *domicile*. At birth, a child normally acquires the same domicile as that of his or her father. If father changes his domicile while the child is a minor, the child's domicile will normally follow that of the father. Once the child is an adult, the individual is free to choose his or her own domicile. To effect a change of domicile, there must be physical presence in a new jurisdiction with the intent to make that place his or her home, and with no present intention of departing. Unlike the UK rules, you never revert to your domicile of origin.

A MARRIED WOMAN'S DOMICILE

A married woman traditionally takes the domicile of her husband but she is capable of changing her domicile for some purposes. For example, a woman separated from her husband can establish a separate domicile in a state for the purpose of bringing an action for divorce or dissolution of marriage against her husband. It is not clear that a married woman living with her husband can establish a separate domicile for federal estate and gift tax purposes.

THE TAXPAYER HAS THE BURDEN OF PROOF

Although an individual can have only a single domicile at one time, there have been some well-publicized cases in which several states or countries claimed to be the domicile of the same individual. There is nothing to stop different courts in different places from reaching different decisions as to an individual's domicile as long as there is a reasonable basis on which each court can base its determination. The taxpayer always has the burden of proof in a civil tax case. If you become a tax exile and you hope to avoid US gift and estate taxes, you must be prepared to prove that you were not domiciled in the US at the relevant time. It is harder for a US citizen moving abroad to prove that he has established a new domicile than to prove abandonment of his residency or citizenship. Here are some guidelines:

- If you were born in the US of parents then living in the US your domicile of origin was in the relevant US state. You must prove subsequent changes in domicile from one state to another or from one country to another.
- If you were born outside the US but subsequently moved to America and became a US citizen, you were certainly domiciled in the US at the time you became naturalized; you would have to prove a change to any later foreign domicile.
- If you lived in the US as an alien with a *green card* for any material period of time, you will probably be considered to have been domiciled in the US for that period of time and you would have to prove a later foreign domicile.
- If you were never a US citizen and you never had a *green card*, but you spent a substantial period of time in the US with a nonimmigrant visa, you should be prepared to show that you never took steps that might be used by the IRS to claim that you were domiciled. The US Supreme Court has ruled that it is not impossible for a nonimmigrant alien to be domiciled in the US [*Elkins v. Moreno*, 435 US 647 (1978)]. If you have spent substantial time in the US with a nonimmigrant visa you need professional advice to make sure that you cannot be considered to be domiciled there. The answer may depend on the visa category and its requirements.

PITFALLS FOR A PT

If you leave the US, abandon your residency and your citizenship or *green card*, and take up a new permanent residence in a foreign country, you or your estate must be able to prove the establishment of a new domicile in that country. If, however, you abandon them to become a *perpetual tourist (PT)*, wandering around from place to place with no new permanent home, you run a serious risk that you will still be considered to be domiciled in the US. That, of course, means that your estate will still be liable for confiscatory US estate taxes.

FEDERAL LAW SHOULD CONTROL

It would make better sense if the determination of whether an individual is domiciled in the US for federal estate and gift tax purposes was made under federal law rather than under state law. There should be a uniform rule. There may not be much difference between the laws of the various states on this subject, but there could be. If the federal government doesn't act, some forward-thinking state should take steps to improve the present archaic rules.

SUGGESTED NEW RULES

Congress should examine the entire question of who is domiciled in the US for purposes of the federal estate, gift, and generation-skipping transfer taxes. It should adopt these new rules:

- A married woman should be allowed to choose her own domicile.
- An individual who is a *lawful permanent resident* of the US should be deemed to be domiciled in the US for purposes of these taxes after a specified period of time, except as otherwise provided in a US treaty. At present the holder of a green card may be able to argue successfully that he is resident but not domiciled. Such a dispute can easily involve millions of dollars of potential tax liability and, under present rules, no one can be sure of the outcome. The result could differ depending on whether the alien first moved to New York or to Nevada.
- An individual who is neither a US citizen nor a lawful permanent resident of the US should not be domiciled for purposes of these taxes unless he has been a US resident alien under the *substantial presence* test for eight out of the most recent ten years. This too would provide some certainty.
- If more than one state claims that any individual is domiciled for purposes of state gift, inheritance, estate or generation-skipping transfer taxes, that individual's domicile should be determined by *compulsory arbitration*.

STATES MIGHT ALSO RESOLVE THE PROBLEM

I would not like to hold my breath waiting for Congress to act on the foregoing suggestions. There is another way to get a suitable change. Since state law now governs, one or more forward-thinking states might enact some changes. Florida, for example, could enact a law giving every married woman the right to choose her own domicile.

Florida might also provide that an individual who is neither a US citizen nor a US lawful permanent resident is not domiciled in Florida unless such person has been a US resident for federal income tax purposes in at least eight of the most recent ten years. This would automatically exempt aliens without green cards who are not long-term residents for US income tax purposes from possible domicile in the US if their only US home is in Florida. It would attract wealthy nonimmigrant aliens and encourage them to spend their time and money in Florida instead of in other states. Florida already enjoys great success in attracting wealthy Americans to change their domicile to Florida from northern states. This would give the state a similar attraction for wealthy foreigners who like to own a home in the US. Even a simple change like this could bring a huge windfall of new investment to Florida.

17. *US* CITIZENSHIP RULES

US citizenship is acquired by birth in the US, birth outside the US with at least one US parent, or naturalization. You are fully subject to US federal income, estate, gift and generation-skipping transfer (GST) taxes on your worldwide income and assets if you are a US citizen. An exception may apply for estate, gift and GST tax purposes if you acquired your US citizenship solely by birth or naturalization in a US possession such as the US Virgin Islands. This chapter is unchanged from last year's edition.

CITIZENSHIP FOR TAX PURPOSES

It is important for you to understand these basic rules concerning US taxation of its citizens:

- All US citizens, wherever resident, are liable to federal income tax on their income and capital gains from both US sources and foreign sources.
- Similarly, all US citizens, wherever domiciled, are liable to federal estate, gift and generation-skipping transfer taxes on their worldwide assets.
- Every person born or naturalized in the US and *subject to its jurisdiction* is a US citizen for federal tax purposes.
- A dual-national individual who is a US citizen and also a citizen of one or more other countries is a US citizen for tax purposes.
- A foreigner who has filed a declaration of intention to become a citizen, but who has not yet been granted citizenship by a final order of a naturalization court, is still an alien.

THE *USVI* OFFERS AN INTERESTING EXCEPTION

An interesting exception to these basic rules applies if you were either born or naturalized in the US Virgin Islands (USVI) and you are domiciled there at the time you die. Despite your US citizenship, you will be treated as a non-domiciled alien for federal estate tax purposes. This means that only your US assets will be subject to federal estate tax. Although this rule would also apply to any US possession it works especially well in the USVI which does not impose any local inheritance tax. If you plan to become a naturalized US citizen, consider establishing your residence and domicile in the USVI, obtain your US citizenship by naturalization there, and maintain your domicile there permanently even if you will also live in one of the states. You won't save any income tax, but you can legally avoid the estate tax on your non-US assets. This exception will not work if you are already a US citizen -- you must acquire your citizenship solely by birth or naturalization in a US possession.

CITIZENSHIP-BASED TAX IS CONSTITUTIONAL

The US Supreme Court decided more than 70 years ago that the US Congress has the power to tax a citizen on his worldwide income solely by reason of his citizenship [*Cook v. Tait*, 265 US 47 (1924)]. The amount in controversy was less than $300 out of a total tax assessment of less than $1,200 under the 1921 Revenue Act, involving tax levied at rates between four and eight percent. I find it hard to believe that such a decision from another era now subjects an estimated three million US citizens living abroad to tax at regular rates on billions of dollars of foreign-source investment income and gains. No other major country in the world attempts to tax its nonresident citizens on their foreign-source income.

ARE YOU A *US* CITIZEN?

For many American readers of this report the answer to this question is obvious. They were born in the US or have been naturalized, and they have never done anything to lose their American citizenship. The rest of this chapter is intended primarily for those who are less certain of their status.

HOW *US* CITIZENSHIP IS ACQUIRED

US citizenship is acquired either by birth or by naturalization. American citizenship is acquired by birth in the US even if both parents are aliens. US citizenship can also be acquired by birth abroad if at least one of the parents is a US citizen and has met minimum US residence requirements. In other cases, citizenship must be acquired by naturalization after at least five years of permanent residence. The nationality rules as stated herein are intended for general guidance only. The rules have been changed many times. Your actual citizenship will normally depend on the law in effect at the time you were born.

BIRTH IN THE *US*

Anyone born in the US and *"subject to its jurisdiction"* is a US citizen by birth even if neither of his parents was a US citizen or a US resident. The only children born in the US who are not *subject to its jurisdiction* are the children of ambassadors or other representatives of a foreign country.

Assume, for example, that Marcel Morgon and his wife, Marie, arrived in the US as tourists for a visit when Marie was seven months pregnant. Both were French citizens and residents. By accident or design they remained in the US until after their son, Maurice, was born. Whether Maurice is a French citizen is a matter of French law and is immaterial to his status for US purposes. From the moment of his birth, Maurice is a US citizen. He is entitled to and will receive a US passport for the return trip to France. If Maurice has income he is a US taxpayer. He will remain a US citizen even if he spends the rest of his life in France unless and until he loses his US citizenship by some act of expatriation. He may not be able to give up his US citizenship until he is 18 years old even if he and his parents want to do so.

CHILDREN BORN ABROAD

A child born outside America is a US citizen at birth if both parents were US citizens when the child was born and at least one of the parents had resided in the US sometime before the child's birth. If one parent is a US citizen and the other is an alien, recent amendments make a child born outside America a US citizen if the citizen parent was physically present in the US for at least five years and at least two of those years were after the citizen parent was 14 years old. The child may be able to obtain US citizenship even if the citizen parent did not spend five years in the US if the child moves to the US with the citizen parent.

NATURALIZATION

A person who does not acquire US citizenship at birth may become a citizen through naturalization. Some persons born as non-citizens in Puerto Rico, the US Virgin Islands, Guam and the Panama Canal Zone have become US citizens through collective naturalization. Most other aliens who acquire citizenship do so by individual naturalization.

To be eligible for naturalization, an alien must have been lawfully admitted to the US for permanent residence. He must intend to reside permanently in the US. He must have resided in the country for at least five years and he must have been physically present in the US for at least two and a half years. In addition, he must be of good moral character and he is supposed to understand the English language and US history. Children under 18 may not apply separately, but they will generally derive citizenship through the naturalization of a parent.

18. THE *US* PERMITS DUAL NATIONALITY

The US permits its citizens to hold more than one nationality. An American can lose his US citizenship by committing an expatriating act, but only if he does so *with the intention of relinquishing US nationality*. The US State Department now presumes that a potentially expatriating act such as the voluntary acquisition of another citizenship was performed with the intention of retaining US citizenship. Thus, an American can safely acquire another citizenship without losing his US citizenship. This chapter is unchanged from last year's edition.

The world is full of dual nationals because each country has its own rules for determining citizenship. Many of these rules, including those of the US, are archaic and peculiar. For example, Maurice Morgon, discussed in the previous chapter, would be a US citizen by birth because he was born in the US. He would probably also be a French citizen by birth since both of his parents were French. Thus he would be a dual national. If his father was Swiss and his mother was French, Maurice would probably have three nationalities -- American, French and Swiss.

Most countries continue to recognize dual nationality acquired at birth at least until the child becomes an adult. A country might require him to make a choice when he attains his majority. Or, he might lose one of his nationalities if he fails to meet certain requirements such as military service. US law does not require a US citizen who is born with dual nationality to choose one nationality or the other when he becomes an adult.

NEW STANDARDS OF EVIDENCE

The law states that a US citizen loses his US nationality by voluntarily obtaining naturalization in a foreign country upon his own application *with the intention of relinquishing US nationality [Immigration and Nationality Act of 1952, § 349(a)(1)]*. The key question is how the State Department determines that a US citizen intended to give up his US citizenship when he voluntarily obtains another citizenship. In a typical situation, a US consul in Ottawa learns from Canada and notifies the State Department that Charles Chardonnay has voluntarily obtained Canadian citizenship and a Canadian passport. The State Department then brings a case to adjudicate Chardonnay's loss of nationality. In it, the State Department must prove that Chardonnay voluntarily obtained Canadian nationality with the intention of relinquishing his US citizenship.

In 1990, the State Department issued new standards of evidence to be used in such cases. It is now presumed that Charles Chardonnay wants to retain his US citizenship. The new policy is retroactive. According to a Canadian newspaper article, some 282,000 Canadians who used to be US citizens can now apply to regain their US citizenship [*Montreal Gazette*, 7 July 1990]. Some will; others cannot or will not, fearing re-entry into the US tax system.

AN IMPORTANT STATE DEPARTMENT ANNOUNCEMENT

The US State Department published an important announcement in 1990 entitled *Advice About Possible Loss of U.S. Citizenship and Dual Nationality*. The text of that announcement is set forth at the end of this chapter. Here are some of its highlights:

- Any of several different acts can result in loss of US citizenship if done voluntarily and with the intent to relinquish US citizenship.
- There is a new premise that a US citizen intends to retain US citizenship when he is naturalized in a foreign country, takes a *routine* oath of allegiance to a foreign country, or accepts non-policy level employment with a foreign government. A citizen planning to commit one of these acts need not submit a statement that he intends to retain US citizenship since that intention is now presumed.
- When a consul learns of such an act he asks the citizen to complete a questionnaire. Unless the citizen affirmatively asserts that he intended to relinquish US citizenship, the consul must certify that the citizen intended to retain his US citizenship.
- The new premise does not apply when a US citizen formally renounces US citizenship before a consul, takes a policy-level position in a foreign government or is convicted of treason.
- If a citizen performs any of the acts and wishes to relinquish his US citizenship, he may affirm in writing to a consul that the act was done with the intent to relinquish US citizenship.
- Individuals who previously lost US citizenship may be able to have their cases reconsidered under the new rules.
- The US does not favor dual nationality, but it recognizes its existence in individual cases.

ROUTINE OATH OF ALLEGIANCE

The State Department announcement did not explain what is meant by a *routine oath of allegiance*. It apparently means an oath which does not require you to renounce other nationalities. Always obtain professional advice before signing an oath of allegiance to any country.

RELINQUISHING US CITIZENSHIP

One of the best ways to be sure that you are giving up US citizenship is for you to formally renounce US citizenship before a consul. You could, however, achieve the same result by giving the consul a completed questionnaire in which you concede that you were naturalized in a foreign country with the intention of relinquishing your US nationality. You should obtain professional advice to help you decide which of these courses of action is best for you.

TAX IMPACT OF RESTORED CITIZENSHIP

The IRS has published a ruling that spells out the tax consequences for those who succeed in having their citizenship retroactively restored as a result of the new policy [*Revenue Ruling 92-109*]. Assume that you performed an expatriating act in 1981 and that the State Department determined that you lost your citizenship as of that time. In 1990, you applied to have your citizenship restored and the State Department restored it retroactively. You are not liable for taxes for the years 1982 through 1989, the year before your citizenship was restored. If you have not yet applied for restoration of your citizenship but you do so at any time in the future you will in any case be liable for taxes for 1993 and all later years.

GET A SECOND CITIZENSHIP AND PASSPORT NOW

If there is any possibility that you might want to become a tax exile from the US at any time in the future, you should get another citizenship and a second passport now. All countries hate stateless persons and you will find it difficult, if not impossible, to relinquish your US citizenship unless you have another nationality. It takes time to get another nationality. You do not want to be under pressure to obtain another citizenship quickly. The cost of getting another citizenship and passport can double or triple if you wait until you need one urgently.

Under the new State Department policy it is perfectly safe for you to have another nationality and a second passport. If you obtain them when you are not in a hurry you can be selective and choose the best for you. If, for example, you would like to live in Europe, you might look into the possibility of obtaining citizenship in an EU member country. It is not easy, but it is not impossible either. An EU passport would give you the right to live and work in any of the 15 member countries of the European Union. I work closely with colleagues throughout the world to obtain citizenship and passports for clients. For details, see Chapter 67 entitled *Resource List*.

USING YOUR SECOND PASSPORT

When can you use your second passport? With rare exceptions, an American citizen who is a dual national must use his US passport when entering or leaving the US. There should be no problem if you use your second passport in other countries.

TEXT OF STATE DEPARTMENT ANNOUNCEMENT

Set forth on the next four pages is the text of the 1990 State Department announcement discussed earlier in this chapter. It is an important document and you should read it carefully.

United tes Department of State

Washington, D.C. 20520

ADVICE ABOUT POSSIBLE LOSS OF U.S. CITIZENSHIP AND DUAL NATIONALITY

The Department of State is responsible for determining the citizenship status of a person located outside the United States or in connection with the application for a U.S. passport while in the United States.

POTENTIALLY EXPATRIATING STATUTES

Section 349 of the Immigration and Nationality Act, as amended, states that U.S. citizens are subject to loss of citizenship if they perform certain acts voluntarily and with the intention to relinquish U.S. citizenship. Briefly stated, these acts include:

(1) obtaining naturalization in a foreign state (Sec. 349(a)(1) INA);

(2) taking an oath, affirmation or other formal declaration to a foreign state or its political subdivisions (Sec. 349(a)(2) INA);

(3) entering or serving in the armed forces of a foreign state engaged in hostilities against the U.S. or serving as a commissioned or non-commissioned officer in the armed forces of a foreign state (Sec. 349(a)(3) INA);

(4) accepting employment with a foreign government if (a) one has the nationality of that foreign state or (b) a declaration of allegiance is required in accepting the position; (Sec. 349(a)(4) INA);

(5) formally renouncing U.S. citizenship before a U.S. consular officer outside the United States (sec. 349(a)(5) INA);

(6) formally renouncing U.S. citizenship within the U.S. (but only "in time of war") (Sec. 349(a)(6) INA);

(7) conviction for an act of treason (Sec. 349(a)(7) INA).

84

ADMINISTRATIVE STANDARD OF EVIDENCE

As already noted, the actions listed above can cause loss of U.S. citizenship only if performed voluntarily and with the intention of relinquishing U.S. citizenship. The Department has a uniform administrative standard of evidence based on the premise that U.S. citizens intend to retain United States citizenship when they obtain naturalization in a foreign state, subscribe to routine declarations of allegiance to a foreign state, or accept non-policy level employment with a foreign government.

DISPOSITION OF CASES WHEN ADMINISTRATIVE PREMISE IS APPLICABLE

In light of the administrative premise discussed above, a person who:

(1) is naturalized in a foreign country;
(2) takes a routine oath of allegiance; or
(3) accepts non-policy level employment with a foreign government

and in so doing wishes to retain U.S. citizenship need not submit prior to the commission of a potentially expatriating act a statement or evidence of his or her intent to retain U.S. citizenship since such an intent will be presumed.

When such cases come to the attention of a U.S. consular officer, the person concerned will be asked to complete a questionnaire to ascertain his or her intent toward U.S. citizenship. Unless the person affirmatively asserts in the questionnaire that it was his or her intention to relinquish U.S. citizenship, the consular officer will certify that it was not the person's intent to relinquish U.S. citizenship and, consequently, find that the person has retained U.S. citizenship.

DISPOSITION OF CASES WHEN ADMINISTRATIVE PREMISE IS INAPPLICABLE

The premise that a person intends to retain U.S. citizenship is not applicable when the individual:

(1) formally renounces U.S. citizenship before a consular officer;
(2) takes a policy level position in a foreign state;
(3) is convicted of treason; or
(4) performs an act made potentially expatriating by statute accompanied by conduct which is so inconsistent with retention of U.S. citizenship that it compels a conclusion that the individual intended to relinquish U.S. citizenship. (Such cases are very rare.)

Cases in categories 2, 3, and 4 will be developed carefully by U.S. consular officers to ascertain the individual's intent toward U.S. citizenship.

PERSONS WHO WISH TO RELINQUISH U.S. CITIZENSHIP

An individual who has performed any of the acts made potentially expatriating by statute who wishes to lose U.S. citizenship may do so by affirming in writing to a U.S. consular officer that the act was performed with an intent to relinquish U.S. citizenship. Of course, a person always has the option of seeking to formally renounce U.S. citizenship in accordance with Section 349(a)(5) INA.

APPLICABILITY OF ADMINISTRATIVE PREMISE TO PAST CASES

The premise established by the administrative standard of evidence is applicable to cases adjudicated previously. Persons who previously lost U.S. citizenship may wish to have their cases reconsidered in light of this policy. A person may initiate such a reconsideration by submitting a request to the nearest U.S. consular office or by writing directly to:

Director, Office of Citizens Consular Services
(CA/OCS/CCS), Room 4811 NS
Department of State
Washington, DC 20520-4818

Each case will be reviewed on its own merits taking into consideration, for example, statements made by the person at the time of the potentially expatriating act.

DUAL NATIONALITY

When a person is naturalized in a foreign state (or otherwise possesses another nationality) and is thereafter found not to have lost U.S. citizenship the individual consequently may possess dual nationality. It is prudent, however, to check with authorities of the other country to see if dual nationality is permissible under local law. The United States does not favor dual nationality as a matter of policy, but does recognize its existence in individual cases.

QUESTIONS

For further information, please contact the appropriate geographic division of the Office of Citizens Consular Services:

Europe and Canada Division	(202) 647-3445
Inter-American Division	(202) 647-3712
East Asia and Pacific Division	(202) 647-3675
Near Eastern and South Asia Division	(202) 647-3926
Africa Division	(202) 647-4994

Sept. 1990

19. THE *US* TAXES ITS CITIZENS LIVING ABROAD

The US is one of only three countries in the world to tax the foreign income of its nonresident citizens. An American citizen working abroad can exclude a limited housing allowance and up to $70,000 a year of earned income from his foreign personal services, but he is fully taxable on any other income. He is also fully subject to US estate, gift and generation-skipping transfer taxes on his worldwide assets. This chapter is unchanged from last year's edition.

Australia, Britain, Canada, France, Germany, Japan and most other high-tax countries have at least one thing in common. None of them even tries to impose taxes on its citizens who live and work overseas, except those who work for the government.

The US is the only country in the world that makes a serious effort to collect substantial taxes from its nonresident citizens. The Philippines is one of only two other countries in the world that even tries to collect income taxes from its nonresident citizens, and it charges them a maximum rate of three percent on their foreign-source income. The other country is Eritrea which in 1995 began charging its nonresident citizens a two percent tax on their foreign-source earnings. A few other countries join the US in trying to collect death taxes and gift taxes from their overseas citizens.

THE FOREIGN EARNED-INCOME EXCLUSION

If you are an American citizen living and working overseas you may be able to eliminate some US taxes on your *income earned from performing foreign personal services*:

- You may be able to exclude up to $70,000 a year of your foreign salary or other income you earn by performing personal services abroad.
- You may also be able to deduct excess *housing expenses* you incur abroad to the extent they exceed a base amount that is now about $9,500 a year. These too must come out of your foreign earned income.
- To get the earned income exclusion and the housing expense deduction you must generally be a *bona fide resident* of a foreign country for at least one full year. You could also qualify if you are *physically present* in one or more foreign countries for 11 out of 12 months.
- You must also have your *tax home* in a foreign country. This generally requires you to have your principal place of business abroad.
- The earned income exclusion and the housing expense deduction apply only to the income tax. You will still have to pay social security taxes to the US or, in some cases, to the foreign country.
- You must also pay US income tax on the income you earn on any days on which you work in the US.
- You cannot take a foreign tax credit for foreign taxes you pay on the excluded income.

This may make the exclusion worthless if you are working in a high-tax country.

- A husband and wife can both qualify for the earned income exclusion.
- You risk losing the exclusion altogether if you do not file a tax return within two years from its original due date.

FULL TAX ON OTHER INCOME

The exclusion and housing expense deduction apply only to your *foreign earned income*. As a citizen, you must pay regular US tax on your earned income from US sources and on all dividends, interest, capital gains and other *unearned income*. You can take a foreign tax credit for the foreign taxes paid on the income that is not excluded if it comes from foreign sources. Typically you end up paying the foreign tax or the US tax, whichever is higher, on such income.

EXCLUSION THREATENED

The foreign earned-income exclusion is like a cat with nine lives. First enacted in 1926, it has been around in one form or another for most of the last 70 years. Unfortunately, it may now be nearing the end of its ninth life. In January 1996, President Bill Clinton proposed repeal of the exclusion for 1996 and later years as part of his latest balanced-budget proposal. American-based multinational companies employing Americans abroad are fighting to keep the exclusion, contending that it is critical to the US export program. Treasury officials respond that there is little evidence that the exclusion has led to higher exports. Check the latest developments.

ESTATE AND GIFT TAXES APPLY

A US citizen who lives abroad remains fully liable for the US gift, estate and generation-skipping transfer taxes. There is no exclusion for the transfer of foreign property.

ALIENS WITH GREEN CARDS

An alien with a green card or one who meets the substantial presence test must pay US income tax on his worldwide income even if he really lives and works abroad. He may be able to qualify for the earned income exclusion and housing expense deduction if he meets the physical presence test. He can qualify under the bona fide residence test only if the country of which he is a citizen has a tax treaty with the US.

MANY AMERICANS ABROAD DON'T FILE RETURNS

A 1985 report by a US Congressional subcommittee estimated that *61 percent* of Americans living abroad don't file US tax returns. The figure was based on a study by the government's General Accounting Office (GAO) which refused to reveal the data on which it based its estimate. The estimate may or may not have been accurate but it led to a 1986 law change that now requires a US citizen's passport renewal application to provide certain information that is given to the IRS.

PASSPORT APPLICATION FORMS

An application to renew a US passport, or for a new one, now requires the applicant to furnish the following information which is routinely furnished by the State Department to the IRS:
- full name;
- mailing address;
- date of birth; and
- social security number.

A federal tax law notice on the back of the passport application form says that if you have not been issued a social security number, you are to enter zeroes. It adds: *Any applicant who fails to provide the required information is subject to a $500 penalty enforced by the IRS.*

The State Department now provides this information to the IRS but it has been unwilling to deny passports to citizens who refuse to supply an identification number. Some reports have indicated that the State Department has been rather slow in getting the information to the IRS but the process is expected to be speeded up in the future. The IRS is apparently using the information to check for non-filers. In addition to the specific $500 penalty for failure to furnish the required information, anyone who does not comply will almost certainly be investigated and may also face criminal penalties for failure to comply with IRS reporting requirements. US passports are now valid for ten years so it will take some time before anyone knows whether the new requirement has substantially increased compliance by delinquent overseas Americans. Some non-filers may be dual nationals who can freely travel around the world on another passport. They can even enter the US from time to time without a current US passport if they do so from Canada or the Caribbean where a birth certificate or any other proof of US citizenship suffices.

IRS RULES FOR PASSPORT APPLICANTS

Proposed IRS regulations require all persons filing applications for passports after January 1987 to answer certain questions relating to their tax liability. They require the State Department to pass this information on to the IRS and to identify those who refuse to comply. In addition to routine identifying information, including your country of residence, you must answer these questions *if required to do so on the passport application form*:
- What is the last year for which you filed a US tax return?
- Are you self-employed?
- What is your occupation?
- Were you required to file a federal income tax return for any of your three most recent years?

•   If so, were such returns filed and, if not, why not?

The new rules are intended to improve tax compliance, particularly by US citizens living abroad. I assume that the passport application form will soon be amended to require the answers to the questions listed above. Similar questions are being asked of all aliens applying for green cards.

THE IRS NON-FILER PROGRAM

An IRS Commissioner recently estimated that between five million and ten million US taxpayers have not filed tax returns for a year or more. Most of them must be in the US since there are not nearly that many Americans living overseas. No one really knows how many Americans are living abroad since the US census does not count them. This makes the GAO estimate of the percentage of overseas Americans who do not file returns highly suspect. Whether the 61 percent non-filing rate is accurate, there are almost certainly a large number of Americans living overseas who do not file US tax returns. It is becoming harder and harder for them to claim that they didn't know they had to file. Many of them would like to get back into the system if they could figure out how to do so without becoming bankrupt or going to jail. Others will probably become permanent tax exiles.

The IRS began a *non-filer program* in 1992. It is designed to bring delinquent taxpayers in the US and abroad back into the system. It is technically not an amnesty program. There is no absolute assurance that a non-filer who comes forward voluntarily will not be prosecuted criminally. The IRS does say, however, that it has had a longstanding practice not to recommend criminal prosecution of an individual for failure to file tax returns where:

•   He voluntarily informs the IRS of his failure to file *before* he is notified by the IRS that he is under criminal investigation.

•   None of his income was earned from activities that are illegal under state or federal law.

•   He files true and correct delinquent tax returns and pays the amounts due (including interest and penalties) or makes bona fide arrangements to pay on an installment basis.

The IRS has also liberalized its rules concerning possible loss of the annual $70,000 exclusion. It previously denied the exclusion to those taxpayers who filed more than a year late. This hampered many delinquent taxpayers working abroad from getting back into the system. Some who would have owed little or no tax had they filed on time found themselves liable for taxes, interest and penalties that exceeded their total earnings. The IRS now gives a taxpayer two years to file before he risks possible loss of the exclusion. Moreover, it has established a procedure under which those who are more than two years delinquent can obtain relief allowing the exclusion for additional years.

Although more than 200,000 delinquent taxpayers came into the IRS voluntarily during the first six months of the non-filer program, this was four percent or less of the estimated total non-filers. Others are apparently still deterred by the fact that they must pay interest and late-filing penalties which typically add 50 percent or more to their tax bills. The IRS hopes that its new "nice-guy" approach will bring more delinquent taxpayers back into the fold voluntarily. It expects that its "tough-guy" approach, as evidenced by programs requiring information from those who obtain green cards and passports, will enable it to catch most of those who do not come forward voluntarily.

TEXT OF PASSPORT APPLICATION FORM

Set forth on the next two pages is the text of the front and back of the US passport application form discussed earlier in this chapter. Note particularly the *federal tax law* notice on the back of the form. The passport renewal application form contains the same requirement.

UNITED STATES DEPARTMENT OF STATE

APPLICATION FOR ☐ PASSPORT ☐ REGISTRATION
SEE INSTRUCTIONS—TYPE OR PRINT IN INK IN WHITE AREAS

1. NAME FIRST NAME   MIDDLE NAME

LAST NAME

2. MAILING ADDRESS

STREET

CITY, STATE,
ZIP CODE

COUNTRY   IN CARE OF

☐ 5 Yr.   ☐ 10 Yr.   Issue
Date _____
R   D   O   DP
End. # _____   Exp. _____

3. SEX   **4. PLACE OF BIRTH** City, State or Province, Country   **5. DATE OF BIRTH**   **6. SEE FEDERAL TAX LAW NOTICE ON REVERSE SIDE** SOCIAL SECURITY NUMBER

Male   Female   Mo.   Day   Year

7. HEIGHT   **8. COLOR OF HAIR**   **9. COLOR OF EYES**   **10. (Area Code) HOME PHONE**   **11. (Area Code) BUSINESS PHONE**

Feet Inches   **12. PERMANENT ADDRESS (Street, City, State, ZIP Code)**   **13. OCCUPATION**

FOLD

14. FATHER'S NAME   BIRTHPLACE   BIRTH DATE   U.S. CITIZEN ☐ YES ☐ NO   **16. TRAVEL PLANS** *(Not Mandatory)* COUNTRIES   DEPARTURE DATE

15. MOTHER'S MAIDEN NAME   BIRTHPLACE   BIRTH DATE   U.S. CITIZEN ☐ YES ☐ NO   LENGTH OF STAY

17. HAVE YOU EVER BEEN ISSUED A U.S. PASSPORT?   YES ☐   NO ☐   IF YES, SUBMIT PASSPORT IF AVAILABLE.   ☐ Submitted

IF UNABLE TO SUBMIT MOST RECENT PASSPORT, STATE ITS DISPOSITION: COMPLETE NEXT LINE

NAME IN WHICH ISSUED   PASSPORT NUMBER   ISSUE DATE (Mo., Day, Yr.)   DISPOSITION

SUBMIT TWO RECENT
IDENTICAL PHOTOS

2" × 2"   FROM 1" TO 1-3/8"

18. HAVE YOU EVER BEEN MARRIED? ☐ YES   ☐ NO   DATE OF MOST RECENT MARRIAGE   Mo.   Day   Year

WIDOWED/DIVORCED?   ☐ YES   ☐ NO   IF YES, GIVE DATE   Mo.   Day   Year

SPOUSE'S FULL BIRTH NAME   SPOUSE'S BIRTHPLACE

19. IN CASE OF EMERGENCY, NOTIFY *(Person Not Traveling With You)* *(Not Mandatory)*   RELATIONSHIP

FULL NAME

ADDRESS   (Area Code) PHONE NUMBER

FOLD

20. TO BE COMPLETED BY AN APPLICANT WHO BECAME A CITIZEN THROUGH NATURALIZATION

I IMMIGRATED TO THE U.S. (Month, Year)   I RESIDED CONTINUOUSLY IN THE U.S. From (Mo., Yr.)   To (Mo., Yr.)   DATE NATURALIZED (Mo., Day, Yr.)

PLACE

21. DO NOT SIGN APPLICATION UNTIL REQUESTED TO DO SO BY PERSON ADMINISTERING OATH

I have not, since acquiring United States citizenship, performed any of the acts listed under "Acts or Conditions" on the reverse of this application form (unless explanatory statement is attached). I solemnly swear (or affirm) that the statements made on this application are true and the photograph attached is a true likeness of me.

Subscribed and sworn to (affirmed) before me.   (SEAL)   X _____

Month   Day   Year

☐ Clerk of Court or
☐ PASSPORT Agent
☐ Postal Employee
☐ (Vice) Consul USA. At _____

_____ (Signature of person authorized to accept application)

(Sign in presence of person authorized to accept application)

22. APPLICANT'S IDENTIFYING DOCUMENTS ☐ PASSPORT ☐ DRIVER'S LICENSE ☐ OTHER (Specify)   No.

ISSUE DATE   EXPIRATION DATE   PLACE OF ISSUE   ISSUED IN THE NAME OF

Month   Day   Year   Month   Day   Year

23. FOR ISSUING OFFICE USE ONLY (Applicant's evidence of citizenship)

☐ Birth Cert.   SR   CR   City   Filed/Issued:
☐ Passport   Bearer's Name:
☐ Report of Birth
☐ Naturalization/Citizenship Cert.   No.:
☐ Other:
☐ Seen & Returned
☐ Attached

APPLICATION APPROVAL

Examiner Name

Office, Date

24.

FEE _____ EXEC. _____ POST _____

FORM DSP-11 (12–87)   (SEE INSTRUCTIONS ON REVERSE)   Form Approved OMB No. 1405-0004 (Exp. 8/1/89)

94

PASSPORT APPLICATION

FEDERAL TAX LAW:

Section 6039E of the Internal Revenue Code of 1986 requires a passport applicant to provide his/her name (#1), mailing address (#2), date of birth (#5), and social security number (#6). If you have not been issued a social security number, enter zeroes in box #6. Passport Services will provide this information to the Internal Revenue Service routinely. Any applicant who fails to provide the required information is subject to a $500 penalty enforced by the IRS. All questions on this matter should be referred to the nearest IRS office.

ACTS OR CONDITIONS

(If any of the below-mentioned acts or conditions has been performed by or applies to the applicant, the portion which applies should be lined out, and a supplementary explanatory statement under oath (or affirmation) by the applicant should be attached and made a part of this application.)

I have not, since acquiring United States citizenship, been naturalized as a citizen of a foreign state; taken an oath or made an affirmation or other formal declaration of allegiance to a foreign state; entered or served in the armed forces of a foreign state; accepted or performed the duties of any office, post, or employment under the government of a foreign state or political subdivision thereof; made a formal renunciation of nationality either in the United States or before a diplomatic or consular officer of the United States in a foreign state; or been convicted by a court or court martial of competent jurisdiction of committing any act of treason against, or attempting by force to overthrow, or bearing arms against, the United States, or conspiring to overthrow, put down, or to destroy by force, the Government of the United States; or having been naturalized, within one year after such naturalization, returned to the country of my birth or any other foreign country to take up a permanent residence.

WARNING: False statements made knowingly and willfully in passport applications or in affidavits or other supporting documents submitted therewith are punishable by fine and/or imprisonment under provisions of 18 USC 1001 and/or 18 USC 1542. Alteration or mutilation of a passport issued pursuant to this application is punishable by fine and/or imprisonment under the provisions of 18 USC 1543. The use of a passport in violation of the restrictions contained therein or of the passport regulations is punishable by fine and/or imprisonment under 18 USC 1544. All statements and documents submitted are subject to verification.

PRIVACY ACT STATEMENT

The information solicited on this form is authorized by, but not limited to, those statutes codified in Titles 8, 18, and 22, United States Code, and all predecessor statutes whether or not codified, and all regulations issued pursuant to Executive Order 11295 of August 5, 1966. The primary purpose for soliciting the information is to establish citizenship, identity, and entitlement to issuance of a United States Passport or related facility, and to properly administer and enforce the laws pertaining thereto.

The information is made available as a routine use on a need-to-know basis to personnel of the Department of State and other government agencies having statutory or other lawful authority to maintain such information in the performance of their official duties; pursuant to a court order; and, as set forth in Part 171, Title 22, Code of Federal Regulations (see *Federal Register,* Volume 42, pages 49791 through 49795).

Failure to provide the information requested on this form may result in the denial of a United States Passport, related document, or service to the individual seeking such passport, document, or service.

HOW TO APPLY FOR A U.S. PASSPORT. U.S. passports are issued only to U.S. citizens or nationals. Each person must obtain his or her own passport.

IF YOU ARE A FIRST-TIME APPLICANT, please complete and submit this application in person. (Applicants under 13 years of age usually need not appear in person unless requested. A parent or guardian may execute the application on the child's behalf.) Each application must be accompanied by (1) PROOF OF U.S. CITIZENSHIP, (2) PROOF OF IDENTITY, (3) TWO PHOTOGRAPHS, (4) FEES (as explained below) to one of the following acceptance agents: a clerk of any Federal or State court of record or a judge or clerk of any probate court accepting applications; a designated postal employee at a selected post office; or an agent at a Passport Agency in Boston, Chicago, Honolulu, Houston, Los Angeles, Miami, New Orleans, New York, Philadelphia, San Francisco, Seattle, Stamford, or Washington, D.C.; or a U.S. consular official.

IF YOU HAVE HAD A PREVIOUS PASSPORT, inquire about eligibility to use Form DSP-82 (mail-in application).

Address requests for passport amendment, extension of validity, or additional visa pages to a Passport Agency or a U.S. Consulate or Embassy abroad. Check visa requirements with consular officials of countries to be visited well in advance of your departure.

(1) PROOF OF U.S. CITIZENSHIP.

(a) APPLICANTS BORN IN THE UNITED STATES. Submit previous U.S. passport or **certified** birth certificate. A birth certificate must include your given name and surname, date and place of birth, date the birth record was filed, and seal or other certification of the official custodian of such records. A record filed more than 1 year after the birth is acceptable if it is supported by evidence described in the next paragraph.

IF NO BIRTH RECORD EXISTS, submit registrar's notice to that effect. Also submit an early baptismal or circumcision certificate, hospital birth record, early census, school, or family Bible records, newspaper or insurance files, or notarized affidavits of persons having knowledge of your birth (preferably with at least one record listed above). Evidence should include your given name and surname, date and place of birth, and seal or other certification of office (if customary) and signature of issuing official.

(b) APPLICANTS BORN OUTSIDE THE UNITED STATES. Submit previous U.S. passport or Certificate of Naturalization, or Certificate of Citizenship, or a Report of Birth Abroad, or evidence described below.

IF YOU CLAIM CITIZENSHIP THROUGH NATURALIZATION OF PARENT(S), submit the Certificate(s) of Naturalization of your parent(s), your foreign birth certificate, and proof of your admission to the United States for permanent residence.

IF YOU CLAIM CITIZENSHIP THROUGH BIRTH ABROAD TO U.S. CITIZEN PARENT(S), submit a Consular Report of Birth (Form FS-240) or Certification of Birth (Form DS-1350 or FS-545), or your foreign birth certificate, parents' marriage certificate, proof of citizenship of your parent(s), and affidavit of U.S. citizen parent(s) showing all periods and places of residence/physical presence in the United States and abroad before your birth.

(2) PROOF OF IDENTITY. If you are not personally known to the acceptance agent, you must establish your identity to the agent's satisfaction. You may submit items such as the following containing your signature AND physical description or photograph that is a good likeness of you: previous U.S. passport; Certificate of Naturalization or of Citizenship; driver's license (not temporary or learner's license); or government (Federal, State, municipal) identification card or pass. Temporary or altered documents are not acceptable.

IF YOU CANNOT PROVE YOUR IDENTITY as stated above, you must appear with an IDENTIFYING WITNESS who is a U.S. citizen or permanent resident alien who has known you for at least 2 years. Your witness must prove his or her identity and complete and sign an Affidavit of Identifying Witness (Form DSP-71) before the acceptance agent. You must also submit some identification of your own.

(3) TWO PHOTOGRAPHS. Submit two identical photographs of you alone, sufficiently recent to be a good likeness (normally taken within the last 6 months), 2 × 2 inches in size, with an image size from bottom of chin to top of head (including hair) of between 1 and 1-3/8 inches. Photographs must be clear, front view, full face, taken in normal street attire without a hat or dark glasses, and printed on thin paper with a plain light (white or off-white) background. They may be black and white or color. They must be capable of withstanding a mounting temperature of 225° Fahrenheit (107° Celsius). Photographs retouched so that your appearance is changed are unacceptable. Snapshots, most vending machine prints, and magazine or full-length photographs are unacceptable.

(4) FEES. Submit $42 if you are 18 years of age or older. The passport fee is $35. In addition, a fee of $7 is charged for the execution of the application. Your passport will be valid for 10 years from the date of issue except where limited by the Secretary of State to a shorter period. Submit $27 if you are under 18 years of age. The passport fee is $20 and the execution fee is $7. Your passport will be valid for 5 years from the date of issue, except where limited as above.

Pay the passport and execution fees in one of the following forms: checks—personal, certified, traveler's; bank draft or cashier's check; money order, U.S. Postal, international, currency exchange; or if abroad, the foreign currency equivalent, or a check drawn on a U.S. bank.

Make passport and execution fees payable to Passport Services (except if applying at a State court, pay execution fee as the State court requires) or the appropriate Embassy or Consulate, if abroad. No fee is charged to applicants with U.S. Government or military authorization for no-fee passports (except State courts may collect the execution fee). Pay special postage if applicable.

FORM DSP-11
12-87

20. ABANDONING *US* CITIZENSHIP

An American seeking to lose his US citizenship can either *renounce* his citizenship before an American consul abroad or *relinquish* it by confirming to an American consul that he has committed an expatriating act such as obtaining another citizenship with the intention of relinquishing his US nationality. These acts have different consequences and you should obtain professional advice before doing either of them. This chapter is basically unchanged from last year's edition, but the impact of 1996 legislation on Americans who expatriate is discussed in the *1997 Update* preceding the sample forms at the end of the chapter.

You can intentionally lose your US citizenship through voluntary renunciation. Congress has also provided that certain other acts will result in loss of citizenship if they are done with the intent to relinquish citizenship. Normally these can occur only when a US citizen is living abroad. The US Supreme Court has held that some of the provisions that used to result in loss of nationality were unconstitutional.

VOLUNTARY RELINQUISHMENT

About 30 years ago, the US Supreme Court held that depriving an American citizen of his citizenship for voting in a foreign political election was unconstitutional [*Afroyim v. Rusk*, 387 US 253 (1967)]. The Court also stated that every US citizen has a constitutional right to remain a citizen *unless he voluntarily relinquishes that citizenship*. This rule applies to both citizens by birth and those that have been naturalized. The Supreme Court did not define *voluntary relinquishment*. In a later case, the Supreme Court held that the US government has the burden of proving that an expatriating act was done with the intent to relinquish citizenship [*Vance v. Terrazas*, 444 US 252 (1980)].

ACTS THAT MAY RESULT IN LOSS OF CITIZENSHIP

Under guidelines promulgated by the US Attorney General, it was clear that voluntary relinquishment was not confined to a written renunciation of citizenship. Certain acts are highly persuasive evidence of an intention to relinquish citizenship and will result in loss of citizenship if the requisite intention is found. These include:
- Naturalization in a foreign country.
- Taking a meaningful oath of allegiance to a foreign country.
- Serving in foreign armed forces engaged in hostilities against the US.
- Serving in an important political post in a foreign government.
- Formally renouncing US citizenship before a US diplomat or consul abroad.
- Conviction of committing an act of treason.

REVOKING NATURALIZATION

The Supreme Court has held that mere residence abroad by a naturalized citizen cannot result in loss of citizenship [*Schneider v. Rusk*, 377 US 163 (1964)]. However, until 1994, it was possible for a naturalized citizen to have his naturalization revoked if he established permanent residence abroad within one year after he was naturalized. Departure from or remaining outside the US in time of war for the purpose of evading military service cannot result in loss of citizenship [*Kennedy v. Mendoza-Martinez*, 372 US 144 (1963)].

DUAL NATIONALS

A dual national now loses his US citizenship only in the same way that other US citizens do. However, a dual national residing in his other country of citizenship and who has been physically present in that other country for ten years immediately before committing one of the statutory acts of expatriation is *conclusively presumed* to have done so voluntarily This conclusive presumption may not be constitutional under the cases discussed above. And, as we have seen in previous chapters, a dual national is a US citizen for tax purposes.

VOLUNTARY RENUNCIATION OFFERS CERTAINTY

US citizenship can be lost by committing one of the designated acts of expatriation, but US Supreme Court decisions require proof that citizenship has been voluntarily relinquished. A US citizen can lose his US nationality voluntarily by signing an oath of renunciation before a US consul in some foreign country. That way he can be certain that he is no longer a US citizen. You should discuss with your professional adviser whether it is better for you to renounce your citizenship or to concede that you committed some act of expatriation with the intent to relinquish your US citizenship.

THE FOREIGN AFFAIRS MANUAL

The *Foreign Affairs Manual* is the *"bible"* given by the US State Department to its consuls telling them what to do and what not to do. My law firm has obtained a copy of Chapter 1200 of the Foreign Affairs Manual under the Freedom of Information Act. The chapter is entitled: *Loss and Restitution of U.S. Citizenship*. It runs about 75 pages. Although we obtained this information in 1991, most of the material in the chapter was last updated by the State Department in 1984. I have prepared a summary of the chapter, setting forth the key things in it that you should know.

Expatriation means loss of US citizenship. More than 125 years ago, the *Expatriation Act of 1868* established the principle of expatriation as the right of the people. An American has the right to give up his US citizenship if he really wants to do so. The manual explains several important US Supreme Court decisions dealing with expatriation.

LEADING SUPREME COURT CASES

In *Nishikawa v. Dulles* [356 US 129 (1958)], the Supreme Court held that the government must prove by clear, convincing and unequivocal evidence that a *potentially expatriating act* was done *voluntarily*. Congress then tried to shift the burden of proof to the citizen by creating a *rebuttable presumption* that a potentially expatriating act was performed voluntarily. In effect, Congress said that if an American citizen commits an act that could cause expatriation, he must prove that he didn't do so with the intent to give up his US citizenship.

Afroyim v. Rusk [387 US 253 (1967)] held that a US citizen has a constitutional right to remain a citizen unless he voluntarily relinquishes his citizenship. This requires a determination that he intended to relinquish his US citizenship at the time he committed the potentially expatriating act.

Vance v. Terrazas [444 US 252 (1980)] upheld the constitutionality of the rebuttable presumption that a potentially expatriating act was done voluntarily. There must be something more than merely committing such an act. There must be evidence of his intent to relinquish US citizenship from his words or as a fair inference from his proven conduct.

CONSUL INFORMS STATE DEPARTMENT

A US consul stationed abroad informs the State Department whenever he believes a person has lost his US citizenship. Consuls frequently learn about these cases when they are notified by the foreign government that a US citizen has been naturalized. In some countries, the names and former nationalities of newly naturalized individuals are published in an official gazette. These gazettes are required reading for US consuls.

EXPATRIATING ACT MUST BE VOLUNTARY

The basic question to be determined by a consul is whether the potentially expatriating act was performed *voluntarily* by the citizen. His motive or reason for performing the act is not material. If the citizen suggests that the act was not performed voluntarily, the consul must decide the issue and show the State Department the evidence relied on for his decision. The key issue is the citizen's intent *when the act was performed*.

A consul who learns that a US citizen has performed a potentially expatriating act asks the citizen to complete a questionnaire entitled: *Information for Determining U.S. Citizenship*. A sample questionnaire taken from the manual appears at the end of this chapter. If the consul is satisfied that the citizen lacked the intent to relinquish US citizenship he submits a finding to that effect to the State Department.

CERTIFICATE OF LOSS OF NATIONALITY

The consul uses a form entitled *Certificate of Loss of Nationality* to certify that a citizen has lost his citizenship. A sample of this form, taken from the manual, appears at the end of this chapter. The consul sends the form to the State Department for approval. Copies of the approved form are returned to the consul who must furnish a copy to the expatriate by hand delivery or by registered mail.

SHOWING INTENT TO RELINQUISH CITIZENSHIP

The manual sets forth numerous acts that may be used by a consul to show a person's intent to relinquish citizenship. These include:
* Making a statement of renunciation in connection with a potentially expatriating act.
* Surrendering a US passport to foreign authorities or returning it to US authorities.
* Making statements in connection with tax returns.
* Requesting a US visa or entering the US on a foreign passport.
* Using a foreign passport exclusively.
* Failing to fulfil obligations of US citizenship, such as filing tax returns.

THE FINAL DECISION IS MADE IN WASHINGTON

The consul cannot make the final decision that a person has lost US citizenship. That decision is made by the State Department in Washington. The consul transmits the facts to the State Department together with a proposed *Certificate of Loss of Nationality*. The State Department gives its consent by approving the proposed *Certificate of Loss of Nationality* prepared by the consul.

RENOUNCING US CITIZENSHIP

A citizen can formally renounce his US nationality before a US diplomat or consul in a foreign country. He must complete and sign a *Questionnaire and a Statement of Understanding*, samples of which appear at the end of this chapter. He must then sign an *Oath of Renunciation* in the precise form prescribed by the Secretary of State. A sample of the oath also appears at the end of this chapter.

Unless the person is physically unable to travel, the renunciation is normally administered only at an American embassy or consulate. The consul must first be satisfied that the individual is a US citizen and that he is taking the oath of renunciation voluntarily. The consul may suggest that the individual defer the contemplated act for a period of time to permit reflection on its gravity and consequences.

It is difficult, but possible, for a minor under 18 to renounce his citizenship. As a practical matter it is virtually impossible for a child to do so unless he is at least 14 years old. Even then, he must satisfy the consul that he understands what he is doing and that he is not acting under duress.

1997 UPDATE

Significant new US legislation was enacted during 1996. Revised expatriation tax rules generally apply to an American citizen who renounces or relinquishes US citizenship after 5 February 1995. An immigration law amendment authorizes the US Attorney General to treat an individual who renounces citizenship to avoid taxes after 29 September 1996 as *excludable*; it apparently does not cover relinquishments. These rules are discussed in Chapter 21 below.

SAMPLE FORMS FROM FOREIGN AFFAIRS MANUAL

Set forth on the next 11 pages is the text of several sample forms discussed earlier in this chapter. These forms are taken from the State Department's *Foreign Affairs Manual*. The first of these is a six-page *Questionnaire* used by a consul to determine whether or not an individual is still a US citizen. Next is a sample of the *Certificate of Loss of Nationality* that is to be completed by the consul and submitted by him to the State Department for final approval. It is followed by a three-page sample of a *Statement of Understanding* to be signed by an individual who wants to renounce US citizenship. Finally, there is the *Oath of Renunciation*.

Sample Questionnaire: "Information for Determining U.S. Citizenship"

QUESTIONNAIRE

INFORMATION FOR DETERMINING U.S. CITIZENSHIP

The following information is needed to determine your present citizenship status and your entitlement to consular services as a United States citizen. You may wish to consult an attorney before completing this form. If you have any questions about the form, you should discuss them with a member of our consular staff before completing the form. Use extra paper as needed and attach any supporting documents to this form.

1.   Name Dongieux,   Jane   B.
          (Last)   (First)   (Middle)

2.   Last U.S. passport issued at Toronto on 6-30-82
                                   (Place)   (Date)

3.   Date and place of birth 5-23-49 at Burlington, Vermont

4.   If not born in the United States, citizenship was acquired by naturalization on_____ before the_____
                                  (Date)   (Name of court)

court at _____, or birth outside the
                  (City)

United States to U.S. citizen parent(s).

5.   Dates and countries of residence outside the United States since birth.

Dates (From - to)	Country
1963 to present	Canada

If more space is needed, use additional paper.

6. Answer this question only if at birth you became a citizen of the United States and of another country (for example, if by your birth in the United States you became a U.S. citizen and, because one or both of your parents were citizens of another country, you also acquired that country's citizenship at birth):

Have you sought or claimed the benefits of the nationality of a foreign state between December 24, 1952, and October 10, 1975 (examples of such benefits are possession or use of that country's passport, owning property in an area where noncitizens cannot own property, or obtaining employment for which noncitizens are ineligible)? Circle one: Yes   No

If you answered "yes," please explain the benefits you sought or claimed:

_____
_____
_____
_____
_____
_____

7. Please circle "Yes" or "No". Have you--

   a. Been naturalized as a citizen of a foreign state?   (Yes)   No

   b. Taken an oath or made an affirmation or other formal declaration of allegiance to a foreign state?   (Yes)   No

   c. Served in the armed forces of a foreign state?   Yes   (No)

d. Accepted, served in, or performed the duties of any office, post or employment under the government of a foreign state? (Yes)   No

e. Renounced U.S. nationality at a U.S. Consulate or Embassy?   Yes   (No)

8. If your answer to all the questions asked in item 7 above is "No," please sign here:

Signature_____Date_____

and return this form to the person who asked you to complete it. If you are completing this form at home, mail it in the enclosed envelope to the Embassy or Consulate.

9. You should be aware that under United States law a citizen who has performed any of the acts specified in item 7 with the intention of relinquishing United States citizenship may have thereby lost United States citizenship. If you voluntarily performed an act listed in item 7 with the intent to relinquish United States citizenship, you may sign the Statement below and return this form to us, and we will prepare the forms necessary to document your loss of U.S. citizenship. If you believe expatriation has not occurred, either because the act you performed was not voluntary or because you did not intend to relinquish U.S. citizenship, you should skip to item 10, and complete the remainder of this form.

STATEMENT OF VOLUNTARY RELINQUISHMENT OF U.S. NATIONALITY

I, _____, performed the act of expatriation indicated in item 7_____voluntarily and
                                        (a, b, c, d, or e)
with the intention of relinquishing my U.S. nationality.

Signature_____Date_____

10. Please circle "Yes" or "No":

    a. Are you a national or citizen of any country other than the United States? (Yes) No

    b. If yes, of what country? *Canada*

    c. If yes, did you acquire that citizenship

       by birth in the foreign country? Yes No

       by marriage? Yes No

       by naturalization or registration

       on *March 8, 1983* (Yes) No
           (Date)

       Other (explain)?_____

       _____

       _____

       _____

11. a. When did you first become aware that you might be a United States citizen (give approximate date)?_____

    I always knew.

    b. How did you find out that you were a citizen of the United States? (For example, did you always know you were a U.S. citizen? If not, when did you learn about your citizenship? Did someone tell you that you were a U.S. citizen?)_____

    Yes, my parents

    _____

12. a. Describe as specifically as you can the act or acts you performed as indicated in item 7 above. For example, by what means or in what sort of proceeding were you naturalized as a citizen of a foreign state? What was the nature of the oath you took? In what foreign army did you serve? What rank did you hold?

What employment did you have and what were your responsibilities? Indicate precisely when and where the act was performed.

I applied for Canadian citizenship. I attended a ceremony and took an oath in which I promised to obey the laws. Also, I have worked as a teacher employed by the provincial government.

b. Describe in detail the circumstances under which you performed the act or acts indicated in item 7 above. Did you perform the act or acts voluntarily? If not, in what sense was your performance of the act or acts involuntary? What was your intent in performing the act or acts?

I became a Canadian citizen because I've lived in Canada a long time. Also, Canadian citizens are given a preference in being hired as teachers. I did this voluntarily but I didn't want to lose my U.S. citizenship.

13. Did you know that by performing the act described in item 7 you might lose U.S. citizenship? Explain your answer.

I was not certain. I did not want to lose my U.S. citizenship.

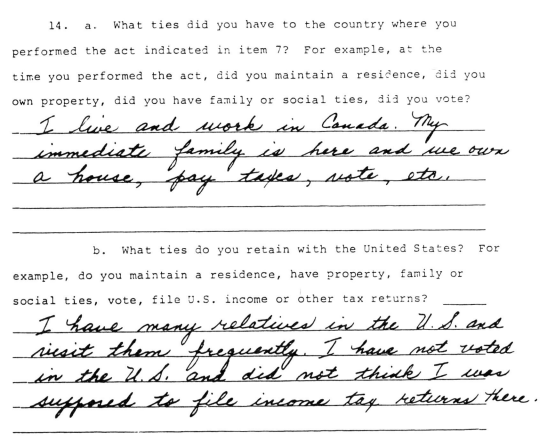

14. a. What ties did you have to the country where you performed the act indicated in item 7? For example, at the time you performed the act, did you maintain a residence, did you own property, did you have family or social ties, did you vote?

I live and work in Canada. My immediate family is here and we own a house, pay taxes, vote, etc.

b. What ties do you retain with the United States? For example, do you maintain a residence, have property, family or social ties, vote, file U.S. income or other tax returns?

I have many relatives in the U.S. and visit them frequently. I have not voted in the U.S. and did not think I was supposed to file income tax returns there.

Your answers on this form will become part of the official record in your case. Before signing this form, read over your answers to make certain that they are as complete and accurate as possible. If you would like to provide additional information you believe relevant to a determination of your citizenship status, you may attach separate sheets with that information.

Jane B. Dougieux _____   *May 4, 1983* _____
(Signature)   (Date)

After signing, return this form to the American Embassy or Consulate in the enclosed envelope. If completing it at a post, return it to the person who asked you to complete it.

Sample: "Certificate of Loss of Nationality of the United States"

DEPARTMENT OF STATE

FOREIGN SERVICE OF THE UNITED STATES OF AMERICA

CERTIFICATE OF LOSS OF NATIONALITY OF THE UNITED STATES

This form is prescribed by the Secretary of State pursuant to Section 501 of the Act of October 14, 1940 (54 Stat. 1171) and Section 358 of the Act of June 27, 1952 (66 Stat. 272).

DEPARTMENT USE ONLY

Consulate __General__ of the United States of America

ss:

at __Toronto, Canada__

I __George J. Sanders, Consul__
(Name)

hereby certify that, to the best of my knowledge and belief,

__Jane B. Dongieux__
(Name)

was born at __Burlington__, __Vermont__,
(Town or City)   (Province or County)

__U.S.A.__, on __May 25, 1949__,
(State or Country)   (Date)

That she ~~XXXXX~~ resided in the United States; from birth to 1960;

That she resides at 26 Spring Street, Downsview, Ontario, Canada M3M 2S3;

That she acquired the nationality of the United States by virtue of __her birth in__
__the United States__

That she acquired the nationality of __Canada__ by virtue of __her naturalization in Canada__

That she __was naturalized as a citizen of Canada on March 8__
(The action causing expatriation should be set forth succinctly)

That she thereby expatriated __herself__ on __March 8, 1983__ under the provisions of
Section __349 (a) (1)__ of (the Nationality Act of 1940)* (the Immigration and Nationality Act of 1952)*

That the evidence of such action consists of the following:

As below

That attached to and made a part of this certificate are the following documents or _____
copies thereof:

Statement of March 10, 1983 from Canadian Citizenship Authorities.

In testimony whereof, I have hereunto subscribed my name and affixed my office seal this __12th__
day of __May__, 19__83__.

George J. Sanders

George J. Sanders
(Signature)

(SEAL)

Consul
(Title)

* Strike out inapplicable item.

FORM
9-72 FS-348

SEE REVERSE FOR APPEAL PROCEDURES

Sample: "Statement of Understanding"

STATEMENT OF UNDERSTANDING

I, _John J. LaSalle_ , understand that:
  (Name)

1. I have a right to renounce my United States citizenship.

2. I am exercising my right of renunciation freely and voluntarily without any force, compulsion, or undue influence placed upon me by any person.

3. Upon renouncing my citizenship I will become an alien with respect to the United States, subject to all the laws and procedures of the United States regarding entry and control of aliens.

4. My renunciation may not affect my military or Selective Service status, if any, and may not exempt me from income taxation. I understand that any problems in these areas must be resolved with the appropriate agencies.

5. My renunciation may not affect my liability, if any, to prosecution for any crimes which I may have committed or may commit in the future which violate United States law.

6. If I do not possess the nationality of any country other than the United States, upon my renunciation I will become a stateless person and may face extreme difficulties in traveling internationally and entering most countries.

". The extremely serious and irrevocable nature of the act of renunciation has been explained to me by (Vice) Consul George J. Sanders

(Name)

at the American Consulate General at

(Fill in rank of post)

Toronto , and I fully understand its consequences.

(City)

I (do not) choose to make a separate written explanation of my reasons for renouncing my United States citizenship. I (swear, affirm) that I have (read, had read to me) this Statement

(Circle one verb)   (Circle one verb)

in the English language and fully understand its

(Name the language)

contents.

John J. LaSalle

(Signature)

John J. LaSalle

(Renunciant's typed name)

CONSULAR OFFICER'S ATTESTATION

___John J. LaSalle___ appeared personally and (read, had read to him)
    (Name)   (Circle one verb)

this Statement after my explanation of its meaning and the conse-

quences of renunciation of United States citizenship and signed

this Statement (under oath, by affirmation) before me this
                          (Circle one)

___12th___ day of ___May___ ___1983___.
(Day of month)   (Month)   (Year)

Seal   *George J. Sanders*
                    (Vice) Consul of the United States of America

WITNESSES' ATTESTATION

The undersigned persons certify that they witnessed the personal

appearance of ___John J. LaSalle___ before the consular officer
               (Name)

___George J. Sanders___, who explained the seriousness and
        (Name)

consequences of renunciation of United States citizenship and the

meaning of the attached Statement of Understanding, after which this

Statement was signed (under oath, by affirmation) before the named
                         (Circle one)

consular officer and undersigned witnesses this ___12th___ day of
                                (Day of month)

___May___ ___1983___.
(Month)   (Year)

Richard B. Roebuck
Witness ___Richard B. Roebuck___ ___650 Elm St., Toronto, Canada___
        (Full name)   (Complete address)

Susan Adams
Witness ___Susan Adams___ ___3012 Maple St., Toronto, Canada___
        (Full name)   (Complete address)

OATH OF RENUNCIATION OF THE NATIONALITY
OF THE UNITED STATES

(This form has been prescribed by the Secretary of State pursuant to Section 349(a)(5) of the Immigration and Nationality Act, 66 Stat. 268, as amended by Public Law 95-432, October 10, 1978, 92 Stat. 1046.)

Consulate General of the United States of America at

Toronto, Canada _____ , ss:

     I, John J. LaSalle _____ , a national of the United States,
             (Name)
solemnly swear that I was born at _____ Denver _____ ,
                          (City or town)

_____ , _____ Colorado _____ , on June 8, 1945 .
(Province or country)   (State or country)   (Date)
     That I formerly resided in the United States at 133 King Street
                                      (Street)
_____ Denver, _____ Colorado _____ .
   (City)   (State)
     That I am a national of the United States by virtue of

_____ . birth in the United States _____ .
(If a national by birth in the United States, or abroad, so state; if

naturalized, give the name and place of the court in the United States before

which naturalization was granted and the date of such naturalization.)

     That I desire to make a formal renunciation of my American nationality, as provided by section 349(a)(5) of the Immigration and Nationality Act and pursuant thereto I hereby absolutely and entirely, without mental reservation, coercion or duress, renounce my United States nationality together with all rights and privileges and all duties of allegiance and fidelity thereunto pertaining.

_John J. La Salle_____
                  (Signature)

Subscribed and sworn to before me this __12th__ day of _May_____ ,

19_83_, in the American Consulate General at Toronto, Canada.

_George J. Sanders_____
         (Signature of officer)

SEAL

         George J. Sanders
         (Typed name of officer)

       Consul of the United States of America
           (Title of officer)

21. *US* EXPATRIATION TAX RULES ARE REVISED

Under expatriation tax rules originally enacted in 1966, a US citizen who expatriated to avoid taxes could remain subject to full US taxes for ten years, but only on his US income, gains and property. These old rules had loopholes which were discussed in earlier editions of this report. In February 1995, President Clinton proposed replacing the old rules with a new set of rules under which a wealthy expatriate would have to pay a departure tax at the time he left. Congress instead revised the old expatriation tax rules, closing some of the loopholes contained in the prior law. This chapter has been substantially revised from last year's edition.

Citizens of most of the major industrial nations can solve their tax problems merely by moving abroad. Most high tax countries levy worldwide income taxes and death taxes only on residents. The US imposes these taxes on all persons who are either citizens or residents. To avoid these taxes, an American must not only move out of the US permanently, but he must also give up his US citizenship, an act we generally call *expatriation*.

Unfortunately, the word *expatriation* has more than one meaning. Sometimes it means the act of abandoning citizenship. However, the word *expatriate* is often used to describe a citizen of a country who lives abroad, retaining his citizenship. In this chapter, when we use the words *expatriate* or *expatriation* in reference to an American citizen, we mean a former American citizen who has surrendered his US citizenship either to become a tax exile or for some other reason. As a result of changes made by 1996 legislation, the word *expatriate* now also covers a long-term lawful resident alien who has surrendered his green card after holding it for eight out of the most-recent 15 years.

If an American citizen or long-term green card holder is treated as having surrendered his US citizenship or residency *for tax avoidance reasons*, he remains liable for some federal income, estate, and gift taxes for a ten-year period. An American citizen or resident who expatriated after 5 February 1995 is automatically treated as having surrendered his US citizenship or residency for tax avoidance reasons if he meets either a *tax liability test* or a *net worth test*. He meets the tax liability test if he has paid an average federal income tax of more than $100,000 per year for the five taxable years preceding expatriation. He meets the net worth test if his net worth as of the date of expatriation was at least $500,000.

Congress taxes all US residents regardless of their citizenship, all US citizens regardless of their place of residence, and many former citizens and long-term residents even though they are no longer residents.

RULES COVER ONLY *US* INCOME AND *US* PROPERTY

Many people think that a tax-motivated expatriate is taxed for ten years in the same way as a US citizen. That is just not so. The US expatriation tax rules generally apply only to income from US sources and to property located in the US. With proper planning, a former citizen or long-term resident can achieve substantial tax benefits even if his expatriation is treated as being tax motivated.

PRIOR RULES DID NOT COVER RESIDENT ALIENS

One aspect of the pre-1995 expatriation tax rules made no sense and, as expected, was changed by the 1996 legislation. The US generally taxes its citizens and its resident aliens in the same way. In this instance it treated them differently, discriminating against citizens. Until 1995, a long-term resident alien could make his fortune in the US and then abandon his US residence permanently without any unfavorable tax consequences. This unequal application of the prior expatriation tax rules encouraged some well-advised wealthy resident aliens to refrain from ever acquiring American citizenship. Under the pre-1995 rules, a resident alien who never became an American citizen was able to leave the US and immediately obtain the beneficial tax status of a nonresident alien unless he reacquired US residency within the next three years.

PRIOR RULES BLOCKED SOME EXCHANGES

Even under the pre-1995 rules, a US taxpayer could not make a tax-free exchange of US property for foreign property. Even if he could do so, the anti-expatriation rules would have taxed an expatriate on gains from selling foreign property if its basis was determined in whole or in part by reference to US property. This rule covered not only real estate, but also stock of a US corporation and debt issued by a US person.

THE PRE-1995 RULES

The pre-1995 rules still apply to a former US citizen who expatriated prior to 6 February 1995. Let us take a closer look at these pre-1995 rules. The prior anti-expatriation rules were set forth in three different sections of the US Internal Revenue Code (IRC), all of which were originally enacted as part of the *Foreign Investors Tax Act of 1966*. They were:

> income tax rules ....IRC § 877
> estate tax rules ....IRC § 2107
> gift tax rules...................................IRC § 2501

The significant points of each of these pre-1995 provisions are summarized below.

PRE-1995 INCOME TAX RULES

Under the pre-1995 rules, a nonresident alien individual who had previously been a US citizen at any time within the preceding ten years was subject to a less favorable tax system if one of the principal purposes for the loss of citizenship was the avoidance of US income, estate or gift taxes. Such a former citizen (*tax-motivated expatriate*) was taxed on his US-source income at the rates applicable to citizens, but only if that resulted in greater tax than would be imposed on him as a nonresident alien.

- *US-source income* was expanded to include capital gains from the sale of US shares, US debt or US property. It also included stock, debt or property whose basis was determined by reference to any of the foregoing. This was supposed to prevent a tax-motivated expatriate from generating nontaxable foreign-source income on the sale of US shares or US debt, or from exchanging US property for foreign property after expatriation and then later selling the foreign property without US tax.
- Gain on the sale of foreign property whose basis was determined in whole or in part by reference to the basis of US property or US securities was treated as gain from selling US property. Thus, a gain from selling that foreign property within ten years after tax-motivated expatriation was still subject to US tax.
- As indicated above, these anti-expatriation rules applied to a tax-motivated expatriate for ten years following loss of citizenship. They applied to a former resident alien during his period of nonresidency only if he became a nonresident alien and then resumed US residency within three years. They did not apply to a former resident alien who left permanently.

The IRS never issued any regulations under the pre-1995 income tax anti-expatriation rules. The rules were apparently not self-executing. They did not apply without action by the IRS, unless the expatriate conceded that his loss of US citizenship had as one of its principal purposes the avoidance of US taxes. No former citizen conceded that he had expatriated to avoid taxes. He did not file US tax returns reporting income that was not taxable to a nonresident alien who was not a tax-motivated expatriate. This left it to the IRS to identify the person and raise the issue. If the IRS did so, the expatriate had the usual taxpayer burden of proof and also had a special burden of proof.

If the IRS established that loss of US citizenship had resulted in a substantial reduction in the expatriate's taxes on his probable income for that year, the expatriate had to prove that his loss of citizenship did not have for one of its principal purposes the avoidance of US income, estate or gift taxes. Since a taxpayer always has the burden of proof anyway, this special burden of proof did not add much. For example, in the cases discussed in the next chapter, Max Kronenberg lost his case even without the special burden of proof and Princess von Furstenberg won her case despite the fact that she had to overcome the special burden of proof. In a typical case, however, an expatriate would have had difficulty meeting either burden of proof.

The most significant item covered by the pre-1995 income tax anti-expatriation rules was *US-source capital gains* from the sale of securities. Such gains were not ordinarily taxed to a nonresident alien unless he spent more than half the year in the US. The issue was normally raised only when the IRS learned that a former citizen had attempted to sell tax-free the shares of a large closely-held business that he had built up over many years. Since the enactment of the *Foreign Investment in Real Property Tax Act (FIRPTA)*, capital gains from the sale of US real estate or US real property holding companies were taxable in any event.

A tax-motivated expatriate also lost the exemptions on US bank-deposit interest and portfolio interest, but a well-advised expatriate generally arranged his affairs so that he received any such interest from foreign sources, making the interest exempt from tax regardless of his motivation.

PRE-1995 ESTATE TAX RULES

The pre-1995 estate tax anti-expatriation rules worked in a similar way. A non-domiciled alien who lost US citizenship within the ten years preceding his death was subject to less favorable estate tax rules if one of the principal purposes for his loss of citizenship was the avoidance of US income, estate or gift taxes. Such a tax-motivated expatriate was taxed on his US-situs property as though he were still a US citizen.

- For many years after this rule was enacted, US citizens and tax-motivated expatriates had to pay a much higher US estate tax rate than ordinary non-domiciled aliens. Since 1988, however, non-domiciled aliens also had to pay these confiscatory rates.
- An ordinary non-domiciled alien was not taxed on shares of a foreign corporation even if it owned US property. For a tax-avoidance expatriate, *US-situs property* was expanded to include his *pro rata* share of the US assets of a foreign corporation which he owned when he died, or which he had previously transferred with a retained interest, if he was deemed to own at least ten percent of its stock and more than half of its voting power.
- A tax-avoidance expatriate was given a unified credit of $13,000, the same as that given to an ordinary non-domiciled alien. It was the equivalent of only a $60,000 exemption. A US citizen or domiciled alien receives a unified credit of $192,800, equivalent to a $600,000 exemption, but is subject to estate tax on his worldwide assets.
- If the IRS established that loss of US citizenship had resulted in a substantial reduction in the expatriate's total death taxes on his estate, the executor had to prove that the decedent's loss of citizenship did not have for one of its principal purposes the avoidance of US taxes.

The only significant item covered by the pre-1995 estate tax anti-expatriation rules was US property owned through a foreign corporation. Had the expatriate remained a US citizen, he would have been subject to US estate tax not only on that property but also on all his foreign property.

Wherever possible an expatriate avoided the US estate tax by restricting his assets to foreign-situs property. He also avoided using a foreign corporation to own US property until ten years had elapsed after his expatriation. There were also many ways to plan around these rules.

PRE-1995 GIFT TAX RULES

Under the pre-1995 gift tax anti-expatriation rules, a non-domiciled alien donor who lost US citizenship within the preceding ten years was subject to slightly less favorable gift tax rules than an ordinary non-domiciled alien if one of the principal purposes for his loss of citizenship was the avoidance of US income, estate or gift taxes. Such a tax-avoidance expatriate was taxed on his gifts of US-situs *intangible property* as though he were still a US citizen. Normally a non-domiciled alien is not subject to US gift tax on the gift of such property. To avoid potential gift tax problems, a non-domiciled alien avoided making gifts of US-situs property other than intangible property. If there was even a remote possibility that a former citizen could be treated as a tax-avoidance expatriate, he also avoided making gifts of US intangible property.

USELESS EXEMPTIONS

The pre-1995 income tax, estate tax and gift tax anti-expatriation rules all theoretically exempted an expatriate who lost his citizenship under any of three sections of the Immigration and Nationality Act. This had become absolute nonsense since all three of these sections of the Immigration and Nationality Act had been repealed by Congress many years ago, in 1978.

REVISED EXPATRIATION TAX RULES ENACTED

President Clinton's February 1995 budget proposal would have required wealthy US tax exiles to pay a departure tax. A bill to that effect, sponsored primarily by Senator Daniel Patrick Moynihan, was passed by the Senate several times. The House of Representatives instead approved provisions contained in a bill introduced by Congressman Bill Archer, Chairman of the House Ways and Means Committee, designed to close some of the loopholes in the pre-1995 anti-expatriation rules. The House version survived and was eventually included in the *Health Insurance Portability and Accountability Act* that was passed by Congress and signed by the President in August 1996 [Public Law 104-191]. As expected, the revised expatriation tax rules apply *retroactively* to persons who expatriated after 5 February 1995.

HOW THE REVISED RULES WORK

Instead of imposing a departure tax on the date of expatriation, the revised rules have tightened up the prior anti-expatriation rules enacted 30 years earlier under which an expatriate remains taxable on US-source income for ten years. Here are the highlights of the new expatriation tax rules enacted in August 1996, generally retroactive to February 1995:

1. ***The revised rules cover both departing citizens and long-term residents.*** The pre-1995 law applied anti-expatriation rules only to citizens who lost their US citizenship. The new rules also apply to long-term residents who lose their green cards after holding them for at least eight years. They also apply to a long-term resident who claims to be nonresident under the tie-breaker rules of a tax treaty.

2. ***A tax-avoidance motive is now immaterial.*** The pre-1995 law applied only if the IRS claimed that expatriation was tax-motivated. The new rules apply automatically to almost every departing individual who has a net worth of at least $500,000, without any inquiry as to his motive for losing his citizenship or residency. A limited category of departing citizens (not resident aliens) can try to show the absence of a tax-avoidance motive. Those eligible to do so must request an IRS ruling within a year after expatriation.

3. ***The new rules still cover only US-source income and gains.*** As under the prior law, an expatriate's ongoing tax liability generally applies only to his US-source income and gains. Thus, an expatriate citizen or resident still generally has no US tax liability on foreign-source income or gains.

4. ***The new rules cover more income and gains.*** More categories of income and gains are treated as from US sources and are therefore taxable under the new rules for ten years after expatriation. Some of the loopholes that existed under the prior law have been closed. Thus, for example, the new rules prevent the tax-free exchange of assets producing US-source income for assets that produce foreign-source income.

5. ***A balance sheet and other information are required.*** New information reporting requirements are imposed on every departing citizen and long-term resident, with penalties for failure to comply. In addition to routine identifying information, an expatriate is required to furnish a balance sheet if his net worth is at least $500,000. A departing citizen has to comply with these reporting requirements when he goes to a US consulate to relinquish his citizenship.

6. ***The removal of artwork and other property may be taxed.*** The new rules authorize the IRS to issue regulations treating the removal of artwork and other tangible personal property from the US as taxable transactions.

7. ***CFC income may be covered.*** The new rules treat as US income any income and gains derived from the stock of a *controlled foreign corporation (CFC)* if the expatriate owns directly or indirectly more than 50 percent of the vote or value of the CFC stock. It apparently does not cover other types of income derived by an expatriate from a CFC, such as salaries or other compensation.

8. ***An expatriate remains taxable on income or gains from US property he contributes to a foreign company.*** A special rule applies to an expatriate who contributes US property to a foreign corporation in which he would have been a US shareholder of a CFC if he had remained a US person. He is treated as receiving the income or gains

received by the foreign corporation from the contributed property or any property substituted for it. If he sells the foreign corporation's stock or part of it, he is taxed on the gain he would have recognized if the foreign corporation had sold the contributed property or a pro rata portion thereof. This rule can be avoided if the expatriate sells the US property to the foreign corporation. This freezes his US tax liability.

9. *The new rules override tax treaties.* These rules override any conflicting tax treaty provisions until August 2006.

10. *Estate and gift taxes remain covered.* An expatriate, including a departing long-term resident, remains subject to US estate and gift taxes for ten years following expatriation on some transfers of US assets that would not be taxed if made by other non-domiciled aliens. As before, however, these taxes do not apply to the transfer of *foreign property.*

11. *The new rules are retroactive to February 1995.* The new rules apply retroactively to any citizen or long-term resident who expatriates after 5 February 1995. The key date for loss of citizenship is the date of the expatriating act if that act occurred before 6 February *1994.* If the expatriating act occurred between 6 February 1994 and 5 February 1995, the key date is the date on which the former citizen applied for a *certificate of loss of nationality (CLN)* at a US consulate or embassy abroad.

IRS NOTICE 97-19

As this edition went to press in late February 1997, the IRS issued *Notice 97-19* which details how the IRS will apply the revised expatriation tax rules. This 16,000-word notice states that the IRS plans to issue regulations incorporating the guidance set forth in the notice, and it requires taxpayers to comply with the guidance set forth in the notice until the regulations are issued. Because of its importance, the full text of Notice 97-19 is published in an appendix to this report.

NEW LAW — NEW LOOPHOLES

The revised expatriation tax rules enacted in 1996 were originally introduced by House Ways and Means Committee Chairman Bill Archer as H.R. 1812 in mid-1995. They were promptly approved by the Republican-controlled Ways and Means Committee, but the minority Democratic members of the committee issued a blistering dissenting report. At a hearing shortly thereafter, Leslie Samuels, then Assistant Secretary of the Treasury for Tax Policy, attacked H.R. 1812 as unworkable. In an appendix to his testimony, he listed these three *Possible Tax Planning Techniques for Expatriates to Avoid Tax Under H.R. 1812 on US Source Income and Gains*:

1. Under H.R. 1812, taxpayers can effectively dispose of their US assets during the ten-year period through installment sales. If an expatriate sells a US asset to a foreign

purchaser for an installment note that will mature in eleven years, it appears that no tax will be imposed on the sale under H.R. 1812. However, during the ten year period he would be able to receive interest on the installment note without US tax because the interest would be from foreign sources.

2. Property which produces US source income can be transferred to a foreign corporation without recognition of gain. As long as that corporation does not sell the property or make any distribution of income to the expatriate within the ten-year window, there will be no US tax imposed by reason of H.R. 1812 on income from those assets. After the ten-year period, the expatriate can withdraw the income without US tax. Also, an expatriate will always have an incentive to contribute his US assets to a foreign corporation, because any resulting gain is only taxed to the extent of preexpatriation gains. In contrast, if he continued to own the assets directly, he could be subject to tax on all gains.

3. An expatriate may reduce tax under H.R. 1812 by incurring interest expenses which would reduce domestic income. For example, assume that an expatriate will earn $20 million of domestic source dividends each year. The expatriate could borrow $200 million (secured by his US stock) and invest the loan proceeds in foreign instruments. After this transaction, the expatriate will earn $20 million of domestic dividends, pay $20 million of interest expense, and earn $20 million of foreign income. Despite the fact that the expatriate may not have significantly changed his overall economic position, the interest expense may be allocated (in whole or in part) against US income, thereby minimizing his US tax obligations under H.R. 1812.

H.R. 1812 subsequently became the revised expatriation tax rules, with one significant change that affects the second of these three suggested tax planning techniques. We thank Secretary Samuels for pointing out these possible loopholes in the revised expatriation tax rules. Secretary Samuels also suggested that there were probably other loopholes in this legislation. He was right; there are. I suggest that you review Secretary Samuels' loopholes with your tax adviser and inquire about others that may be even more helpful.

GIFTS AND INHERITANCES MUST BE REPORTED

Another provision enacted in 1996 requires a US citizen or resident who receives a gift or inheritance from any foreign person (not just an expatriate) exceeding $10,000 in value during a year to report the gift and to give the IRS such other information about the gift as the IRS may require [IRC Section 6039F(a)]. There is an exception covering transfers for tuition or medical care. If the recipient fails to report a gift, the IRS could recharacterize the gift as income. It could also impose a penalty of up to 25 percent of the value of the gift. If the gift is from a trust, then any amount, even $5, is reportable.

NEW IMMIGRATION LAW PROVISION

Warning! In September 1996, Congress enacted new immigration legislation that contained a provision under which the US Attorney General could make *excludable* a former citizen who renounced citizenship to avoid US taxation. It provides that:

"Any alien who is a former citizen of the United States who officially renounced United States citizenship and who is determined by the Attorney General to have renounced United States citizenship for the purpose of avoiding taxation by the United States is excludable."

The provision affects only those individuals who *renounce* US citizenship after 29 September 1996. It apparently does not apply to those who *relinquish* (rather than renounce) their US citizenship. There has been no announcement yet as to how this amendment may be applied, so it is too early to tell what impact, if any, it will have on those who expatriate after the effective date. Consult your professional adviser for any new developments.

SENATOR MOYNIHAN'S BILL

Although the Republican version proposed by Chairman Archer prevailed in 1996, it is still too early to write off completely Senator Moynihan's bill. One reason is that President Clinton, the Treasury Department and Congressional Democrats have been highly critical of Chairman Archer's bill. They contend that it will not work. They continue instead to support Senator Moynihan's bill which the Senate passed twice. Fortunately, however, President Clinton did not repropose this legislation in his February 1997 budget message. Even though Chairman Archer's bill was enacted during 1996, some future Congress may resurrect the Moynihan bill, although they probably could not do so retroactively. Here are the highlights of that earlier proposal:

1. *General principles of proposed departure tax.* A US citizen or a long-term resident (green card holder) who expatriates would be treated as having sold his worldwide property at fair market value immediately before the expatriation date. He would recognize gain or loss at that time. His net gain on the deemed sale would be taxed to the extent it exceeds $600,000. What constitutes an expatriate's property would be determined by applying estate tax rules, but US real estate and qualified retirement plans would be excluded on the theory that they will be taxed later. Special rules would determine what part of a trust an expatriate is deemed to own.

2. *Departure tax would be due 90 days after expatriation.* Unless he makes other arrangements with the IRS, an expatriate would have to pay as a tentative tax the tax that would be due for a hypothetical short tax year that ended on the expatriation date. The tentative tax would be due within 90 days after expatriation. It would be based on all his income, gain, loss and credits for the year through the expatriation date, including amounts realized from the deemed sale of property. He would also have to

file a tax return for that year on which he would receive a credit for the tentative tax paid. He could delay paying some or all of the tentative tax and the expatriation tax by reaching an agreement with the IRS to postpone payment of the tax or by electing to continue to be taxed as a US citizen.

3. ***Deferrals and extensions would terminate.*** Any deferral of income or gain would terminate on the expatriation date. Thus, for example, if an expatriate had sold his principal residence but had not yet acquired a replacement home, the period to do so would end and he would be taxed on the gain from the original sale. Any extension of time for paying tax would also terminate on the expatriation date.

4. ***Some anti-expatriation rules would be replaced.*** The existing income tax anti-expatriation rules would not apply to a former citizen who expatriated after the effective date of the new rules. Those rules would continue to apply to persons not covered by the new rules. The existing estate tax and gift tax anti-expatriation rules would, however, apply to all expatriates for ten years after expatriation.

5. ***Gifts and inheritances from an expatriate would become taxable.*** The latest version of the Moynihan proposal in effect provides that a US citizen or resident who receives a gift or inheritance from an individual subject to the departure tax would have to include the value of the gift or inheritance as taxable income. Such a provision would be totally irrational and may be unconstitutional. As noted above, however, Congress has already enacted a provision requiring the US recipient of a gift or inheritance exceeding $10,000 from a foreign person to report the gift to the IRS.

6. ***Balance sheet and other information required.*** As under the revised expatriation tax rules enacted in 1996, special information reporting requirements would be imposed on every departing citizen and long-term resident, with penalties for failure to comply.

7. ***New rules would be retroactive to February 1995.*** As under Chairman Archer's bill, the new rules would apply retroactively to any citizen or long-term resident who expatriates after 5 February 1995. However, the key date for purposes of determining liability for the expatriation tax would be the date on which he applied for a *certificate of loss of nationality (CLN)* at a US consulate or embassy abroad, not the date on which he committed an expatriating act.

THE BOTTOM LINE

Revised expatriation tax rules were enacted during 1996, retroactive to February 1995. The new rules apparently have some significant loopholes. Congress also enacted a provision requiring the US recipient of a gift or inheritance from a foreign person to report the gift to the IRS and an immigration provision under which a tax-avoidance expatriate could be declared excludable. The Moynihan bill is not dead and it could re-emerge in the future.

22. *US* ANTI-EXPATRIATION RULES--THE CASES

There have been relatively few court decisions dealing with the pre-1995 expatriation tax rules. These decisions are analyzed. This chapter is basically unchanged from last year's edition.

It is now 30 years since Congress enacted the original anti-expatriation rules. The courts have had only a few opportunities to examine these rules. Most of the reported cases have been tried by different judges in the US Tax Court and there is a great deal of helpful discussion in their published opinions. In this chapter, I will try to summarize some of the most significant points in these cases. The case citations are given so that you can locate the full text of these decisions if you or your advisers wish to explore the subject in further detail. We begin with two cases that arose before the anti-expatriation rules were enacted.

WHAT CONSTITUTES EXPATRIATION?

Upon her marriage to a Mexican citizen, American-born *Dorothy Gould Burns*, daughter of financier Jay Gould, executed a Mexican certificate of nationality. She continued to pay US income taxes and she applied for and received a US passport. A court determined that obtaining a Mexican certificate of nationality was merely a routine act of dual citizenship since she automatically became a Mexican citizen upon her marriage. Subsequent representations by her on the acquisition of a US passport prevented her from denying her continued US citizenship and her resultant US tax liability. Her estate was therefore subject to more than $3 million of US estate tax [*US v Matheson*, 532 Federal 2d 809, *certiorari denied* by the Supreme Court, 429 US 823 (1976)].

TAXPAYER LOST DESPITE HIS EXPATRIATION

In 1963, *William Dillin* moved from the US to Nassau, became a resident of the Bahamas, and renounced his US citizenship. Later that year and in the two following years he received payments totalling about $660,000 for services he had performed in 1958. Until 1963, Dillin had been resident and domiciled in Texas, a state that has community property rules. Dillin's wife, Patrea, moved to the Bahamas with him but she retained her US citizenship.

The *Dillin* case covered income received in years before the enactment of the anti-expatriation rules. The Tax Court judge accepted that Dillin was a nonresident alien when he received the payments. Dillin had to prove not only that he had established residency in the Bahamas but that he had abandoned his US residency. The judge found that he met this burden of proof. Since (like most US individuals) he was a cash basis taxpayer, he was not taxable as a US citizen merely because he had been a citizen when the work was done and the money was earned. A cash basis taxpayer was at that time taxable only when his income was actually or constructively received. His status at the time it was earned was then immaterial. The income was, however, taxable for other reasons. Dillin was taxable because the income was held to be from US sources. And, his wife had a vested interest in half of his income under Texas law from the time it was earned in 1958. Thus, she was taxable as a US citizen on that half and Dillin was only taxable on the other half [*Dillin v. Commissioner*, 56 Tax Court 228 (1971)].

Judge Sterrett indicated that Congress has every conceivable power to tax. In theory, it could enact a law taxing everyone in the world on income earned anywhere in the world. If someday Congress were to decide to expand its anti-expatriation rules to cover *foreign-source income* earned by a former US citizen or resident, the courts would probably uphold such a law.

The remaining cases discussed in this chapter arose after the enactment of the existing anti-expatriation rules in 1966.

US LIQUIDATING DIVIDEND WAS TAXED

Max Kronenberg was born in Switzerland in 1922. He immigrated to the US in 1949. He became a naturalized American citizen in 1955, but he retained his Swiss citizenship. Kronenberg owned most of the stock of a US importing business. His wife and children owned the remaining shares.

The corporation agreed to sell its assets in 1966 and it adopted a one-year plan of liquidation. Under the law then in force, there was no tax to the corporation and a capital gain to the shareholders if they received the liquidating dividend within one year. Shortly before the year was up, Kronenberg's accountants told him that the liquidating dividend would be tax free if he lost his US citizenship before he received the dividend. Just before the year ended, Kronenberg and his family moved to Switzerland and he and his wife renounced their US citizenship. The next day, a liquidating dividend of about $500,000 was paid. The IRS claimed a tax deficiency of about $100,000, contending that the liquidating dividend was taxable because Kronenberg was a tax-motivated expatriate.

Tax Court Judge Simpson found that the timing of Kronenberg's activities was too perfect to be unplanned. At least one of his principal reasons for expatriation was to try to secure the liquidating dividend free of US tax. Therefore, the anti-expatriation rules applied and the gain was taxable since it came from US sources [*Kronenberg v. Commissioner*, 64 Tax Court 428 (1975)]. The decision was not based on the special burden of proof rule provided in the anti-expatriation rules because that issue was not raised in a timely manner by the IRS. However, the judge said it didn't matter since he would have reached the same conclusion in this case with or without the special burden of proof.

PRINCESS WON DESPITE EXPATRIATION

Cecil von Furstenberg was an American heiress born in Texas in 1919. Her father was a founder of Humble Oil & Refining Co., the predecessor of Exxon Corp. She traveled extensively in Europe and spoke French and other languages like a native. She moved to Paris in 1970 and was a French resident from 1970 through 1977. She married Prince von Furstenberg in Paris in 1975. Austria's Ambassador to France granted her Austrian naturalization the same day she applied for it and she thereby lost her US citizenship that day under the 1952 Immigration and Nationality Act. (That might not be the case if she did so today unless she conceded in writing to a US Consul that she had acquired Austrian citizenship with the intention of losing her US citizenship). At the time of trial (about 1983) she and the Prince had been married for over eight years and they both planned at their deaths to be buried at the von Furstenberg family burial plot in Austria.

The IRS claimed tax deficiencies of over $5 million for the years 1975 to 1977, mostly from capital gains of over $10 million. Judge Featherston found that there was no tax-avoidance motive [*Furstenberg v. Commissioner*, 83 Tax Court 755 (1984)]. The judge believed her when she testified that tax avoidance was neither a principal purpose nor any purpose whatsoever in her decision to adopt Austrian citizenship.

She had the special burden of proof under the anti-expatriation rules after the IRS met its initial burden of showing that her taxes were substantially reduced. She had to show that tax avoidance was not one of her principal purposes in expatriating. This is a purely factual issue. She met the burden. She had lived abroad for years and she had agreed to follow the general European aristocracy custom of adopting her husband's nationality.

The judge compared her conduct with that of Max Kronenberg whose activities had been described as "too perfect to be unplanned." In contrast, her activities "were too imperfect from a tax standpoint to have been planned." For example, she did nothing to delay distributions until after her expatriation. Since the judge found that tax avoidance was not one of her principal purposes in expatriating, she was taxable as a regular nonresident alien.

The saving clause in the French-US income tax treaty did not cover tax-motivated expatriates until 1979. The judge found it unnecessary to decide the issue of whether the more general saving clause applied as claimed by the IRS based on its *Revenue Ruling 79-152*. This issue was decided against the IRS a year later in the *Tedd Crow* case, discussed below. Thus, she would probably have won her case anyway.

I am intrigued by two facts that were ignored by Judge Featherston. The von Furstenbergs had moved from France to Monte Carlo as of the time her Tax Court petition was filed, in 1980. Also, any discussions she may have had with her tax lawyer prior to expatriation was a privileged communication. She could not be required to waive that privilege and nothing could be inferred from her refusal to do so. Thus, the IRS could not refute her claim that at the time she agreed to adopt her husband's nationality as "expected" of her, she did not know what the tax consequences would be.

CAPITAL GAIN WAS EXEMPT UNDER A TREATY

In 1978, *Tedd Crow* moved to Canada and renounced his US citizenship. Shortly after he moved to Canada, he sold all of the stock of a US corporation for a $6.3 million note payable over 20 years without interest. The IRS claimed about $1.6 million tax for the capital gain in the year of sale and imputed interest income in later years.

The old 1942 Canada-US income tax treaty was in force during the year of sale. It exempted from US tax US capital gains derived by a Canadian resident with no US permanent establishment. The IRS conceded that Crow had become a nonresident alien and that he had no US permanent establishment. The IRS claimed, however, that Crow was taxable under the anti-expatriation rules. Crow conceded that the avoidance of US taxes was a principal purpose of his expatriation. The IRS relied on *Revenue Ruling 79-152* which contained almost identical facts. (I suspect that the IRS issued the revenue ruling after it became aware of what Crow had done).

Judge Cohen noted that the US traditionally insists upon maintaining its right to tax its citizens who reside in a country with which it has a tax treaty. It does so by including a saving clause in each tax treaty. The IRS did not argue that the anti-expatriation rules overrode the treaty. It could not do so because the 1966 Act that introduced the anti-expatriation rules stated that the Act's provisions would not apply in any case where they would be contrary to any treaty obligation. Instead, the IRS argued that as provided in its revenue ruling the reference to citizens in the treaty's saving clause should include former citizens who had expatriated. The legislative history of the 1966 Act stated that a treaty obligation *in force on the date of enactment* would prevail over the Act. The judge decided in favor of Crow, indicating that the issue was not what Congress could have done but what it did [*Crow v. Commissioner*, 85 Tax Court 376 (1985)]. Judge Cohen also determined that the treaty would not prevent the IRS from taxing Crow on imputed interest, apparently at a 15 percent treaty rate. Although Crow won, the move to Canada no longer works. The current Canada-US income tax treaty contains a saving clause that specifically covers *former citizens*. A list of those pre-1966 US income tax treaties that are still in force appears in the next chapter.

AUTHOR WAS TAXED ON PRE-EXPATRIATION INCOME

US-born *Norman Dacey*, the author of a best-selling book on *How to Avoid Probate*, moved to Ireland in 1980 and subsequently expatriated. The Tax Court held that he remained taxable as a US citizen until he formally renounced his US citizenship in 1988 [*Dacey v. Commissioner*, Tax Court Memo 1992-187].

Dacey claimed that he had written a letter to the US State Department in 1981 in which he renounced his US citizenship. The State Department was unable to locate any such letter. The court held that, in any event, it was not possible to renounce US citizenship by means of such a letter. Moreover, Dacey had renewed his US passport by mail in 1985 and he was bound by statements in his passport renewal application to the effect that he had not been naturalized in a foreign country and that he had not renounced his US citizenship. Dacey obtained an Irish passport in 1986 and formally renounced his US citizenship before a US consul in Dublin in 1988. The IRS successfully argued that Dacey remained a US citizen until 1988 and that he was therefore liable for income tax and self-employment (social security) tax on the royalty income he received from 1981 through 1985, plus penalties and interest. The court also approved an IRS assessment on one-half of the social security benefits he received during two of those years.

Dacey had not filed US tax returns for any of the years in question. He was not allowed any deductions for expenses since he had not claimed any. His income for the five years was determined to be about $372,000, on which he was assessed taxes of about $172,000 (an average of about 46 percent), plus penalties of some $52,000. In addition he would owe interest and a further penalty of 50 percent of the interest on the tax deficiency for most of the years. My rough calculation is that the total would come to about $494,000 (about 133 percent of the income). Dacey has since died. Presumably the IRS sought to collect by levying on any further royalties that were due to him.

23. IMPACT OF *US* TAX TREATIES

Some US tax treaties can still override the expatriation tax provisions, but only for those who expatriated before the 1996 amendments took effect. The amended provisions override all tax treaties for those who have expatriated after 5 February 1995. This chapter has been revised from last year's edition to reflect new treaties and the impact of the treaty override. The tables at the end of the chapter have also been updated.

SOME TREATIES MAY OVERRIDE THE TAX LAW

An expatriate American residing in a country that has a tax treaty with the US may be able to escape the impact of the special anti-expatriation rules because treaty provisions frequently take precedence over the US tax laws passed by Congress. The anti-expatriation provisions were originally enacted in the Foreign Investors Tax Act of 1966. No amendment made by that Act can apply in any case where its application would be contrary to any US treaty obligation.

The US Treasury later began to incorporate the anti-expatriation rules into US tax treaties. Many recent US tax treaties authorize either country to tax its former citizens for ten years when loss of citizenship had as one of its principal purposes the avoidance of tax.

1942 TREATY PREVAILED OVER TAX LAW

In 1979, the IRS issued *Revenue Ruling 79-152*, a questionable ruling in which it took the position that the anti-expatriation rules apply to a tax-motivated expatriate residing in a treaty country even when the applicable treaty does not specifically give the US the right to tax its former citizens. That ruling was sharply criticised by many tax practitioners, including me. We were vindicated in 1985 by the decision in the Crow case, discussed in the preceding chapter. Crow admitted that he had moved to Canada and renounced his US citizenship to avoid US taxes. He argued that the 1942 Canada-US income tax treaty (then still in force) precluded the US from taxing him on capital gains. The Tax Court agreed and Crow prevailed. By the time the case was decided, the 1942 treaty had been replaced by the current Canada-US income tax treaty under which Crow and similarly situated taxpayers would now lose.

Princess von Furstenberg had raised the same issue in her Tax Court case decided a year earlier. Her case, also discussed in the preceding chapter, involved the 1967 France-US income tax treaty. Since she won on another issue it was unnecessary for Judge Featherston to decide the treaty question in her case. Had she lost on the other issue, she might well have won on the treaty issue for reasons similar to those later given in the Crow case. Once again, by the time her case was decided, the 1967 France-US treaty had been amended by a 1978 protocol under which she and similarly situated taxpayers would have lost.

PRE-1966 TREATIES PREVAIL

In his opinion in the *Crow* case, Judge Cohen analyzed the legislative history of the anti-expatriation rules as they were originally enacted by the *Foreign Investors Tax Act of 1966*. He concluded that a treaty obligation *in force on the date of enactment*, 13 November 1966, would prevail over the Act. Now, over 30 years later, only seven pre-1966 income tax treaties are still in force and several of them will be replaced in the next year or two.

REMAINING PRE-1966 INCOME TAX TREATIES

As of early 1997, the remaining pre-1966 US income tax treaties still in force are with Austria, Denmark, Greece, Ireland, Luxembourg, Pakistan and Switzerland. These are the only treaties that fall squarely within the holding in the *Crow* case. Some of these treaties exempt capital gains; others do not. None of them is likely to work as favorably as the 1942 Canada-US treaty did for *Tedd Crow*. If you are planning to move to any of these countries, you should consult with your tax adviser to see if you can possibly obtain benefits similar to those enjoyed by Crow. New treaties with Austria, Luxembourg and Switzerland have been signed but are not yet in force.

SOME LATER TREATIES BLOCK FORMER CITIZENS

Prior to 1977, the typical saving clause in a US income tax treaty permitted either country (or just the US) to tax its residents and its citizens as if the treaty had not come into effect. The 1977 US model income tax treaty, Treasury's starting point in treaty negotiations, introduced new language to the saving clause. It would extend the saving clause to include a *former citizen* whose loss of citizenship had as one of its principal purposes the avoidance of income taxes, for ten years following such loss. This clause was generally consistent with the statutory income tax anti-expatriation rule. However, it covered only avoidance of income tax whereas the law covers avoidance of *any* tax, and it therefore also applies if the taxpayer's purpose is to avoid gift or estate taxes.

Treasury included a clause like the one contained in its 1977 model treaty in protocols with France, Norway and Jamaica signed between 1978 and 1981. It kept the same clause in its 1981 draft US model income tax treaty. However, most new treaties and protocols signed since 1982 cover former citizens whose principal purpose is to avoid any tax.

I believe that the courts would uphold these clauses as valid. Former citizens residing in these countries should assume that they are subject to the anti-expatriation rules for ten years following their loss of citizenship. There are now 25 US income tax treaties with saving clauses expressly covering former citizens. These treaties are with Australia, Barbados, Canada, Cyprus, the Czech Republic, Finland, France, Germany, Hungary, India, Indonesia, Israel, Italy, Jamaica, Kazakstan, Mexico, the Netherlands, New Zealand, Norway, Portugal, Russia, Slovakia, Spain, Sweden and Tunisia.

There are some minor variations in these provisions. For example, the 1989 Germany-US income tax protocol covers only income tax avoidance but there is a clause in the 1980 Germany-US estate and gift tax treaty covering avoidance of any tax. The 1990 protocol with Spain requires the two governments to consult together on the purposes of the loss of citizenship. The Tunisia-US provision applies only if the avoidance motive is either acknowledged by the taxpayer or determined by a court decision. The 1992 Netherlands-US treaty does not permit the US to tax a former US citizen who is a *Dutch national.*

LATER TREATIES WITHOUT SPECIFIC PROVISIONS

Although the *Crow* decision specifically covered only pre-1966 treaties, each of 14 post-1966 US income tax treaties contains a saving clause that fails to mention any right of the US to tax its former citizens. These treaties are with Belgium, Bermuda, China, the CIS (most of the countries that formerly comprised the USSR), Egypt, Iceland, Japan, Korea, Morocco, the Philippines, Poland, Romania, Trinidad and Tobago and the United Kingdom. It is certainly arguable that the result under each of these treaties should be the same as that under the *Crow* case. The Bermuda-US treaty covers only insurance enterprises. The Malta-US treaty was terminated at the end of 1996; it had presented a special problem. The treaty itself didn't mention former citizens but the Senate Foreign Relations Committee's report on the treaty gratuitously suggested that the IRS position was that the treaty's saving clause was intended to cover former citizens. This suggestion was based on *Revenue Ruling 79-152* which was later discredited by the *Crow* case.

THE BOTTOM LINE FOR INCOME TAX TREATIES

An income tax treaty is most likely to be of significant benefit to someone whose tax motive for expatriation is to escape a large capital gains tax on the sale of a family-owned business. Using a combination of the old Canada-US income tax treaty and internal Canadian rules, Tedd Crow apparently escaped taxes in both countries. Most of those treaties remaining are unlikely to give you that good a result. There are, however, some possibilities that might be considered. These should be discussed with your tax adviser. As noted below, the recently enacted revised expatriation tax rules override all tax treaties.

PRE-1966 ESTATE TAX TREATIES

Pre-1966 estate and gift tax treaties should similarly prevail over the existing anti-expatriation rules. As of early 1997, the remaining pre-1966 US estate tax treaties still in force are with Australia, Finland, Greece, Ireland, Italy, Japan, Norway, South Africa and Switzerland. There are two separate treaties with Australia, one covering estate tax and the other covering gift tax. These treaties have never been terminated even though Australia no longer imposes such taxes. The treaty with Japan also covers both the estate and gift taxes.

The others cover only estate or other death taxes. None of them expressly covers the generation-skipping transfer tax.

LATER ESTATE TAX TREATIES

All but one of the seven post-1966 US estate tax treaties also cover the gift tax and the generation-skipping transfer tax. The exception is the Netherlands in which only the estate tax is covered. The others are with Austria, Denmark, France, Germany, Sweden and the United Kingdom.

The saving clause in each of the estate tax treaties with Austria, Denmark, Germany and Sweden expressly denies coverage of some treaty provisions to a former citizen who is a tax-motivated expatriate. The treaties with France, the Netherlands and the United Kingdom do not appear to do so.

THE BOTTOM LINE FOR ESTATE TAX TREATIES

If you are moving to any of the mentioned countries, review the situation carefully with your tax adviser. The absence of a specific provision covering tax-motivated expatriates in the post-1966 estate and gift tax treaty with France, for example, may exempt a former US citizen domiciled in France from US estate, gift and generation-skipping transfer taxes on transfers of shares of a US corporation. To the extent that the applicable French taxes are lower than those imposed by the US, this could result in a saving. As noted below, the recently enacted revised expatriation tax rules override all tax treaties.

1997 UPDATE

Congress has stated that the recently amended expatriation tax provisions will override any conflicting tax treaty provisions until 21 August 2006. Thus, a former US citizen or a former long-term resident who has expatriated after 5 February 1995 cannot benefit from any favorable tax treaty provisions. Former citizens who expatriated before that date can generally still benefit from favorable tax treaty provisions; however, any former citizen who attempted to expatriate by committing an expatriating act, such as obtaining another citizenship with the intent to lose US citizenship, after 5 February 1994 is subject to the new provisions unless he perfected his expatriation before a US consul prior to 6 February 1995.

TABLES OF RELEVANT TAX TREATIES

Set forth below are six tables showing the current status of US income tax and estate tax treaties and their potential impact on former US citizens. These tables provide information concerning pre-1966 US income tax treaties still in force, post-1966 US income tax treaties with saving clauses that do not expressly mention former citizens and those with saving clauses that do, pending US income tax treaties that are not yet in force, pre-1966 US estate and gift tax treaties still in force, and post-1966 US estate and gift tax treaties. These tables have been updated as of March 1997.

IMPACT OF US TAX TREATIES ON FORMER CITIZENS

1. *Pre-1966 US Income Tax Treaties Still in Force* - The table below lists the pre-1966 US income tax treaties that were still in force as of March 1997:

Country/Treaty	Signed	Amended
Austria-1 [1]	1956	
Denmark-1 [2]	1948	
Greece-1	1950	1953
Ireland-1	1949	
Luxembourg-1 [1]	1962	
Pakistan-1	1957	
Switzerland-1 [1]	1951	

1   A proposed new treaty was signed in 1996, but it has not yet entered into force.

2   A proposed new Denmark-2 treaty was signed in 1980 and amended in 1983 but it is unlikely to enter into force without further amendments.

2. *Post-1966 US Income Tax Treaties With Saving Clauses That Do Not Expressly Mention Former Citizens* - The table below lists such treaties that were in force as of March 1997:

Country/Treaty	Signed	Amended	Article
Belgium-2	1970	1987	23(1)
Bermuda-1 [1]	1986		4(1)
China-1	1984	1986	1984 Protocol ¶ 2
CIS/Former USSR-1 [2]	1973		VII
Egypt-1	1980		6(3)
Iceland-1	1975		4(3)
Japan-2	1971		4(3)
Korea-1	1976		4(4)
Morocco-1	1977		20(3)
Philippines-1	1976		6(3)
Poland-1	1974		5(3)
Romania-1	1973		4(3)
Trinidad-3	1970		3(3)
United Kingdom-2	1975	1976-79	1(3)

1 The Bermuda-1 treaty is limited and generally covers only insurance enterprises.

2 The CIS/Former USSR-1 treaty now applies in all of the CIS states, except Russia and Kazakstan. It covers Armenia, Azerbaijan, Belarus, Georgia, Kyrgyzstan, Moldova, Tajikistan, Turkmenistan, Ukraine and Uzbekistan. New Russia-2 and Kazakstan-2 treaties are now in force with those countries. A proposed new Ukraine-2 treaty has been signed, but it has not yet entered into force.

3. *Post-1966 US Income Tax Treaties With Saving Clauses That Expressly Apply to Former Citizens* - The table below lists such treaties that were in force as of March 1997:

Country/Treaty	Signed	Amended	Article	Avoidance of
Australia-2	1982		1(3)	tax
Barbados-2	1984	1991	1(3)	tax
Canada-3	1980	1983-95	XXIX(2)	tax
Cyprus-2	1984		4(3)	tax
Czech Republic-1	1993		1(3)	unlimited
Finland-3	1989		1(3)	tax
France-4	1994		29(2)	income tax
Germany-2	1989		Protocol ¶ 1(a)	income tax
Hungary-1	1979		1(2)	unlimited
India-1	1989		1(3)	tax
Indonesia-1	1988	1996	28(3)	tax
Israel-1 [1]	1975	1980-93	6(3)	tax
Italy-2	1984		1(2), Protocol Art 1(1)	tax
Jamaica-2	1980	1981	1(3), 13(7)	income tax, gains
Kazakstan-2	1993		1(3)	unlimited
Mexico-1	1992	1994	1(3)	tax
Netherlands-2 [2]	1992	1993	24(1)	income tax
New Zealand-2	1982		1(3)	tax
Norway-2	1971	1980	22(3)	income tax
Portugal-1 [1]	1994		Protocol ¶ 1(b)	tax
Russia-2	1992		1(3)	unlimited
Slovakia-1	1993		1(3)	unlimited
Spain-1 [1]	1990		1(3), Protocol ¶ 1	tax
Sweden-2	1994		1(4)	tax
Tunisia-1 [3]	1985	1989	22(2)	tax

1   Consultations may be required before treaty benefits are denied.

2   The clause does not permit the US to tax a former US citizen who is a *Dutch national*.

3   The Tunisia-1 treaty requires a court decision if the taxpayer does not concede a tax-avoidance motive.

4.   *Pending US Income Tax Treaties With Saving Clauses That Expressly Apply to Former Citizens* - The table below lists treaties that were signed but not yet in force as of March 1997:

Country/Treaty	Signed	Article	Avoidance of
Austria-2	1996	1(4)	tax
Luxembourg-2	1996	1(3)	tax
South Africa-2 [1]	1997	1(4)	tax
Switzerland-2	1996	1(2)	unlimited
Thailand-1 [1]	1996	1(2)	tax
Turkey-1	1996	1(3)	tax
Ukraine-2	1994	1(3)	unlimited

1   The proposed South Africa-2 and Thailand-1 income tax treaties would allow the US to tax both its former citizens *and its former long-term residents* whose loss of citizenship or residence was to avoid tax *as defined under US law*.

5.   *Pre-1966 US Estate and Gift Tax Treaties Still in Force* - The table below lists the pre-1966 US estate and gift tax treaties that were still in force as of March 1997:

Country	Signed	Effective	Taxes Covered
Australia	1953	1953-54	estate/gift
Finland	1952	1952	estate
Greece	1950-53	1953	estate
Ireland	1949	1951	estate
Italy	1955	1956	estate
Japan	1954	1955	estate/gift
Norway	1949-51	1951	estate
South Africa	1947-52	1952	estate
Switzerland	1951	1952	estate

6. *Post-1966 US Estate and Gift Tax Treaties in Force* - The table below lists the post-1966 US estate, gift and generation-skipping transfer (GST) tax treaties that were still in force as of March 1997:

Country	Signed	Effective	Taxes Covered	Former Citizen Covered?
Austria	1982	1983	estate+gift+GST	yes
Denmark	1983	1984	estate+gift+GST	yes
France	1978	1980	estate+gift+GST	no
Germany	1980	1979	estate+gift+GST	yes
Netherlands	1969	1971	estate	no
Sweden	1983	1984	estate+gift+GST	yes
United Kingdom	1978	1979	estate+gift+GST	no

24. LEAVING AMERICA (THE *US*)

People leave the US for both tax and non-tax reasons. Except as to gains from the sale of US real estate, a nonresident alien is generally taxed much more favorably than either a US citizen or resident. The recently amended expatriation tax provisions generally require a former US citizen or a former long-term green card holder to pay the same tax as an American on all of his US-source income and gains, but he can still escape US tax on most of his foreign income and gains. This chapter has been substantially revised from last year's edition.

An estimated 250,000 Americans move out of the US each year but most of them are not true tax exiles. The vast majority of them retain their American citizenship and therefore remain liable for US taxes, at least at the federal level.

WHY AMERICANS ARE LEAVING

Articles in mainstream publications such as *Forbes* and *Money* have begun to take notice of the fact that many Americans don't like the direction the US has been taking during recent years. Some are leaving; others are thinking about doing so. An article entitled *Escape From America*, by Gary Belsky [*Money*, July 1994, pages 60-70], noted the following points:

- The US is facing a brain drain.
- 60 percent of Americans say the US quality of life is getting worse.
- Record numbers of Americans are moving abroad each year to seek better lives.
- Those leaving include some of the country's wealthiest and best-educated native-born citizens.
- Some 250,000 people now emigrate from the US each year (up from 160,000).
- About half of them are native-born Americans (up from 20 percent a few years ago).
- About 25 percent of college-educated Americans and 25 percent of those earning $50,000 or more a year have considered emigrating.
- More skills are draining from the US than are entering it.
- One family who left says: "We've finally captured the American dream. It's just a shame that we had to come to New Zealand to do it."

Significantly, the *Money* article did not deal with those who may be leaving to avoid what they consider to be confiscatory taxes. Although tax relief may be one of the reasons why some Americans are leaving, I believe that the vast majority of them would stay if they were satisfied with the quality of life in their country. Once they really decide to go, some of them become interested in the possible tax benefits they could enjoy if they became tax exiles rather than mere emigrants.

BECOMING A *TAX EXILE*

The only way a US citizen can legally eliminate all US income and estate taxes is by cutting off all of the tentacles of the dreaded tax octopus discussed in Chapter 3 above. To become an American tax exile you must:

- Move abroad so that you are no longer a US resident for federal income tax purposes.
- Change your domicile from some American state to a suitable foreign country so that you are no longer a US domiciliary for federal estate tax purposes.
- Give up your US citizenship so that you are no longer subject to federal income and estate taxes based on your citizenship.
- Make certain that your status is not tainted by that of your spouse. You can accomplish this in either of two ways. One is for your spouse to take all of the same steps that you do. The other is to make sure that none of your property or income is jointly owned or subject to community property rules.
- Make sure that most or all of your income is derived from foreign sources under the US income tax rules.
- Make sure that most or all of your assets are foreign-situs property under the US estate and gift tax rules.
- Coordinate the timing of all of these changes and be sure that you know when each of them will be fully effective.
- Determine whether your beneficiaries will also become tax exiles and, if not, the likely tax impact on them when they eventually inherit your estate.

In the remainder of this chapter we will take a closer look at some of these steps.

ABANDONING *US* RESIDENCY

It generally doesn't matter very much whether a US citizen is also a US resident. He is taxable on his worldwide income anyway because of his citizenship. The only exception is that an American citizen working abroad may qualify to exclude up to $70,000 a year of earned income for foreign personal services from US income tax, but not from social security taxes. He may be able to increase the foreign earned income exclusion by a housing allowance if he is paying a high amount of rent abroad. In any case he is fully subject to US tax on his unearned income and capital gains derived anywhere in the world. He gets a foreign tax credit for the foreign taxes he pays on his foreign-source income, except for taxes paid on any excluded income.

From the standpoint of estate taxes, the US citizen who lives overseas has precisely the same liability as the US citizen living at home. The rates are progressive and reach a maximum of 55 percent on taxable estates of more than $3 million. All of his US and foreign assets are fully included in his taxable estate.

HOW A *US* CITIZEN OR RESIDENT ALIEN IS TAXED

Whether an *alien* is resident or nonresident is a critical issue of tax law. If you are either a US citizen or an alien who is resident for income tax purposes, the following rules apply:

- You pay federal income tax at rates up to 39.6 percent on all of your US-source income except for tax-free interest from US municipal bonds.
- You are also subject to US income tax on all of your foreign-source income, but you may generally take a foreign tax credit for foreign taxes paid.
- Shares you own in a foreign corporation may subject you to current US tax on your pro rata share of its undistributed earnings if the foreign corporation is either a foreign personal holding company (FPHC) or a controlled foreign corporation (CFC).
- Your shares in foreign corporations may be subject to the passive foreign investment company (PFIC) rules.
- Transfers of appreciated property to a foreign corporation or a foreign trust are subject to a 35 percent excise tax.
- You pay US tax at regular rates up to a maximum of 28 percent on capital gains derived from both US and foreign sources. Gain is determined by reference to your historic cost, even if you acquired the property many years before you moved into the US.

HOW A NONRESIDENT ALIEN IS TAXED

If you are a nonresident alien for income tax purposes, you are subject to a substantially different taxing system. If you are a nonresident alien but you were a US citizen or a long-term US resident alien with a green card at any time during the past ten years and you are treated as having expatriated for tax-avoidance reasons, you are taxed under a special system which denies you some of the beneficial tax treatment accorded to nonresident aliens generally, *but only with respect to US-source income*.

Listed below is the treatment accorded to you if you are a nonresident alien. The special rules that apply for ten years if you are a former American citizen or long-term resident who has expatriated to avoid taxes are shown in *italics*.

- You pay US income tax at regular rates up to 39.6 percent on any income that is effectively connected with the conduct of a US trade or business.
- You are subject to a maximum 30 percent US withholding tax on dividends, interest, and other investment income that you derive from US sources; the 30 percent tax rate may be reduced or eliminated by favorable income tax treaty provisions. *If you are treated as a tax-motivated expatriate you might have to pay the higher regular income tax rate, up to 39.6 percent; you would not be entitled to benefits under any US income tax treaties.*
- Your interest income derived from some US bonds and from US banks and savings

institutions would be completely tax free. *A tax-motivated expatriate would be taxable on this income.*

- You are not subject to any US income tax on your foreign-source income except under a few very limited circumstances.

- You are not subject to the FPHC, CFC or PFIC rules. Thus, you are not subject to any US tax on your share of undistributed earnings of a foreign corporation. *A tax-motivated expatriate remains taxable on dividends and gains derived from shares of his former CFC.*

- Your transfers of appreciated property to a foreign corporation or a foreign trust are not subject to excise tax.

- You are not ordinarily subject to any US tax on your capital gains derived from foreign sources. Moreover, you do not ordinarily pay any US tax on your capital gains from US sources unless they relate to US real estate or a US business. *If you are a tax-motivated expatriate, you may have to pay a maximum 28 percent tax on your capital gains from US sources. This treatment would also apply to foreign property and securities that you acquired through tax-free exchanges of US property for foreign property.*

FOUR HYPOTHETICAL EXAMPLES

A detailed explanation of the *US residency rules* is set forth in Chapter 15 above. A tax exile leaving the US is likely to fall into one of several categories that are illustrated by these hypothetical examples:

- *Alvin Almaden* was born in the US and has always lived there. He plans to move abroad and to abandon his US citizenship as soon as he can acquire another one.

- *Bruno Brunello* was born abroad, but he moved to the US many years ago and has since become a naturalized US citizen. He plans to move back to his country of birth, reacquire citizenship there which he can do on demand, and give up his American citizenship.

- *Charlton Chablis* was born abroad. He came to America as a lawful immigrant with a green card several years ago, but he never became a US citizen. He plans to leave America and become resident in a tax haven.

- *Doris Dole* is an American citizen. She has already lived and worked abroad for the past several years, and she now plans to give up her US citizenship as well.

If we assume that Almaden, Brunello and Chablis all plan to move out of the US during 1997, we need to examine their residency status for US income tax purposes for the years 1997, 1998 and later years. Dole's situation is simpler since she is already living abroad.

Even if Almaden moves abroad at the beginning of 1997, he will probably remain a US taxpayer for that year both because of the substantial presence test under the residency rules and because of his citizenship. He will need time to acquire another citizenship and to abandon his US citizenship. Regardless of his residency status, Almaden will remain taxable until he loses his US citizenship. Even if he is able to complete the expatriation process early in 1997, he may still be a resident for that year because of the substantial presence test. In determining his residency for 1997, Almaden must count all the days he spends in the US in 1997, plus one-third of the days he spent in the US in 1996 and one-sixth of the days he spent there in 1995. If he spent all of 1995 and 1996 in the US, he may already be resident for 1997. Even if he spent only 330 days in the US in each of the prior years, he would have to count 55 days for 1995 and 110 days for 1996, giving him 165 days, all but 17 of his allowable 182 days. One rule could help Almaden for the year 1997. He could move abroad in January 1997 and remain out of the US for the balance of that year. The substantial presence test would not apply to him that year if, after eliminating excluded days, he is in the US for less than 31 days during that year. Thus, Almaden can avoid US residency for 1997 if he is present in the US that year for 30 days or less. He might be able to spend some additional days in America that year if they are excluded days because he is, for example, a qualified student, teacher or diplomat, but this is unlikely. If he does spend only 30 days in the US during 1997, he can spend substantially more time in the US during 1998 and later years. During 1998, for example, he would count 10 days for 1997 (one-third of 30 days) and 61 days at most for 1996. That would allow him another 111 days during 1998. As a practical matter, he should thereafter be able to spend safely between 100 and 120 days a year in the US without running into residency problems under the substantial presence test.

Brunello can control his timing more easily since he can reestablish his prior foreign residency and citizenship at will. He too should move at the beginning of the year and he should spend a maximum of 30 days in the US during 1997.

Chablis will likewise meet the substantial presence test for 1997 unless he departs permanently at the beginning of the year and he spends no more than 30 days in America that year. He should abandon his green card when he leaves or promptly thereafter. Until he does so he will remain a US resident under the green card test. If he merely puts his green card into a desk drawer or cuts it in half and throws it away, he would remain a US resident for income tax purposes. There must be an official administrative determination that Chablis has abandoned his green card. Time permitting, the best procedure would be for him to complete his move abroad and then immediately turn in his green card at an American Consulate. He should request a receipt for the green card and a multiple-entry B-1/B-2 visa permitting him to visit the US for business or pleasure.

Dole should have the least problem with timing since she already lives abroad. If she has been spending less than four months a year in the US, she can continue to spend up to 120 days each year there without running into problems under the substantial presence test. Like Almaden, she will remain a US taxpayer until she actually relinquishes her US citizenship.

ABANDONING *US* DOMICILE

Most Americans don't know or care where they are domiciled. Under US law the place where an individual is domiciled is determined by state rather than federal law. Although the rules tend to be similar, there can be minor technical differences in the rules governing domicile from one state to another. Even for affluent Americans the issue of where they are domiciled is relatively insignificant except when they make a will, get divorced, move overseas, make large gifts or die owning substantial assets. Domicile does not affect an American's liability for federal income taxes. Whether an American is domiciled in the US is also immaterial for federal estate and gift tax purposes. He is fully subject to these taxes on his worldwide assets because of his citizenship.

If you want to leave America to become a tax exile, *you must establish a new domicile in a suitable foreign country*. You don't want to go out of the frying pan and into the fire. You have to make sure that your new place of domicile is suitable for the purpose. You will want a country that does not increase your income tax burden or impose high death taxes by reason of your domicile there. In Part VI of this report, Chapters 36 to 64, I will review for you the tax consequences of citizenship, residency and domicile in many of the foreign countries to which you might consider moving. If you have to give up a US domicile, you must limit your choice to a place in which you can establish a new domicile without thereby creating new tax problems.

ABANDONING *US* CITIZENSHIP

Suppose that you decide to give up your US citizenship. Unless you are already living abroad, you must first find a place that is willing to accept you as a resident and in which you and your family are willing to live. You must apply for and obtain the required residence permits. If you plan to work, you will probably also need a work permit. Most countries will require you to be a resident for several years before you can even apply for citizenship. Since it is difficult for a stateless person to travel from country to country, you should not relinquish your existing citizenship without first obtaining some other citizenship and passport. A US consul may balk at accepting your voluntary renunciation of citizenship unless you can satisfy him that you have another citizenship. Neither the US nor any other country wants you to be stateless. They want you to belong to some country so they can send you back if you *"misbehave."*

Most countries offer passports only to citizens. However, if you plan to give up your US citizenship, you can probably obtain citizenship and a passport somewhere if you are willing to pay for these privileges. Let us assume that the country you have chosen to live in will not give you either citizenship or a passport for several years. You may be able to obtain another citizenship because of your religion or ethnic origin. You may already be entitled to some other citizenship because of where your spouse or parents or grandparents were born. You may be able to acquire *economic citizenship* by making an acceptable investment in another country. Information concerning several such programs is contained in Part VI of this report, Chapters 36 to 64. You should be certain that the passport is legally issued and is not subject to possible revocation. I have consulted with many clients on the subject of obtaining an additional or alternative citizenship and passport. In cases where I have not been able to help a particular client, I have worked with or referred them to other reliable consultants. *The Passport Report*, published by Scope International, also contains useful information on obtaining passports.

AMENDED EXPATRIATION TAX PROVISIONS

President Clinton's February 1995 budget proposal would have required wealthy US tax exiles to pay a departure tax. Senator Moynihan's bill to that effect was passed by the Senate twice, but the House of Representatives instead approved amendments introduced by Chairman Archer of the House Ways and Means Committee that closed some of the loopholes contained in the prior expatriation tax provisions. The House version survived and was included in the *Health Insurance Portability and Accountability Act* that was enacted in August 1996 [Public Law 104-191]. As I predicted in the previous edition of this report, the 1996 amendments to the expatriation tax provisions were made retroactive to February 1995. They generally require a former US citizen or a former long-term green card holder who expatriated after 5 February 1995 to pay the same tax as an American on all of his US-source income and gains, but he can still escape US tax on most of his foreign income and gains.

AN ALIEN WHO GIVES UP HIS GREEN CARD IS AN EXPATRIATE

A resident alien who surrendered his *green card* before 6 February 1995 is treated as an ordinary nonresident alien. A long-term resident alien who surrenders his green card after 5 February 1995 is subject to the amended expatriation tax provisions if he has held his green card for eight out of the preceding 15 years. He must generally pay the same tax as an American on all of his US-source income and gains for ten years following his expatriation, but he can escape US tax on most of his foreign income and gains. In determining gains on property that he held on the date he first became a resident alien, however, he may use as his basis the fair market value of the property on that date. He is treated as a tax-motivated expatriate and is subject to the amended expatriation tax provisions if his net worth at the time he surrenders his green card is at least $500,000 *or* he has paid US income taxes averaging over $100,000 a year in the five years preceding his expatriation.

25. LEAVING BRITAIN (THE *UK*)

You must abandon your residence and ordinary residence in Britain to escape UK income and capital gains taxes. You also need to change your domicile so as to reduce or eliminate your potential liability to the 40 percent UK inheritance tax. The minor changes to this chapter from last year's edition are reflected in the *1997 Update* at the end of the chapter.

It is much easier to establish residence in Britain than to abandon it. Any one of several different tests may continue to make you a resident of the UK for income tax purposes. It is even harder to abandon your UK domicile, particularly if it was your domicile of origin.

ABANDONING RESIDENCE AND ORDINARY RESIDENCE

The UK has two sets of residency rules. If you are to succeed in avoiding UK income tax and capital gains tax, you must abandon both *residence* and *ordinary residence*. Generally, if you spend too many days in Britain during any given tax year you will be *resident* for that year. And, if you have been habitually resident in Britain year after year, you will be *ordinarily resident*. It is not unusual for someone to be a UK resident without being an ordinary resident. The converse does not generally occur. To abandon both residence and ordinary residence, you must:

- Avoid being physically present in the UK for more than 182 days in any tax year. For individuals, the tax year begins on 6 April and ends on the following 5 April.
- Avoid regular visits to Britain exceeding an average of 90 days a year for four years.
- Be able to show that you have set up a permanent home abroad. A *perpetual tourist (PT)* will have great difficulty in establishing that he has abandoned residency for UK tax purposes.
- Be able to show that you are working or self-employed full-time abroad and that your visits to the UK are for a temporary purpose.
- Until 1993, you had to avoid having *available accommodation* in the UK. Otherwise, even one day in the UK during a year could make you resident that year. This rule was a real stinker when it applied. You didn't even have to own a house or flat; the rule applied if you had a place set aside for you, such as a bedroom in someone's home. Fortunately, there were some exceptions to the available accommodation rule. For example, it did not apply if you were employed or self-employed *full-time* abroad and none of your duties were carried out in the UK. You could then have accommodation available or even own property in the UK and still be nonresident. The 1993 UK Finance Act eliminated the available accommodation rule for later years.

A few years ago the UK considered adopting new residency rules similar to those now in force in the US. The proposal was abandoned by the Tory government after strong protests by some of those who benefit from the present system. It remains to be seen what will happen to these rules if Labour replaces the Tories in the next general election which must take place by May 1997.

HOW DOMICILE AFFECTS YOUR TAX LIABILITY

As in the US, you can only have one domicile at any given time. If your *domicile of origin* is in some part of the UK, you remain domiciled there until you convincingly establish a new *domicile of choice*. British courts put a heavy burden on anyone who claims that an individual has changed his domicile, particularly if it was his domicile of origin. This helps a newcomer to Britain to avoid establishing a domicile in the UK; it makes it much harder for a Briton to leave.

A green paper on *Residence in the United Kingdom* published in 1988 by the UK Board of Inland Revenue suggested that domicile can be capricious in its effects. For example, an individual may be domiciled in a country which he has never visited. He may not be domiciled in the UK even if he was born there, has lived in the UK all his life, and he holds a British passport. He will be taxed differently from his neighbor who is in all respects the same except that he has a UK domicile.

To establish a foreign domicile of choice, you must sever your ties with the UK and settle in another country with the clear intention of making your permanent home there. If you are not careful, under present rules you might later revive your domicile of origin without intending to do so. Let us look at a hypothetical example:

Edward Emilion's domicile of origin is England since that was his father's domicile when he was born and throughout his childhood. Ten years ago he moved out of Britain, established his permanent home on the Costa del Sol in Spain, and made Spain his domicile of choice. He is now planning to leave Spain and to wander around the world as a *perpetual tourist (PT)* with no fixed home. Under UK rules, if Emilion abandons his domicile of choice in Spain and he does not establish a new domicile of choice somewhere else, his English domicile of origin will be revived, complete with all its nasty tax consequences.

The UK has considered changing some of its domicile rules, but the change is not imminent. Under the proposed rules, he would never revert to his domicile of origin. Instead, he would retain his current domicile of choice until he acquired a new one. See Chapter 40 below for a more-detailed discussion of the proposed rules.

WIFE CAN HAVE A SEPARATE DOMICILE

In 1973, the UK adopted a very civilized law that permits a married woman to acquire a separate domicile from that of her husband. A wife leaving Britain should make certain that she adopts her own domicile if she is unsure of or not happy with her husband's domicile.

CITIZENSHIP IS IRRELEVANT FOR TAX PURPOSES

Whether you are a British national is generally irrelevant for UK tax purposes. Thus, most Britons leaving the UK retain British nationality.

TAX IMPLICATIONS OF LEAVING BRITAIN

If you are no longer resident or ordinarily resident in Britain and you are no longer domiciled in some part of the UK, you will not be subject to UK income tax except on income arising in the UK. And, if you are neither resident nor ordinarily resident, you will generally also be exempt from UK capital gains tax.

The UK inheritance tax covers your UK property regardless of where you are domiciled. If you are domiciled in some part of the UK, or deemed to be domiciled there for inheritance tax purposes, the inheritance tax is now 40 percent on the value of your worldwide estate exceeding £215,000.

It will take you some time to abandon your UK domicile for inheritance tax purposes. For inheritance tax purposes only, you are deemed domiciled in the UK if at the time of your death you had been a *resident* of the UK for 17 out of the last 20 years *or* you had been *domiciled* in the UK during the preceding three years. After you finish four complete tax years of nonresidence and non-domicile, you can no longer be deemed domiciled in the UK for inheritance tax purposes. If you succeed in abandoning your UK domicile, you will no longer be subject to UK inheritance tax on your foreign property.

1997 UPDATE

The UK inheritance tax allowance has been raised from £200,000 to £215,000 for persons dying after 5 April 1997. A UK general election must be held by May 1997 and Labour has a big lead in the pre-election opinion polls. If they win, a Labour Government may change some or all of the rules discussed in this chapter.

26. LEAVING CANADA

You must abandon your residence and ordinary residence in Canada to escape Canadian income and capital gains taxes. You may keep your Canadian citizenship and you may be able to retain your Canadian domicile but that may be difficult to do while abandoning residence. The only change to this chapter from last year's edition is the addition of the *1997 Update* at the end of the chapter.

The Canadian residency rules are somewhat similar to the UK rules. An individual who is present in Canada for more than 182 days during a year is resident that year. However, an individual present less than half the year may still be resident in Canada if he is ordinarily resident in Canada. Whether you are resident in Canada will be determined based on all of the facts and circumstances. If you leave Canada but keep your house available for your occupancy, you will have difficulty convincing Revenue Canada that you are no longer resident. It will help considerably if you lease it to a third party for a year or two and you have no right to reoccupy it. It may be impossible for you to claim that you are not resident in Canada unless you can show that you have established a new residence someplace else. If you leave Canada and become a *perpetual tourist (PT)* you will probably still be treated as a Canadian resident for tax purposes. In determining whether you have abandoned your residency, Revenue Canada will also look at factors such as the regularity of your visits to Canada, whether your spouse and children are in Canada and whether you own or lease your new home abroad.

If you are resident in Canada, you are taxable on your worldwide income and your worldwide capital gains. If you succeed in becoming nonresident, you will only be taxable on income and capital gains from Canadian sources. However, you may be subject to a *departure tax* when you leave Canada in the form of a capital gains tax on your assets other than taxable Canadian property. If you leave Canada during the year to take up permanent residence abroad, you are taxable on your worldwide income and gains for the period preceding your departure.

CAPITAL GAINS TAX AT DEATH

Canada currently has no federal gift tax and no federal tax at death other than a capital gains tax as though you had sold your assets just before you died. If you have previously abandoned your Canadian residency, this capital gains tax at death will apply only to your taxable Canadian property. For many years, none of the Canadian provinces has imposed any death taxes.

DEPARTURE TAX PLANNING

Canada's departure tax generally applies if you have been a resident of Canada for more than 60 months (five years) out of the ten years preceding your departure. If so, you are deemed to have sold and reacquired your assets other than taxable Canadian property just before you left, subjecting you to a capital gains tax. Your *taxable Canadian property* is not subject to the departure tax since it remains taxable at your death or when you sell it. If you have been in Canada less than five years you do not pay the departure tax on foreign properties you owned when you became a Canadian resident.

When you leave Canada, you can elect to treat property that would be subject to the departure tax as taxable Canadian property. You may have to provide Revenue Canada with a bond or other acceptable security to cover the departure tax that would otherwise have been payable. One advantage of doing so is that you may later be able to reduce or eliminate the capital gains tax under Canada's tax treaty with your new country of residence.

PROVING NONRESIDENCE IS GETTING HARDER

My Canadian colleagues tell me that it is getting harder to convince Revenue Canada that an individual has terminated residence for tax purposes. Revenue Canada now has a *Form NR73(E)* which you can use to show that you are no longer resident. The form is not mandatory; some practitioners think it may be better not to use it.

DOMICILE AND CITIZENSHIP ARE IRRELEVANT

Neither your domicile nor your citizenship has any relevance to your Canadian tax liability. If you can succeed in abandoning your status as a resident and ordinary resident of Canada, you may find it advantageous for purposes of taxation in your new country of residence to show that you have retained your Canadian citizenship and domicile. This may be particularly important if you move from Canada to a country such as the US where these factors have important tax consequences.

The only difficulty I foresee is that there may be some similarity in the Canadian rules determining your ordinary residence and your new country's rules for determining whether you are still domiciled in Canada. This will take some careful planning. You may, for example, keep a burial plot and some non-residential property in Canada.

1997 UPDATE

Reports from Canada indicate that some of the Hong Kong Chinese who had moved to Vancouver and Toronto and obtained Canadian citizenship are now moving out of Canada because of a new Canadian reporting requirement. Revenue Canada now requires every Canadian resident with more than Cdn $100,000 (about US $75,000) of non-Canadian assets to file a detailed report of these assets each year.

27. LEAVING GERMANY

Residence is the key to German taxation and terminating German residence may have serious tax consequences. This chapter has not been changed from last year's edition.

Germany taxes an individual if he is resident there or if his customary place of abode is in Germany. A resident individual is taxed at high rates on his worldwide income and on some capital gains such as short-term gains, those from business and those from holdings of more than 25 percent of the shares of a corporation. Since 1972, a German who emigrates may be subject to special rules designed to inhibit departures.

EXTENDED LIMITED TAX LIABILITY

Germany's *Foreign Tax Law (Aussensteuergesetz)* contains special rules for German citizens and residents who leave Germany and move to a low-tax country. If a German citizen was resident in Germany for income tax purposes for at least five of the ten years preceding his move and he retains substantial economic ties with Germany, he is subject to *extended limited tax liability* if he moves to a low-tax country or he does not establish residence in another country. His new country will be treated as a low-tax country if its income tax rate is less than two-thirds the German rate for a hypothetical single person. It is also treated as a low-tax country if it gives the German emigrant preferential treatment or if it taxes him on a remittance basis. The extended limited tax liability requires the emigrant to pay German income tax on his German-source income at a tax rate that takes into account his worldwide income. He also remains subject to net wealth tax and to inheritance and gift taxes.

DEEMED DISPOSITION OF SUBSTANTIAL HOLDINGS

The Foreign Tax Law also provides that an individual who terminates German residence after more than ten years of residency is treated as having disposed of his holdings in German corporations in which he owns more than 25 percent. He is deemed to have sold such holdings at their fair market value as of the time he left Germany and he is taxable thereon at half the normal German income tax rate.

28. LEAVING HONG KONG

Those who leave Hong Kong are political exiles rather than tax exiles. The PRC takes over Hong Kong on 1 July 1997. This chapter is unchanged from last year's edition.

Hong Kong's countdown to 1997 is nearing its end. On 1 July 1997, Hong Kong will cease to be a British dependent territory and it will become a special administrative region of the People's Republic of China (PRC). Under an agreement between Britain and the PRC, Hong Kong is supposed to remain a self-governing capitalistic enclave for at least another 50 years. Shortly after the agreement was signed, Britain took a survey and proudly announced that 80 percent of Hong Kong's Chinese population planned to remain in Hong Kong. To me that meant that about 20 percent (roughly 1.2 million people) hoped to leave.

POLITICAL EXILES

The Chinese leaving Hong Kong are not tax exiles; they are *political exiles*. In that sense they differ from most of the people discussed in this report. However, their needs are much the same. Those choosing to leave need a new place of residence, a new permanent home or domicile, and a new citizenship and passport. Many of them will retain their business interests in Hong Kong until just before the PRC takes over. Some of them will even risk staying on after the takeover, but they want someplace safe to go when and if the situation in Hong Kong deteriorates. Even those who obtain another citizenship and passport will be taking a gamble if they remain after the takeover. The PRC has indicated that they will be dual nationals. They will be given special PRC passports and they will have to use these PRC passports to enter and leave Hong Kong. This means that the PRC could prohibit them from leaving. If that happens, there is little or nothing that their new country of citizenship will be able to do to get them out.

SUITABLE DESTINATIONS

During the past few years, Hong Kong Chinese have been emigrating at the rate of about 50,000 per year. Many of the wealthier ones have established new homes in other countries. Australia and Canada have been the destinations of choice. Some have also gone to the US despite its unfriendly tax regime. Singapore has become attractive to some because of its program to give them the right to move there anytime within five years.

29. LEAVING THE NORDIC COUNTRIES

Denmark, Finland, Norway and Sweden are all high-tax countries. Each of them makes it difficult for its residents to leave, generally by continuing to tax former residents and citizens on some income after they have left. This chapter is unchanged from last year's edition.

Some of the highest taxes in the world are levied in the Nordic countries. Denmark is fairly typical; a Danish resident is subject to national income tax on his worldwide income, plus two local income taxes, social security tax, church tax and net wealth tax. The overall tax burden of these taxes may amount to as much as 78 percent of taxable income.

It should come as no surprise, therefore, that these countries try to hold on to those of their "customers" who leave. Denmark, Finland, Norway and Sweden all seek to tax former residents living abroad for some period of time after they have departed. Several of them also impose some taxes on citizens living abroad by treating them as though they were still resident.

DENMARK - CONTINUED RESIDENCE AND A DEPARTURE TAX

An individual who leaves Denmark after having been a permanent resident for at least four years remains resident for income tax purposes for up to four more years unless he proves that he is subject to a substantially equivalent income tax in his new country. Denmark also imposes a departure tax on the deemed disposition of bonds or a substantial holding of shares by a departing individual who has been resident for at least five of the preceding ten years. It may be possible to postpone payment of this departure tax until an actual sale or death.

FINLAND TAXES CITIZENS WHO RETAIN TIES

A Finnish *citizen* who leaves the country is deemed to remain a resident for national income tax purposes for three more years unless he proves that he has not maintained *real connections* with Finland.

NORWAY HOLDS ON UNLESS YOU ARE TAXED ABROAD

A departing Norwegian resident does not terminate his *full tax liability* for income tax purposes until he has been absent from Norway for at least four years. However, this four-year extension is reduced to one year if he is taxed as a resident in his new country.

In principle, Norway imposes its inheritance and gift taxes on an individual who is either a Norwegian citizen or resident at the time of the transfer. However, tax based on citizenship is not imposed if the transferor's new country of residence taxes the transfer.

SWEDEN TAXES SOME CITIZENS LIVING ABROAD

Swedish *citizens* and former residents of Sweden remain resident for income tax purposes so long as they *maintain essential ties* with Sweden. If you were a resident of Sweden for at least ten years, you are deemed resident for five years following departure unless you can prove that you have not maintained essential ties with Sweden. After five years the burden of proof apparently shifts to the government. The factors considered in determining whether an emigrant still has essential ties with Sweden include: whether his family is present in Sweden, whether he has a home in Sweden available for year-round use and the extent of his economic activity in Sweden.

Sweden imposes inheritance tax and gift tax at rates up to 65 percent, depending on the relationship of the transferor to the recipient. Property inherited from or given by a Swedish *citizen living abroad or his spouse* is subject to Swedish inheritance tax or gift tax for the first ten years after his departure from Sweden.

30. LEAVING OTHER *EU* COUNTRIES

France, Greece and the Netherlands, all members of the European Union (EU), impose some tax liability on former residents or on citizens living abroad. This chapter is basically unchanged from last year's edition.

FRANCE TAXES CITIZENS WHO MOVED TO MONACO

Under a 1963 tax treaty between France and Monaco, France can tax as a French resident any French *citizen* who moved to Monaco after 1956. France is now also trying to tax Monaco-born children of French citizens who moved to Monaco early enough to escape French taxes under the treaty. If you are French, you can move almost anywhere except Monaco.

GREECE TAXES TRANSFERS BY NONRESIDENT CITIZENS

Greece imposes its inheritance and gift taxes on transfers of personal property by a Greek *citizen* who has been living abroad for less than ten years.

NETHERLANDS PERMITS ESCAPE TO THE ANTILLES

A Dutch *citizen* who moves abroad remains a resident of the Netherlands for ten years for gift and inheritance tax purposes. A former Dutch resident who is not a Dutch citizen remains liable for Dutch gift tax on transfers he makes in the year after he leaves. Dutch emigrants are also taxed on capital gains from the sale of substantial holdings in Dutch companies for five years after they leave the Netherlands. They may be able to escape these rules by retiring to the Netherlands Antilles since it is still a part of the Kingdom of the Netherlands. For details, peak ahead to Chapter 55.

PART V

CHOOSING ONE OR MORE NEW HOME COUNTRIES

31. A TAX EXILE'S WISH LIST

A tax exile must generally establish a new country of residence, a new domicile, and may also need a new citizenship and passport. Some of the *economic citizenship programs* discussed near the end of the chapter have recently been modified. These changes from last year's edition are discussed in the *1997 Update* at the end of the chapter.

Larry and Laura Latour have made a preliminary decision to become tax exiles. Where will they go? Before looking at individual countries, they must determine what they will require. How will they choose one country over another? What do they need and where will they find it?

MORE THAN ONE HOME COUNTRY

Until now, the Latours have been US citizens, and they have been resident and domiciled in the US. There may not be any one other country that will immediately meet all of their needs. Their first choice of a country in which to reside may not permit them to become citizens for many years. Moreover, it may not be suitable as their permanent domicile. They may have to choose more than one new home country -- one, or perhaps several, for residency, one for their permanent home or domicile, and still another for citizenship and passports with which to travel.

A HOME COUNTRY FOR RESIDENCY

The Latours need at least one country in which they can actually live. Eventually, they may want one place where they can spend most of the year. Initially, however, they may choose to divide the year, spending a few months in each of several countries. This will give them the opportunity to try out several places. If they like some of them better than others they can spend more time there.

Any new home country for residency should be a safe place in which to live and it should have a good quality of life. It should also have a fair and reasonable tax system. They may consider any of the following:

• *An island in the Caribbean or Atlantic with little or no taxes and an easy lifestyle.* They should look at the Bahamas, Bermuda, Cayman, St. Kitts and Nevis, and Turks and Caicos. They might also look at Anguilla, Antigua, Costa Rica and either Curacao or St. Maarten in the Netherlands Antilles.

• *An English-speaking base in or near Europe from which they can easily travel.* They should look at Britain, the Channel Islands, Cyprus, Gibraltar, Ireland, the Isle of Man, Israel and Malta.

- *A "real country" in which they can establish roots and eventually obtain citizenship.* They should consider Australia, Britain, Canada, Ireland and New Zealand.
- *A toehold on the European continent from which they can readily travel around Europe by car or train.* They should look at Britain (now that the Channel tunnel is open), Gibraltar, Monaco and Switzerland. They may also look at Andorra and Campione.

A HOME COUNTRY FOR DOMICILE

The Latours need to choose one country that will be their new domicile. For practical purposes, it must be one of the countries that they have chosen for residency. It should be the one place that they will call their permanent home. They should be comfortable with its laws concerning the eventual descent and distribution of their assets. They will want to know whether it has community property and forced heirship rules and whether they can live with those rules. They will also want a place that does not have excessive taxes on lifetime gifts or at death.

Here, they will begin the process by eliminating those countries that impose excessive death taxes on persons who are domiciled there. This will probably eliminate Britain and Ireland. Surprisingly, perhaps, they can probably cope with the gift and death tax structures of any of the other countries. Some, like Canada or Switzerland, may require very careful estate planning.

A HOME COUNTRY FOR CITIZENSHIP AND A PASSPORT

The Latours will need a new citizenship and passports on which they can freely travel without undue hassle. Their new passports should give them visa-free travel to as many as possible of the places they like to visit.

Most of the countries whose citizenship and passports they would like will not give them immediate citizenship or passports. Some of the countries that they may consider for residency or domicile will never allow them to become citizens. Others will grant them citizenship only after several years of residency. Their biggest problem is the time factor. They need citizenship and passports now.

They may be lucky. One of them may have a parent or grandparent who was born in Ireland. If so, he or she would be entitled to Irish citizenship with its first-class passport. The other spouse would also be entitled to Irish citizenship based on the first spouse's citizenship. Similar, less publicized rights, may exist if their parents were born in other countries within the European Union (EU) or the larger European Economic Area (EEA).

If either of them is Jewish, he or she may be entitled to Israeli citizenship under that country's *law of return*. This comes with immediate citizenship and a *laissez-passer*; a full passport is issued after a year. An Israeli passport is a very good travel document for visa-free travel.

If none of these situations exist, they will almost certainly have to consider one of the few countries with *economic citizenship programs*. Those countries with legal programs recently available include:

- *Ireland.* This was by far the most expensive program, but it offered a full EU passport. The required investment was IR£1 million (about US $1.6 million) for seven years at about three percent interest, plus substantial fees and other requirements. Each spouse required a separate investment. Ireland is effectively on hold at this time. Virtually no applications are being approved and this situation is likely to continue at least until after the next Irish general election.

- *Dominica.* This is probably the best legal program at this time. Both spouses and one or two young children can qualify for full citizenship for a total outlay of US $75,000. The applicant donates US $50,000 to the Dominica government. The other US $25,000 covers all government fees, professional fees and miscellaneous expenses. Each eligible family member receives a British Commonwealth passport good for visa-free travel to more than 90 countries, including Canada, Switzerland, Britain and most other British Commonwealth countries. Estimated time: about two months after papers are filed.

- *St. Kitts and Nevis.* Both spouses can qualify for non-voting citizenship by purchasing a condominium costing at least US $250,000 or by investing US $200,000 in 10-year government bonds that pay no interest. Government registration fees and professional fees for the two of them would add about US $70,000 to the cost. Both spouses would receive British Commonwealth passports good for visa-free travel to about 90 countries. Estimated time: about two months after papers are filed.

- *Cape Verde.* This is the least expensive of the legal programs currently available. A US $35,000 donation to a foundation would qualify both spouses for citizenship and passports. Visa-free travel is, however, somewhat limited. Estimated time: about two months after papers are filed.

The Latours must determine how much they need to invest to get a passport that will satisfy their travel requirements. This may depend on how much traveling they plan to do. If they plan to stay in one place most of the time, they may be satisfied with a Cape Verde passport. If they expect to travel extensively, they may need one requiring a larger investment, such as Ireland (if available), Dominica or St. Kitts and Nevis.

1997 UPDATE

Three of the *economic citizenship programs* discussed above have been modified during the past year or so. As already noted, *Ireland* is on hold at this time. *Dominica* used to involve an investment in a proposed luxury hotel project, but the hotel investment project ran into problems as construction of the hotel was stopped twice during the past year. Fortunately, the overall cost has not increased and the replacement program is running smoothly. *St. Kitts and Nevis* has substantially increased both the amount required to be invested and the government registration fees payable by the applicant and each family member. Nevis has taken initial steps to secede from the present two-state federation and may complete the process within the next year or so.

32. PASSPORTS AND VISAS

You should have a passport that enables you to travel to a large number of countries without a visa. If your present passport is unsatisfactory, you may be able to acquire another one through an economic citizenship program. A monthly publication called *TIM* tells you whether your passport requires you to obtain a visa to visit a particular country. This chapter has not been materially changed from last year's edition but some new developments are noted in the *1997 Update* at the end of the chapter.

One of the most important things you must consider when you obtain another citizenship is how easily you can travel on that country's passport. Your goal should be to enjoy as much visa-free travel as possible, especially to those countries that you plan to visit regularly. The next best choice is to have a passport with which you can reasonably expect to obtain multiple-entry visas to those countries. You certainly don't want a passport that will severely restrict your ability to travel.

RATING DIFFERENT PASSPORTS

How do you compare the usefulness of some of the "instant" passports available under economic citizenship programs? If you have a clean record and you are prepared to make the required investment, you should be able to obtain citizenship and a passport from Ireland, Dominica, St. Kitts and Nevis or Cape Verde within a few months. In terms of visa-free travel facilities, someone has suggested that an Irish passport is like a Rolls-Royce, a Dominica or St. Kitts and Nevis passport is like a Ford, and a Cape Verde passport is like a Fiat. The Irish passport, being an EU passport, gets you into most countries without a visa. It also gives you the right to live and work anywhere in the growing European Economic Area (EEA). The Dominica or St. Kitts and Nevis passport, being a British Commonwealth passport, gets you into the UK, Switzerland, Canada and about 90 other countries without a visa, but you would need a visa to visit most EU countries or the United States. The Cape Verde passport gets you into some 15 West African countries that you are unlikely to want to visit. More importantly it also gets you into about 40 other countries that either have liberal visa exemptions or issue visas on arrival. Regardless of which of these programs you use, you should be able to get visas to visit countries that are not on the relevant visa-free list.

DIFFICULT PASSPORTS

I have some clients who find it difficult to travel on their home-country passports. Take, for example, someone who is Russian. He can go to some Eastern European countries or to Cyprus without a visa. He can't travel to Britain (or to any other EU country) without a visa and he can't get a UK visa without an invitation to visit from someone in Britain. It will probably take him several weeks to obtain a visa good for a single entry to Britain. He has to repeat the entire process each time he wants to come to London. He has what I would call a *difficult passport*.

Other countries with a *difficult passport* would include most of the CIS countries that were formerly part of the Soviet Union, some of the new countries that formerly comprised Yugoslavia, China (PRC), Iran, Iraq, Lebanon, Libya, Somalia, Syria, Taiwan, Uganda and Zaire. In general terms, it would also include any country from which everyone wants to flee, such as Haiti, Rwanda or Liberia.

PASSPORTS WITHOUT CITIZENSHIP

Another type of passport may cause difficulties even though it is issued by a country whose normal passports are well respected. It is a passport issued by a country to someone who is not a citizen of that country. An example is an Uruguayan passport issued to a non-citizen who invests in the country. Anyone of good character who is not an Uruguayan citizen can obtain a ten-year Uruguayan passport by investing US $70,000 for ten years. See Chapter 60 below for details of this program. The passport issued under this program looks much like the one issued to an Uruguayan citizen but it contains some special language that could cause you problems. As an example, the March 1997 issue of the *Travel Information Manual (TIM)*, when discussing passport requirements for the United Kingdom, states:

> *Admission and transit restrictions*: The Government of the United Kingdom does not recognize: ...passports issued by the government of Uruguay containing endorsement on page 12/13 in Spanish "this passport is issued by virtue of decree 289/90 the bearer being a legal resident. The issue of this passport does not imply recognition of Uruguayan nationality or citizenship".

The effect of this restriction seems to be that a regular citizenship-based Uruguayan passport gets you into Britain without a visa but a passport issued under the investment program doesn't get you in at all. Nor is Britain the only country to have such a restriction. The Benelux countries (Belgium, Luxembourg and the Netherlands) impose substantial restrictions on the holders of passports issued by the government of any country to persons not holding the nationality of that country.

Considering these restrictions, it does not make sense for you to have a non-citizenship passport as your only travel document. However, you may want to have such a passport as an extra, to be used where it can if your home-country passport causes difficulties in some parts of the world. Thus, it might be used as an extra passport for someone who is a national of Cape Verde, Israel, Lebanon or Taiwan.

VISAS AND VISA-FREE TRAVEL

How do you determine whether you need a visa to go to a particular country? To find the answer you do what airline employees and travel agents do -- you consult the latest monthly issue of the *Travel Information Manual (TIM)*. It is a standard reference manual published jointly by 14 of the world's leading international airlines and used by most of the others. It is a paperback book that runs about 400 pages. You can subscribe for 282 Dutch guilders (about US $150) a year by telephoning TIM's Subscriptions Department at the number shown below. You can save money by arranging for your favorite travel agent to give you last month's edition when he receives the current one, as the information does not change that much from one month to the next.

You have to learn how to use the *TIM*. It does not, for example, tell you where you can travel on your Irish passport. You have to examine the passport and visa requirements for each country you plan to visit. It will tell you whether an Irish citizen needs a passport for visits to that country and whether or not he needs a visa to enter that country. Suppose, for example, that you are an Irish citizen and you plan to visit Turkey. You will find that you need a passport, you need a visa unless you have a diplomatic, official or service passport, and you can obtain a visa on arrival at a cost of about £5, although it is advisable to hold a visa prior to arrival.

If you want to compile a list of all the countries in the world you can visit with your new passport, you will have to go through the entire book, country by country. I have done that for a few of the countries with economic citizenship programs and some of the results are given in the next three chapters. Note, however, that these requirements change from time to time and you should always check the latest situation before actually traveling.

1997 UPDATE

The Irish economic citizenship discussed above is now on hold. The publisher of the *Travel Information Manual (TIM)* has moved to Amsterdam. TIM now costs 282 Dutch guilders (still about US $150) a year. The telephone number of the Subscriptions Department is now (31 20) 316 3714; the fax number is (31 20) 316 3800.

33. VISITING WESTERN EUROPE

Non-European visitors to most EU countries require a *Schengen* visa. The Schengen group now has 15 member countries, but only seven of them have implemented the treaty that permits passport-free travel from one member country to another. This chapter has not been revised from last year's edition but some new developments are noted in the *1997 Update* at the end of the chapter.

If you are about to acquire another citizenship, one of the first things you will want to know is how you will be able to use your new passport to travel to various places. Let us look at the travel requirements imposed by some key countries, starting with Western Europe.

Western Europe is divided into several different groups of countries. The best known of these is now called the *European Union (EU)*. Before the Maastricht treaty took effect, the EU was called the European Community (EC); and, before that, it was generally called the European Economic Community (EEC). It began with six members, grew to 12, and, with the addition of three new members in January 1995, it now consists of 15 member countries.

The *European Free Trade Association (EFTA)* generally consists of Western European countries that are working their way toward membership in the EU. It lost three of its members when they became EU countries at the beginning of 1995. Its members also include countries such as Norway that have chosen not to join the EU.

Adding to the confusion, a third grouping is called the *European Economic Area (EEA)*. It was originally intended to combine the membership of the EU and EFTA into a single bloc of countries whose citizens could freely move from one country to another without restriction. This did not work out as planned when the Swiss people voted against joining the EEA. Switzerland remains a member of EFTA, but it is not within the EEA.

Finally, within the 15-member EU there is a sub-group of countries that are seeking to do away with their common borders entirely. These *Schengen* countries (so-called because their treaty was signed at Schengen, Luxembourg in 1985) are supposed to have one common border around them and no internal borders between them. Traveling from one Schengen country to another is supposed to be like going from one state to another in the United States, completely free of passport controls.

If you are a citizen of any of these Western European countries you already have the right to travel without a visa to any of the others. You may need a passport or, in some cases, only an identity card. In most cases you also avoid the long lines of people waiting for immigration control when you arrive at each airport. You go to the fast-moving special line for EU/EFTA/EEA citizens and simply flash your passport or identity card as you walk by. This ability to travel visa-free and hassle-free virtually anywhere in Western Europe makes citizenship and a passport of any of these countries a valuable asset. It helps to explain why people are anxious to obtain citizenship in countries like Ireland.

We will now look at the impact of these various groupings on your ability to travel to them if you are a citizen of some third country. In doing so we will concentrate on the status of individuals who have acquired a new citizenship under one of the available economic citizenship programs discussed in this report. We will begin by looking at the Schengen countries.

SEVEN SCHENGEN COUNTRIES

Eventually, all of the European Union (EU) countries are supposed to have a single border around them and passport-free travel from one EU country to another. A draft EU treaty to that effect has been pending for several years. Experts tell me, however, that it is unlikely to be approved anytime soon. Recognizing that agreement by all EU countries could take many years, a few EU countries met at Schengen in 1985 and reached an agreement to abolish gradually checks at their common borders. Although most people I know have never heard of the *Schengen Agreement*, its rules are likely to determine your ability to travel to some EU countries for the next several years.

Five EU countries participated originally, but the number has since increased. Despite numerous delays in implementing the agreement, it finally took effect in March 1995. It currently applies to Belgium, France, Germany, Luxembourg, the Netherlands, Portugal and Spain. Austria, Greece and Italy are now also parties to the agreement but they have not yet implemented it. Ireland and the United Kingdom are not part of the Schengen group. Denmark, Finland and Sweden will probably join if non-EU members Norway and Iceland are also permitted to join.

Here are some of the general rules that will determine your ability as a third-country national to travel to the seven EU countries that are already Schengen countries:

- You can visit any or all of the Schengen countries for up to three months with your passport and a Schengen visa if one is required. You could be required to report your entry into each country within three working days, but this is unlikely for most visitors.

- A uniform travel visa valid for all Schengen countries is issued by the consulate of the country of either your principal destination or your first destination. It is valid for multiple visits to any or all Schengen countries that do not total more than three months in any six-month period.

- If you want to visit any Schengen country for more than three months in any six-month period you will need that country's national visa. It will permit transit through the other Schengen countries.

- If some Schengen countries do not recognize the validity of your passport, your visa will be limited to those that do. Thus, for example, a Schengen visa in a non-citizenship Uruguayan passport might not be valid for travel to any of the Benelux countries. To avoid this, you obviously want to have a passport that is valid in all Schengen countries.

- If you have a residence permit in any Schengen country you can transit through any of the other Schengen countries.

PERSONS REQUIRING *EU* VISAS

An annex to the draft EU *Convention on Controls on Persons Crossing External Frontiers* originally listed 126 countries whose nationals would be required to obtain visas under that treaty. That list was modified in 1995 by the Council of the European Union. Council Regulation [EC] No. 2317/95 of 25 September 1995 was published in October 1995. Beginning in April 1996, nationals of every one of the 100 countries on the EU black list must obtain a visa to visit every EU country, including countries that have previously permitted them to visit without a visa. Thus, for example, visitors from Bahrain, the Dominican Republic (not Dominica), Kuwait, Mauritius, Peru, Qatar and the United Arab Emirates will now require UK visas to visit the United Kingdom. An individual visa will be required by nationals of black list countries for visits to non-Schengen countries; a Schengen visa will be required for visits to Schengen countries. Here are some comments on the new EU black list:

- Citizens of most Western European countries, except Turkey, are not subject to the visa requirement.
- In Eastern Europe, citizens of Albania, Bulgaria and Romania require visas, while those from the Czech Republic, Hungary, Poland and Slovakia may not. Citizens of some of the states that formerly comprised Yugoslavia -- Serbia, Montenegro and the Former Yugoslav Republic of Macedonia (FYROM) -- are on the black list, but those from Bosnia Herzegovina, Croatia and Slovenia are not.
- Citizens of most of the 15 independent states that formerly comprised the USSR require visas. However, citizens of the Baltic States -- Estonia, Latvia and Lithuania -- are not on the list.
- Citizens of Israel are not on the black list. However, citizens of most other Middle East countries are.
- Only a few Western Hemisphere countries are on the black list. These are Cuba, the Dominican Republic, Guyana, Haiti, Peru and Suriname.
- The black list includes citizens of most African countries, but it does not include Kenya, Malawi or South Africa.

Looking at some of the countries with economic citizenship programs, we find that Irish citizens obviously do not require EU visas since Ireland is an EU member. Belize, Dominica and St. Kitts and Nevis are not on the black list, but their citizens still require visas to visit some EU countries. Cape Verde is on the black list so its citizens require visas for visits to all EU countries. Holders of Uruguayan passports acquired through investment will probably require EU visas since they are not Uruguayan nationals. Moreover, their passports may not be valid for travel to the Benelux countries or the United Kingdom.

There is no white list as such, but citizens of EU countries and citizens of their dependent territories do not require EU visas. Citizens of third countries not on the black list are not guaranteed visa-free entry to EU countries. For the time being, they remain subject to the visa requirements of each individual EU country. Thus, a third country national may still require a Schengen visa to visit France or Germany even though he or she does not require a visa to visit the United Kingdom.

OTHER WESTERN EUROPEAN COUNTRIES

Norway's people voted in late 1994 not to join the EU. Norway remains in EFTA and the EEA. The Swiss people had voted about a year earlier not to join the EEA, but Switzerland remains in EFTA. Liechtenstein, which has a custom's union with Switzerland, has voted to join the EEA. Iceland remains a member of both EFTA and the EEA. Cyprus and Malta are not yet members of either EFTA or the EEA. Looking at the visa requirements of each of these countries we find:

- Cyprus does not require a visa for citizens of Ireland, Belize, Dominica or St. Kitts and Nevis. It does require a visa for citizens of Cape Verde and Israel.
- Iceland and Malta do not require visas for citizens of Ireland, Israel, Belize, Dominica or St. Kitts and Nevis. They do require visas for citizens of Cape Verde.
- Norway does not require a visa for citizens of Ireland, Israel, Belize or Dominica. It does require a visa for citizens of Cape Verde and St. Kitts and Nevis.
- Switzerland and Liechtenstein have identical visa rules. They do not require a visa for citizens of Ireland, Israel, Dominica or St. Kitts and Nevis. They do require a visa for citizens of Belize and Cape Verde.

Remember! These visa requirements change from time to time; always check the latest available information.

1997 UPDATE

The draft EU treaty permitting passport-free travel between EU countries may be finalized in the next year or two, but it will probably not cover the United Kingdom or Ireland. Denmark, Finland, Sweden and two non-EU countries, Iceland and Norway, have recently become Schengen members, but they have not yet implemented the Schengen treaty.

34. VISITING NORTH AMERICA

Canada, the United States and Mexico each have different visa requirements. There have been no major changes to this chapter since last year's edition, but one new development is noted in the *1997 Update* at the end of the chapter.

We will now look at some of the travel requirements imposed by Canada, the US and Mexico on citizens of Cape Verde, Ireland, Israel, Belize, Dominica and St. Kitts and Nevis. We will look first at Canada and then at the US and Mexico.

CANADIAN VISA REQUIREMENTS

Canada does not require a visa for citizens of Ireland, Israel, Dominica or St. Kitts and Nevis. Canada does, however, require a visa for a person holding an orange-colored travel document issued by Israel, presumably because it is a *laissez-passer* rather than a full passport. Canada also requires a visa for citizens of Belize and Cape Verde.

US VISA REQUIREMENTS

US rules generally provide that visas are required by citizens of all foreign countries other than Canada. However, the US instituted a *visa waiver pilot program* a few years ago and has extended it from time to time since.

Under the visa waiver pilot program, citizens of 25 countries traveling on holiday, for business or in transit can generally enter the US without a visa for a stay of up to 90 days. The countries covered by the program are Andorra, Argentina, Australia, Austria, Belgium, Brunei, Denmark, Finland, France, Germany, Iceland, Ireland, Italy, Japan, Liechtenstein, Luxembourg, Monaco, the Netherlands, New Zealand, Norway, San Marino, Spain, Sweden, Switzerland, and the United Kingdom. The list changes from time to time. For example, Ireland was added to the list on 17 March 1995 (St. Patrick's Day) after considerable pressure from Irish-American politicians.

The US also has a number of special exemptions. For example, citizens of any British Commonwealth country or of Ireland who are permanent residents of either Bermuda or Canada do not require a US visa. This rule covers citizens of Belize, Dominica and St. Kitts and Nevis since they are members of the British Commonwealth. Thus, for example, a citizen of St. Kitts and Nevis who has a Bermuda work permit or permanent residence certificate can enter the US without a visa. The same situation would apply if he was a *landed immigrant* of Canada. This rule applies even if he is entering the US from someplace other than Bermuda or Canada.

A Canadian landed immigrant coming directly from Canada or Mexico can enter the US without a visa on any passport if it contains a *Canadian border crossing identification card*. Thus, for example, a Cape Verde citizen legally resident in Canada as a landed immigrant can enter the US from Canada without a US visa.

The US has recently begun to issue machine-readable visas and it now charges about US $22, or the equivalent in local currency, for each visa application. The new visas contain photographs and they are valid for a maximum of ten years. Anyone who has an indefinite validity visa issued more than ten years ago will be admitted to the US once at which time his visa will be cancelled without prejudice to apply for a new one.

MEXICAN VISA REQUIREMENTS

Mexico requires only a tourist card issued by the airline for citizens of a number of countries, including Ireland, Israel and Belize. Citizens of Cape Verde, Dominica and St. Kitts and Nevis apparently require both visas and tourist cards. Those for citizens of Dominica and St. Kitts and Nevis are supposed to be issued in Jamaica.

Once again, this is a reminder that these visa requirements do change from time to time. Be sure to check the latest available information with your travel agent or airline.

1997 UPDATE

Argentina and Australia are now also covered by the US *visa waiver pilot program* which remains in force.

35. VISITING ASIA AND THE PACIFIC

Some key Asian countries have liberal visa exemptions; these include Hong Kong, Singapore, South Korea and Thailand. Australia, China, Japan and New Zealand require visas for visitors from many countries. This chapter has not been revised from last year's edition.

Let us now briefly examine the travel requirements imposed by some key countries in Asia and the Pacific on citizens of Cape Verde, Ireland, Israel, Belize, Dominica and St. Kitts and Nevis. We will look first at China (the PRC), Hong Kong, Japan, Korea, Singapore and Thailand in Asia, and then at Australia and New Zealand in the South Pacific.

SOME KEY ASIAN COUNTRIES

- The People's Republic of China requires visas for citizens of Cape Verde, Ireland, Israel, Belize, Dominica and St. Kitts and Nevis. China requires visas for most foreign persons who are not traveling on diplomatic passports.
- Hong Kong has one of the most liberal visa requirements of any country in the world. It does not require visas for citizens of Cape Verde, Ireland, Israel, Belize, Dominica or St. Kitts and Nevis.
- Japan does not require a visa for citizens of Ireland or Israel. It does require a visa for citizens of Cape Verde, Belize, Dominica and St. Kitts and Nevis.
- The Republic of Korea (South Korea) has very liberal visa requirements for tourists. It does not require visas for citizens of Cape Verde, Ireland, Israel, Belize, Dominica or St. Kitts and Nevis.
- Singapore similarly has very liberal visa requirements for tourists. It does not require visas for citizens of Cape Verde, Ireland, Israel, Belize, Dominica or St. Kitts and Nevis.
- Thailand does not require a visa for citizens of Ireland or Israel. It also has very liberal requirements for tourists from many other countries. It allows citizens of Cape Verde, Belize, Dominica or St. Kitts and Nevis to obtain a visa upon arrival.

AUSTRALIA AND NEW ZEALAND

- Australia requires visas for citizens of Cape Verde, Ireland, Israel, Belize, Dominica and St. Kitts and Nevis. It requires visas for all foreign persons except New Zealand citizens.
- New Zealand does not require a visa for citizens of Ireland. It does require a visa for citizens of Cape Verde, Israel, Belize, Dominica and St. Kitts and Nevis.

As previously noted, visa requirements change from time to time. Be sure to check the latest available information with your travel agent or airline.

In Part VI, we will look at a number of individual countries and the extent to which each of them may be suitable as a base for your residence, your domicile and your citizenship and passport.

PART VI

SUITABLE COUNTRIES FOR RESIDENCE, DOMICILE, CITIZENSHIP AND PASSPORTS

36. AMERICA (THE *US*)

Moving to America (the US) can be dangerous to your wealth, but you may be able to improve your situation by very careful planning. In most cases, you will be better off visiting the US for less than four months a year. Revised expatriation tax rules were enacted in 1996, retroactive to February 1995; these are discussed briefly in *Expatriation Tax Legislation Enacted* near the end of the chapter. Another new development is noted in the *1997 Update* at the end of the chapter.

If you like to play with fire you can try living in the United States of America (US) as a tax exile, without being taxed on your worldwide income. Moving to the US has to be done the way porcupines make love to each other. You have to do it very carefully. Don't acquire a green card. Make sure you don't become *domiciled* in the US. Get good professional advice and follow it carefully.

PART-TIME VISITING IS BEST

The best way for a *PT* or a tax exile to live in the US is part time -- less than four months a year. If you stay in the US less than 120 days each year you can avoid being a US resident for income tax purposes. That is the *green zone*. Keep a careful record of the exact number of days you spend in the US each year. Be prepared to prove that number if necessary.

LONGER STAYS ARE DANGEROUS

If you stay in the US more than 182 days (roughly six months) in any calendar year you are automatically *resident* for federal income tax purposes that year. That is the red zone.

If you average more than four months a year in the US you will meet the *substantial presence test* and you will be presumed to be a resident for income tax purposes. That is the *amber zone*. If you are only in the amber zone, you may be able to overcome the presumption of residence but it won't be easy. You may be able to avoid residence despite longer stays if you are a full-time student or teacher, or if you are an accredited diplomat.

A tax treaty may help you, but you will have to file a federal income tax return and you may have to disclose information concerning your worldwide income. You will have to file information returns disclosing what you have in foreign bank accounts and foreign securities accounts. You will also have to disclose your interests in foreign companies and foreign trusts. Even if the Internal Revenue Service (IRS) can't tax you on some of your foreign income they may decide to pass on the information you give them to another country.

Some people coming from countries with even higher taxes than those in the US are willing to pay US income taxes. They are prepared to give up more than a third of their income and gains for the privilege of living in the US. If you plan to take that route you need careful professional planning *before* you move to America. If possible, choose one of the few remaining US states that still has no personal income tax at the state or local level. These were listed in Chapter 2 above.

PLANNING IDEA FOR NEW RESIDENTS

Miami attorney Robert F Hudson, Jr has suggested an excellent plan for prospective new US residents. It can be illustrated by the following example:

> Victor Valbuena is moving himself and his family from Panazuela, a mythical Latin American country, to the US. He plans to retain his huge Panazuelan business, Valbuena SA, which provides him with an income of over US $1 million a year. Panazuela taxes that income heavily at the corporate level but it imposes little or no personal income tax on Valbuena. Valbuena's cost basis for his shares in the SA are minimal. Thus, if he were to sell his shares while resident in the US he would have to pay a huge US capital gains tax.

> Before he becomes a US resident, Valbuena will reorganize his Panazuelan corporation from an SA into an SRL, a limited-liability company that exists in all civil law countries. Properly organized, the SRL will be treated as a partnership rather than as a corporation for US tax purposes. It will almost certainly remain a corporation for Panazuelan tax purposes so there should be no unfavorable tax consequences there. For US tax purposes, the conversion from an SA (corporation) to an SRL (partnership) will be treated as a liquidation of the SA. This will give Valbuena a pre-immigration step-up in basis to current fair market value for his shares in the company. It will reduce substantially any future US tax if he decides to sell his shares. More importantly, Panazuelan income tax imposed each year on Valbuena SRL will be treated as tax paid by a partnership so that Valbuena will be entitled to a foreign tax credit for his share of that tax. If Valbuena can avoid becoming domiciled in the US (by retaining his Panazuelan domicile) he can also avoid US gift and estate taxes on these shares, his principal asset.

INVESTORS' IMMIGRATION PROGRAM IS A FLOP

In 1990, the US Congress enacted a new *investors' immigration program*. It grants permanent residence to a foreigner who invests US $1 million in a US business that employs at least ten American workers. The amount can be reduced to US $500,000 for an investment in an economically distressed area. A successful applicant is granted *conditional* permanent residence for himself, his spouse and his children. This is converted to full permanent residence (*a green card*) after two years if the investment is a reality and employs the required number of US workers.

The program was designed to attract up to 10,000 investors. As of late 1992, three years after enactment, the program had attracted only 500 applicants and only 141 of these had been approved. Several factors appear to have contributed to the program's lack of success:

- The program has very restrictive documentary requirements.
- An applicant must provide extensive information about the source of his capital.
- A wealthy immigrant is fully taxable on his worldwide income and, at death, on his worldwide estate.

One US immigration expert has suggested that the benefits of living in the US simply do not outweigh the high cost of taxes to a wealthy migrant. He prefers to spend a few months in the US each year and spend the rest of the year in a tax haven.

CONSIDER MOVING TO THE *US* VIRGIN ISLANDS

If you simply must move to the US and you insist on becoming a US citizen, you can minimize the damage to your family's wealth by moving to the US Virgin Islands (USVI). The income tax hit will be just as bad as if you had moved to the mainland, but you can legally escape the US estate tax. The key factor is to establish and maintain your residency and your domicile in the USVI instead of the US mainland. The USVI, a US possession located near Puerto Rico in the Caribbean, consists of three islands -- St. Thomas, St. Croix and St. John.

A US citizen domiciled in the USVI at the time of his death is treated as a non-domiciled alien for US estate tax purposes if he acquired his US citizenship solely by birth or naturalization in the USVI [US Internal Revenue Code section 2209]. Although this might also work in some other US possession, the USVI gives you a double benefit since it has no estate or inheritance tax of its own.

This plan normally works only for someone who has never been a US citizen and who starts out by moving to the USVI instead of the US mainland. It is of no use to someone who is already a US citizen by virtue of birth or naturalization in the US mainland. If that was not the case the USVI would be overrun with US tax exiles seeking to avoid the estate tax. Despite this, it might be possible for an American who has moved abroad, abandoned US residence and domicile, and terminated US citizenship, to obtain a green card enabling him to move to the USVI. He might then become resident and domiciled in the USVI and even become a US citizen by naturalization in the USVI, thereby meeting the requirements of the provision.

FOR MORE INFORMATION

Read Marshall Langer's book *Practical International Tax Planning*, (looseleaf third edition, updated annually), especially Chapter 6: *Determining Residence Status for Income Tax Purposes*, and Chapter 7: *Determining Domicile for Estate and Gift Tax Purposes*. The book is available in the US from the Practising Law Institute, New York; see chapter 66 for details. For expedited delivery outside the US, you can order the book from Scope International.

EXPATRIATION TAX LEGISLATION ENACTED

Congress enacted revised anti-expatriation rules in August 1996, retroactive to February 1995. These close some loopholes and considerably tighten the prior rules, but they do not impose the departure tax requested in President Clinton's budget proposal. A wealthy foreigner who moves to the US should seriously consider obtaining a non-immigrant visa rather than a *green card*. This may enable him to retain his foreign domicile so as to avoid the US estate and gift taxes on his foreign property; it will also enable him to avoid the revised expatriation tax rules that now apply to a long-term green card holder who surrenders his green card. For further details, see revised Chapter 21 above. Anyone who is considering whether to obtain or keep a green card should carefully read *IRS Notice 97-19* the text of which is set forth in an appendix to this report.

THE BOTTOM LINE

Stay out of the *red zone* and stay out of the *amber zone*. Stay in the *green zone* by averaging less than 120 days a year. In fact, considering the peculiar way days are counted, it is better to plan on staying in the US only about 100 days each year. Avoid becoming a test case by being too close to the line. Pick the right state, and plan carefully. Consider the USVI as a possible alternative.

1997 UPDATE

The IRS has adopted new rules to determine whether a foreign entity will be treated as a corporation or a partnership.

37. AUSTRALIA

Australia is a high-tax country for residents but it no longer imposes death duties. It is a safe place for domicile and you can get citizenship and a passport after two years of residence. This chapter is basically unchanged from last year's edition.

Australia is an attractive destination for tax exiles despite its relatively high income taxes. *Reasons*: It welcomes new immigrants, it offers them citizenship and its first-class passport after only about two years of residence, and it has abolished all death duties. Australia may be suitable for you if:

- You are unhappy with your present citizenship and passport and would like to replace them reasonably quickly. This has made Australia a very attractive destination for some Hong Kong Chinese who desperately want another nationality.
- You prefer an English-speaking country with Anglo-American traditions. You are willing to pay high income taxes in return for a quality lifestyle that you feel you cannot obtain in some exotic tax haven.
- You already have sufficient wealth so that you are more interested in keeping what you have for yourself and your heirs than building up your assets.

REQUIREMENTS FOR BUSINESS MIGRATION

If I can assume that you don't have close family members already living in Australia, you will probably have to qualify for *business migration*. Australia has tightened its immigration rules and procedures. You used to be able to qualify merely by investing substantial funds in Australia. Now there is a point system under which factors such as your age, business experience, English language facility and assets are all considered.

The Australian Embassy will assess whether you, your spouse and your dependents are likely to contribute to Australia's development. Australia favors entrepreneurs who will employ Australians over investors.

IT IS DIFFICULT TO ABANDON RESIDENCE

Once residence is established it is difficult to abandon it. You remain resident for Australian income tax purposes, especially if you are domiciled in Australia, unless your *permanent place of abode* is outside Australia. Detailed rules set forth several factors that are used to determine whether your permanent place of abode is outside Australia. You almost certainly have to select a particular place and spend substantial time there. You cannot escape Australian taxes by becoming a *PT*.

FOR MORE INFORMATION

For helpful information on what it takes to acquire an Australian passport, see *The Passport Report*, published by Scope International.

THE BOTTOM LINE

Australia offers residence, a safe domicile with no death taxes, and a passport and citizenship after a couple of years.

38. THE BAHAMAS

The Bahamas is a traditional tax haven with no income tax and no taxes at death. This makes it a good place for your residence and domicile. You can obtain residence without the right to work by purchasing a home. This chapter has not been materially changed from last year's edition, but a new development is noted in the *1997 Update* at the end of the chapter.

In 1994, the Bahamas launched a *national investment policy* that offers *permanent residence* for a price. You will have to invest at least $250,000 in the purchase of a home or condominium (the Bahamian dollar is at par with the US dollar). The Bahamas may be suitable for you if:

*   You already have a satisfactory citizenship and passport (you cannot expect to obtain either in the Bahamas if you were not born there).
*   You want a new permanent residence.
*   You can show that you have a sufficient personal net worth to maintain yourself and your family.
*   You are willing to invest at least $250,000 to buy or build your place of residence in the Bahamas.

THE NATIONAL INVESTMENT POLICY

You should enter into a contract to buy a home or condominium, subject to approval of your application for permanent residency. The government will apparently not consider your application for permanent residency until your funds for the purchase have been deposited in escrow in the Bahamas. You must come to Nassau for an interview at the Ministry of Justice and Immigration. Once a completed application has been filed, you can expect a decision within about three months. The grant of permanent residence covers you, your spouse and unmarried children under 18. Your permit gives you the right to residence only, with no right to work in the Bahamas. The new national investment policy seems to offer a much better deal than the former investment promotion program. You no longer need to invest additional funds in Bahamian government bonds or in an approved business. Although you are expected to spend some time in the Bahamas, there is no specific minimum-stay requirement. You no longer have to keep your Bahamian home for a minimum number of years.

One company is actively selling townhouses at a price designed to fit the new government investment policy. They offer fully furnished townhouses starting at $250,000 and they will sell you one conditional upon your being granted permanent residency status. For details, contact *Sandy Port Development Company Limited*, P.O. Box N-8585, Nassau, Bahamas. Telephone: (1 242) 327 8500. Fax: (1 242) 327 8665. The Sandyport Marina Village is located near Cable Beach, about six miles east of Nassau.

OTHER ADVANTAGES INCLUDE NO TAXES

The Bahamas is a traditional tax haven with no taxes on income or capital gains and no taxes at death. The Bahamas is a safe place to establish your new residence and domicile. It has lots of sunshine, great beaches and water sports.

Nassau, the capital and principal city, is very close to the US mainland. Flying time to Miami is an hour or less. There are numerous daily flights to Miami, New York and other US cities; you pre-clear US immigration and customs at Nassau International Airport. US newspapers are available on the day they are published. US television is available by cable TV. The Bahamian dollar has been at par with the US dollar for many years.

POSSIBLE DISADVANTAGES

The Bahamas has exchange controls to protect the Bahamian dollar and, as a permanent resident, you will be subject to these controls. You may be required to keep some of your funds in Bahamian dollars and you will need permission to convert them to other currencies. Prices are quite high because practically everything you consume in the islands is imported and is subject to high import duties.

THE BOTTOM LINE

Purchase of a home for $250,000 or more gives you residence and a safe domicile with no taxes at death. There is virtually no chance of obtaining citizenship or a Bahamian passport.

1997 UPDATE

The Bahamas has changed its telephone area code from 1 809 to 1 242.

39. BERMUDA

Bermuda is a traditional tax haven with no income tax and no taxes on foreign property at death. This makes it a good place for your residence and domicile. You can obtain residence without the right to work by purchasing a home, but these are expensive. You may be able to obtain a work permit and residence by establishing an *exempted company* and managing it. This chapter has not been materially changed from last year's edition, but some recent developments have been noted in the *1997 Update* at the end of the chapter.

Bermuda has no formal program to attract new residents but you can obtain permanent residence there if you are retired. However, permits to reside and work in Bermuda are restricted. If you are a retired person with substantial means and you acquire property in Bermuda, you will receive a *residential certificate* that gives you permission to reside in Bermuda indefinitely. To purchase a residential property in Bermuda, you need a license from the Minister of Labour and Home Affairs.

The government's policy is to restrict the acquisition of residential property by non-Bermudians without discouraging them from doing so. Foreigners (non-Bermudians) are permitted to buy only the more expensive properties. You would probably have to spend at least $350,000 for a condominium and at least $1.5 million (but probably much more) for a private house. The Bermuda dollar is at par with the US dollar. Bermuda is already the home of many tax exiles, most of them from Britain and Canada. Bermuda may be suitable for you if:

- You already have a satisfactory citizenship and passport (you cannot obtain either in Bermuda unless you are married to a Bermudian).
- You want a new permanent residence in which you can actually reside as little or as much as you want.
- You are willing to buy a house or condominium unit with a specified minimum *annual rental value*. As of 1994, the house had to have an annual rental value of $43,800; it was likely to cost at least $1.5 million. There are only about 260 qualified houses in all of Bermuda. The minimum annual rental value is set by Parliament and is increased periodically.
- As an alternative, you can buy a condominium unit in one of 17 approved developments that collectively have about 480 units. As of 1994, such a condominium unit had to have a minimum annual rental value of $15,300; it was likely to cost at least $350,000.

OTHER REQUIREMENTS

The license to acquire a private home will cost you a one-time license fee of 22 percent of the purchase price of the property; the comparable license fee for a condominium has been reduced and is now 15 percent. You will also have to pay at least half of the stamp duty on the conveyance, a further stamp duty on any mortgage you may require, and legal fees.

ANOTHER WAY TO BECOME RESIDENT

There is another way to become resident in Bermuda. You can arrange to incorporate a Bermuda *exempted company*, one that is exempt from local ownership requirements. Bermuda has over 7,000 international businesses, mostly exempted companies. Such a company can carry on almost any type of offshore business activity. It should cost less than $5,000 to form such a company with a minimum authorized capital and a similar amount each year to maintain it in good standing. At least two of the company's directors must live in Bermuda. You could be one of them if you live in Bermuda. As the owner of an exempted company you should be able to get an annually renewable permit to live there and manage the company.

As an employee of an exempted company you or your company will have to pay Bermuda's *hospital levy*, a payroll tax like social security. Since books of exempted companies are not open to government inspection, an employee of an exempted company is ordinarily assessed on a notional salary that is adjusted annually, with no reference to the actual salary he is paid. Thus, the hospital levy for an exempted company's employee is usually the same whether his salary is $1 or $500,000, and it is generally paid entirely by the company. However, an exempted company may now elect to pay this tax on its actual payroll. As of a recent date, the hospital levy had been increased to 11.5 percent on a notional annual salary of $66,000 per employee, making the annual tax $7,590 for each exempted company employee unless the election is made. The hospital levy is not imposed on directors and officers of exempted companies unless they also regularly perform managerial functions on a day-to-day basis.

By arranging to manage the company, you subject your company to paying the hospital levy for you, but you also secure the right to live and work in Bermuda. You or your company can then rent a home or condominium instead of having to buy one of the expensive residences available to foreigners.

For further details about exempted companies, see Chapter 59: *Bermuda*, in Marshall Langer's book: *Practical International Tax Planning* (looseleaf third edition, updated annually), available from the Practising Law Institute, New York.

OTHER ADVANTAGES INCLUDE NO TAXES

Bermuda is a traditional tax haven with no income tax or capital gains tax and no gift or death taxes on foreign property. It is therefore a safe place to establish your new domicile. It has a favorable climate throughout most of the year, although it is occasionally buffeted by hurricanes and other Atlantic storms. Bermuda is relatively close to the US mainland. There are numerous daily flights to New York and other US cities, and two flights a week to London. Flying time to New York is about two hours, and you pre-clear US immigration and customs in Bermuda. US newspapers are available in Bermuda the same day they are published. US television is available by cable TV. The Bermuda dollar has been at par with the US dollar for many years. Although Bermuda has exchange controls to protect the Bermuda dollar, new permanent residents can obtain exemptions from these controls. You can have a Bermuda dollar bank account if you wish.

POSSIBLE DISADVANTAGES

Prices are quite high because practically everything you consume in Bermuda is imported and is subject to high import duties. Cars, for example, have an import duty of 150 percent of the FOB price. Each family can have only one car. If you want to replace your old car with a new one you have to scrap the old one. Otherwise you can't buy the new car for a year. Bermuda residents are subject to gift and estate duties of up to ten percent on transfers of Bermuda property.

FOR MORE INFORMATION

The law firm of *Appleby, Spurling & Kempe* has published a helpful 11-page booklet entitled *The Acquisition of Residential Property in Bermuda by Non-Bermudians*. You can obtain a copy by writing to John D Campbell, Appleby, Spurling & Kempe, P.O. Box HM 1179, Hamilton HM EX, Bermuda. Telephone: (1 441) 295 2244. Fax: (1 441) 292 8666.

THE BOTTOM LINE

A $350,000 condominium apartment gets you residence and a safe domicile with no death taxes except on local property. Alternatively, you can become a resident by forming and managing your own exempted company. There is no chance of getting citizenship or a passport.

1997 UPDATE

The one-time license fee for acquiring a private home has been increased from 20 percent to 22 percent; the comparable fee for a condominium remains 15 percent. Bermuda has recently changed its telephone area code from 1 809 to 1 441. The law firm of *Conyers, Dill & Pearman* also publishes a booklet entitled *Acquiring a Residence and Property in Bermuda*, and you can obtain a copy from Michael J McCabe, Conyers, Dill & Pearman, PO Box HM 666, Hamilton HM CX, Bermuda. Telephone (1 441) 295 1422. Fax (1 441) 292 4720.

40. BRITAIN (THE *UK*)

You can move to Britain and live there tax-free by retaining your foreign domicile and living off remittances of capital from abroad. These beneficial rules may change after the UK general election which must be held by May 1997. This chapter is basically unchanged from last year's edition.

I live in the UK and many Britons I know constantly complain about their high taxes. They are right. British taxes are high and they will probably increase dramatically if a Labour government comes to power. There is a secret, however, shared by some 1.7 million foreigners living in Britain. Don't tell anyone but -- many foreigners living in Britain do not have to pay British taxes if they do not want to. *Reason*: British residents who are not domiciled in some part of the UK do not pay UK taxes on their foreign-source income unless they remit that income to the UK. Therefore, Britain may be suitable for you if:

- You can qualify for residence under the new UK immigration rules.
- You already have a satisfactory citizenship and passport (you cannot obtain either in the UK for at least five to seven years).
- You want a new permanent residence and you are willing to make it your main home.
- You have a suitable foreign domicile and you have no problem retaining it.
- All (or most) of your income is earned abroad.
- You have (or can obtain) foreign capital which you keep abroad and you can live primarily off amounts of capital that you remit to the UK from time to time.

CURRENT IMMIGRATION RULES

You need permission to reside and work in the UK. The current UK immigration rules took effect in 1994. There are still numerous categories under which people can qualify for residence. The most significant immigration categories for the typical high-net-worth individual are these:

- A new *investor category* permits anyone with £1 million of disposable assets to acquire residence by investing £750,000 in UK government bonds or shares of active UK companies. Since the money must be invested in the UK, the income it generates will be subject to UK income tax and the capital may be subject to UK inheritance tax even if he retains his foreign domicile. The investor must make the UK his main home; he can be self-employed or run a business, but he cannot be employed. Preliminary reports indicate that very few individuals have applied under this category.
- A person of *independent means* who is over 60 years old can retire in the UK if he has an income of £20,000 a year and a close connection to the UK. The income need not be remitted to the UK so it may not be subject to the UK income tax if he remains non-domiciled. The UK must be his main home and he cannot work or be self-employed.

Unless you are a citizen of an EU country you should employ a solicitor who is expert in UK immigration rules and practice to assist you with your immigration application. After five years of virtually full-time residence, you can apply to the Home Office to become a British citizen. Processing time for citizenship applications now takes from one to two years.

INCOME TAX RESIDENCY RULES RETAINED

The UK Inland Revenue published a green paper in 1988 in which it proposed fundamental changes in the way Britain taxes non-domiciled UK residents. The 60-page paper was entitled *Residence in the United Kingdom: The Scope of UK Taxation for Individuals -- A Consultative Document*. The proposed new rules were very similar to those introduced in the US in 1985. If they had been adopted, individuals regularly spending an average of over four months a year in Britain would have been taxed on their worldwide income. As a result of strong protests and pressure from Greek shipping interests and others who threatened to close down their UK businesses, the British government abandoned the proposed changes in 1989. Thus, non-domiciled individuals remain taxable in Britain on foreign-source income only if it is remitted to the UK. Some changes may still be forthcoming at a later date, but they are unlikely to be as drastic and far reaching as those contained in the abandoned proposals.

In explaining the government's decision to abandon the proposal, Norman Lamont, then Financial Secretary to the UK Treasury (and later Chancellor of the Exchequer), made the following statement to the House of Commons at the time of the 1989 UK Budget:

> Last July, the Government issued a consultative document that considered the possibility of simplifying the rules determining residence in this country for tax purposes and of relating liability for United Kingdom income tax more closely to the degree of an individual's connection with this country.
>
> It has always been recognised that any changes must take account of the wider economic implications and ensure in particular that our tax environment is broadly comparable with that of other developed countries. The United Kingdom derives considerable benefit from people who come here from overseas to carry on business and other activities. We have no wish to see them leave. I am grateful for the many responses that we received. They expressed a variety of views, and considerable concern was expressed about the implications of moving to a world income basis of liability for certain categories of people not domiciled here.
>
> We decided that the world income approach would not provide a satisfactory basis of taxation for non-United Kingdom domiciled foreigners who are resident in this country. Therefore, we do not intend pursuing it, and in those circumstances it is not our intention to bring forward any proposals at this time. I may say that we received representations from members of the Labour party as

well as of the Conservative party on that matter, and they were both in the same direction.

THE MARVELOUS REMITTANCE BASIS

The UK has used the *remittance* basis ever since it first introduced the income tax, about 200 years ago. It originally applied to all taxpayers; since the start of the first world war in 1914, it has applied only to those individuals who are not domiciled in the UK. Relatively few people take advantage of the remittance basis rules and there has been no popular outcry for change.

The rules work well for foreign income items like dividends and interest. You maintain two foreign bank accounts, one for capital and the other for income. You keep the income abroad (in the income account) and you remit only capital (from the capital account). Capital gains can cause a problem, however, since part of what you receive is gain and the rest is recovery of capital. If you remit any of the proceeds you are taxable on at least part of them. You should be able to overcome this problem by using an offshore trust.

UK tax barrister Milton Grundy suggests that neither of the following constitutes a remittance of income to the UK:

1. You use your foreign income account to buy a car abroad which you then drive to London.
2. You use a credit card issued outside the UK to charge a purchase in London, and you pay for it by issuing a check drawn on your foreign income account.

By using the marvelous remittance basis you can live in the UK and pay no taxes other than VAT on your UK purchases, an annual TV license fee and a community charge based on the value of the residence in which you live.

DOMICILE RULES MAY CHANGE

The present UK domicile rules are helpful to foreigners who move to Britain. With a bit of care these new UK residents can easily remain domiciled in one of the places from which they came. By doing so they avoid UK taxation on their unremitted foreign-source income. They also avoid UK inheritance tax on their non-UK property unless they remain in Britain for 17 years.

The UK government may someday change the domicile rules by carrying out recommendations made in a 1987 Law Commission Report. The concept of *domicile of origin* would be eliminated. Your *domicile of choice* would become more significant and, as in the US, it would become easier to trigger a new domicile. Under the proposed rules, a non-domiciled resident would become domiciled in the UK if he were present and he intended to settle there for an *indefinite period*. You would need to show the Inland Revenue when and under what circumstances you intend to leave the UK. Merely buying a burial plot abroad would no longer be sufficient. This, of course, would make it harder for foreigners residing in the UK to retain their beneficial non-domiciled status indefinitely.

UK tax barrister Milton Grundy also suggests that if the new rules take effect a non-domiciled resident seeking to retain that status should be prepared to prove that even though he resides in the UK he does not intend to *settle* there. You should therefore strengthen your ties with the place where you claim to be domiciled by such things as owning land on which you plan to build your retirement home, keeping club memberships and joining societies and committees there. You should also be prepared to show that you are resident in the UK for a *definite period*, not an indefinite one. Show, for example, that when you reach a certain age you plan to retire, move back to the place where you claim to be domiciled, build a retirement home on your land there, and carry out some retirement project. Prime Minister John Major has indicated that his government has no immediate plans to carry out the proposed change. The new rules would not apply to prior years. The proposal did not originate from the Inland Revenue and is not tax driven, but it would have a substantial tax impact.

WHAT IF LABOUR WINS?

Gordon Brown, the shadow chancellor, will be in charge of the UK budget and its tax program if the Labour party wins the next general election. That election must take place no later than 1997 and opinion polls now show Labour with a commanding lead over the Tories who have been in power for over 15 years. We have therefore been examining statements made by Brown for clues as to what might happen if Labour is elected.

At the October 1994 annual conference of the Labour party, Brown attacked the "tax privileges" which he said subsidized "boardroom privilege". According to the *Financial Times*, he reaffirmed that a Labour government would *tighten up residency rules for the rich*, stating that Labour would "rewrite the tax rules for the undeserving rich". One of my colleagues has facetiously suggested that Labour's definition of the undeserving rich may include everyone who is not on the dole. For further thoughts on this subject, see Chapter 66 below.

OTHER ADVANTAGES

London is one of the greatest places in the world in which to live. Britain has no exchange controls. Flights are available from London to almost anywhere in the world.

POSSIBLE DISADVANTAGES

Living costs in the UK are very high, especially in London. You must not change your domicile to one in the UK. That would make you subject to full income taxes on your worldwide income at high rates. It would also subject your estate to inheritance tax on your non-UK property. Thus, you must keep your present domicile or establish a new one somewhere else.

FOR MORE INFORMATION

John Dewhurst has written an excellent 186-page book entitled Migration--United Kingdom, (second edition 1986), available from the publisher, Kluwer, P.O. Box 23, 7400 GA Deventer, Netherlands. Telephone: (31 5700) 47261. Fax: (31 5700) 22244. Or, in the US, Kluwer Law and Taxation Publishers, 6 Bigelow Street, Cambridge, MA 02139. Telephone: (1 617) 354 0140. Fax: (1 617) 354 8595. I also recommend James Kessler's 83-page report entitled *Tax Planning for the Foreign Domiciliary*, published in 1987 by Key Haven Publications, now at 7 Crescent Stables, 139 Upper Richmond Road, London SW15 2TN, England. Telephone: (44 181) 780 2522. Fax: (44 181) 780 1693.

THE BOTTOM LINE

The UK is a great place for residence, but you must avoid being domiciled there. Citizenship and a passport take at least five years.

41. CAMPIONE

Tiny Campione offers the possibility of living "in Switzerland" without paying Swiss taxes, since it is technically a part of Italy. This chapter has not been revised from last year's edition, but some minor changes are noted in the *1997 Update* at the end of the chapter.

Campione is a *back door to Switzerland*. You can live there without paying Swiss taxes, and possibly with no taxes. Yet, for all practical purposes, it is a part of Switzerland. *Campione d'Italia* (meaning sample of Italy) is a tiny enclave on Lake Lugano near the Swiss-Italian border. It is a part of Italy but, except for mountain goats and expert mountain climbers or skiers, it is accessible by land only from Switzerland. You can reach it from Italy only by water. You use Swiss roads to drive there, all local cars have Swiss (Canton of Ticino) license plates, and the 3,000 or so residents use the Swiss postal and telephone systems. The Swiss cannot collect taxes since it is Italian territory. Italy apparently does not bother to do so, especially from non-Italians. Local needs are amply covered by revenues from its famous gambling casino. A number of wealthy European tax exiles now live there. It is relatively easy to establish residency there, particularly if you have a European Union (EU) passport. Campione may be suitable for you if:

- You are retired or semi-retired and have a substantial income; you can't really work or carry on a business there.
- You already have a suitable citizenship and passport, and you are not an Italian citizen.
- You are willing to rent or buy a house or condominium there and spend some time there each year.

HOW CAMPIONE WORKS

You rent or buy an apartment or townhouse in Campione. You then obtain a Campione residence permit by applying to the police in nearby Como (Italy). You should get the permit in about ten days. With it you may obtain a Swiss driving license, Swiss car registration, and Swiss license plates.

Real Estate: You can buy and sell real estate in Campione without problems. Swiss restrictions don't apply since Campione is not Swiss territory. A decent, small one-bedroom apartment with a view of the lake is likely to cost you at least Sfr500,000 (about US $350,000). Double that for a three-bedroom apartment and triple it for a townhouse. You can obtain current information on apartments and townhouses for sale in Campione from Immobiliare Wehner, Viale Marco 27, CH-6911 Campione, Switzerland. Telephone: (41 91) 649 7549. Fax: (41 91) 649 6345.

Taxes: There is no tax collection office in Campione. The tax office in Como, Italy is responsible for assessing and collecting taxes in Campione. As a practical matter, they do not bother to collect taxes from most non-Italians unless they have Italian-source income. If you do have taxable income from Italian sources, they will take your worldwide income into account in calculating the tax rate on that income. Your tax liability is calculated in a strange way that should prove highly beneficial to you. You calculate your income in Swiss francs and convert it into Italian lire at an historical exchange rate of 242 lire to the franc. Since the actual exchange rate (as of March 1997) is about 1,140 lire to the franc, your reportable taxable income will be less than 20 percent of what it really is. As a "resident" of Italy you should be able to take advantage of Italian tax treaties to reduce your tax on income from other countries.

OTHER ADVANTAGES

For all practical purposes, Campione is a suburb of Lugano which is a very nice Swiss city. Since you are technically resident in Italy, you may eventually be able to qualify for Italian citizenship.

POSSIBLE DISADVANTAGES

Campione is a tiny village and there isn't much to do there. Real estate is much more expensive than it is in nearby Swiss and Italian towns.

FOR MORE INFORMATION

Dr WG Hill's *The Campione Report*, available from Scope International, contains useful maps and much helpful information. Hill describes Campione as *Switzerland's Secret Semi-Tropical Tax Haven*.

THE BOTTOM LINE

By renting or buying an apartment you can become a *de facto* resident of Switzerland with no Swiss taxes and little or no Italian taxes.

1997 UPDATE

If you can still get a small apartment in Campione for Sfr500,000, the decline of the Swiss franc would make this about US $350,000. As of March 1997, there were about 1,140 Italian lire to the Swiss franc. The new numbers for Immobiliare Wehner are: Telephone: (41 91) 649 7549; Fax: (41 91) 649 6345.

42. CANADA

Canada is a high-tax country for residents. It no longer imposes death duties but it does impose a capital gains tax at death and upon departure from Canada. It is a safe place for domicile and you can get citizenship and a passport after at least three years of residence. This chapter has not been revised from last year's edition, but some recent developments have been noted in the *1997 Update* at the end of the chapter.

Thousands of new Hong Kong Chinese have been moving to Canada each year, and both Toronto and Vancouver now have huge Chinese communities. Canada is quite attractive for tax exiles as well as political and economic refugees despite its relatively high income taxes. *Reasons*: Like Australia, it welcomes new immigrants, it offers them citizenship and a first-class passport after three full years of residence, and it has abolished death taxes. Canada may be suitable for you if:

- You are unhappy with your present citizenship and passport and would like to replace them, and you can afford to wait three years to do so.
- You prefer an English-speaking country with Anglo-American traditions. You are willing to pay high income taxes in return for a quality lifestyle that you feel you cannot obtain in some exotic island tax haven. If you prefer to speak French you can try Montreal.
- You already have sufficient wealth so that you are more interested in keeping what you have for yourself and your heirs than building up your assets. In effect, you are more concerned with avoiding confiscatory capital and death taxes than high income taxes.

REQUIREMENTS FOR PERMANENT RESIDENCE

If you don't have close family members already living in Canada, you may be able to qualify for permanent residence under an *independent category* or under the *business immigration program*, either as an entrepreneur or as an investor.
- You can be an *entrepreneur* by setting up a properly capitalized business that you run on a full-time basis and that employs at least one Canadian; or
- You can buy your way in as an *investor* by showing that you have over Cdn$500,000 (about US $370,000) and by investing about Cdn$250,000 (US $185,000) as a passive investor.

INVESTMENT POSSIBILITIES

There are some good investment possibilities available, and I have worked with several Canadians who specialize in arranging *landed immigrant* status in Canada for foreigners who invest in Canada. An individual qualifying as an investor must have a proven business record and must have accumulated the required net worth through his own endeavors. There are three tiers of investment:

- Tier 1 requires a net worth of Cdn$500,000 (US $370,000) and an investment of Cdn$250,000 (US $185,000) for five years in one of the seven provinces that receives fewer business immigrants: Alberta, Manitoba, New Brunswick, Newfoundland, Nova Scotia, Prince Edward Island, or Saskatchewan.
- Tier 2 requires a net worth of Cdn$500,000 (US $370,000) and an investment of Cdn$350,000 (US $260,000) for five years in one of the three provinces that receives more business immigrants: British Columbia, Ontario, or Quebec.
- Tier 3 requires a net worth of Cdn$700,000 (US $520,000) and an investment of Cdn$500,000 (US $370,000) for five years in any of the provinces; it allows a third-party guarantee by a Canadian financial institution as to both principal and interest.

Once you are admitted as a *landed immigrant* you can live anywhere in Canada, not just in the province in which you have invested. As a landed immigrant, you are not supposed to leave the country for more than six months at any one time, and you are expected to remain in the country for more than six months each year. Failure to do so may cause serious problems when you apply for Canadian citizenship.

Here is an example of a Tier 1 *immigrant investment fund* that you could have acquired a couple of years ago through one of the big Canadian banks and which would have qualified you for immigration into Canada.

You purchase a Cdn$250,000 (now about US $185,000) promissory note issued by a Prince Edward Island (PEI) company. It pays interest of two percent a year and matures in five years. The fund is divided into two parts: 70 percent is used to finance a real estate project in Charlottetown, PEI; the other 30 percent is invested in bank deposits and government paper. There are various forms of security for the real estate project, including a support agreement of a regional development corporation owned by the provincial and city governments.

For further information about current immigrant investment fund offerings, contact Richard J Marshall, Vice President, or H Arnie Brown, Assistant General Manager, Private Banking, Executive Offices, The Bank of Nova Scotia, 44 King Street West, Toronto, Ontario, Canada M5H 1H1. Telephone: (1 416) 866 3461 or 866 6109. Fax: (1 416) 866 7773.

COMPARING THE *US* AND CANADA

If you are a wealthy tax exile from Europe or Asia and you want to move to North America, you are generally much better off moving to Canada than to the US. Canadian income taxes are about as high as those in the US, but they are much fairer when applied to new residents. Canada gives an incoming resident a new valuation for his assets as of the date he moves in; the US does not. Suppose you move to North America with an asset that originally cost you $10,000 but is now worth $600,000. You later sell the asset for $700,000. Canada would tax you on a $100,000 gain; the US would tax you on a $690,000 gain.

If you continue to hold the asset until you die, Canada will impose its capital gains tax at death as though you had sold the property at that time. There is presently no Canadian estate or inheritance tax at the federal or provincial levels. The US would impose a federal estate tax on the fair market value of your worldwide assets exceeding $600,000, at rates ranging from about 40 percent to 55 percent. Many US states would impose an additional estate or inheritance tax. The US would revalue your unsold assets at death so that future sales by your heirs might escape some of the capital gains tax. The practical result of all of this is that US death taxes are confiscatory for a husband and wife who have combined assets exceeding about $2 million. Your taxable estate includes absolutely everything you own anywhere in the world. As regards US tax, trusts don't help and neither do foreign companies. On estates exceeding about $21 million the US federal estate tax is a flat 55 percent.

Canada gives you citizenship and a passport after three years; the US does the same after five years. If you later move out of North America, Canada would impose a departure tax if you had lived in Canada over five years as though you had sold your assets (other than Canadian properties) just before you moved out. You could thereafter live anywhere in the world as a Canadian with no further tax liability to Canada. The US would continue to tax you fully as a citizen for both income and estate tax purposes unless you relinquished your citizenship, and even then it would try to tax you in part for ten years thereafter.

You can have the best of all worlds if you move to Canada for three or four years (long enough to obtain citizenship and a passport) but less than five years (not long enough to trigger the Canadian departure tax). Moreover, with good tax planning involving the use of pre-immigration offshore trusts, you can minimize your Canadian income taxes during your first five years in Canada. If you are allergic to cold Canadian winters you can do the same thing most wealthy Canadians do -- spend three months or so each winter in warm, sunny Florida, without remaining there long enough to trigger US tax problems.

CANADA NOW COLLECTS *US* TAXES

Warning! Canada and the US recently amended their current income tax treaty; the protocol amending the treaty took effect in late 1995. Among other things, it enables Canada to assist the US in collecting any US tax if the US certifies to Canada that its *revenue claim* has been finally determined. Canada will not assist in collecting a US revenue claim against an individual who was a Canadian citizen when the claim arose. This new provision is retroactive for ten years; it therefore covers revenue claims that became final since 1986.

Assume, for example, that Charles Corton, a US citizen, moved to Canada in 1991 and that he becomes a Canadian citizen in 1999. Canada will now assist the US in collecting all US federal taxes due prior to 1999. If Corton dies before becoming a Canadian citizen, Canada will assist the US in collecting its estate tax. The US may, of course, claim that Corton still owed US estate tax on his US property. However, the IRS might also base its revenue claim on the theory that Corton was still domiciled in the US at the time he died and that his estate was therefore liable for full US estate tax on his *worldwide assets*.

Any US citizen or former citizen who moves to Canada should now carefully consider the fact that Canada will assist the US in collecting any prior US taxes and any future taxes that might arise up to the day on which he becomes a Canadian citizen.

OTHER ADVANTAGES

Canada permits dual nationality. The US Social Security Administration has ruled that, based on reciprocity, a Canadian citizen who is not a US citizen or resident can continue to receive US social security benefits to which he is entitled despite continued absence from the US.

POSSIBLE DISADVANTAGES

Watch out for bureaucratic delays when you apply for Canadian citizenship; it can take a year or more to complete the process. Employ a good immigration lawyer and apply for citizenship as soon as you become eligible to do so. Most of Canada is freezing cold during the winter months, with lots of snow. Canada has high taxes and strict enforcement, leading many long-term Canadian residents to leave Canada as tax exiles.

FOR MORE INFORMATION

H Arnold Sherman and Jeffrey D Sherman have written an excellent 360-page book entitled *Migration-Canada*, (published in 1985), available from the publisher, Kluwer, P.O. Box 23, 7400 GA Deventer, Netherlands. Telephone: (31 5700) 47261. Fax: (31 5700) 22244. Or, in the US, Kluwer Law and Taxation Publishers, 6 Bigelow Street, Cambridge, MA 02139. Telephone: (1 617) 354 0140. Fax: (1 617) 354 8595. You can obtain helpful notes on Canadian immigration rules from Toronto immigration lawyer David Lesperance, 84 King Street West, Suite 202, Dundas, Ontario L9H 1T9, Canada. Telephone: (1 905) 627 3037. Fax: (1 905) 627 9868. Ask your nearest Canadian Embassy or High Commission for a free copy of *Business Immigration Program: Immigration Regulations, Guidelines and Procedures*, published by Employment and Immigration Canada.

THE BOTTOM LINE

Canada offers residence and a safe domicile. Death taxes are limited to a capital gains tax at death on the increased value of your estate over what it was worth when you immigrated. You can apply for citizenship and a passport after three years.

1997 UPDATE

A Canadian resident with more than Cdn $100,000 (about US $75,000) of non-Canadian assets must now file a detailed report of these assets with Revenue Canada each year. Canadian immigration lawyer David Lesperance can now be contacted at 84 King Street West, Suite 202, Dundas, Ontario L9H 1T9, Canada. Telephone: (1 905) 627 3037. Fax: (1 905) 627 9868.

43. CAPE VERDE

You can obtain citizenship for yourself, your spouse and your children under 18 by making a one-time donation of only US $35,000 to a government-sponsored foundation. However, visa-free travel on a Cape Verde passport is more limited than that on passports acquired under some other economic citizenship programs. This chapter has not been revised from last year's edition, but an address change is noted in the *1997 Update* at the end of the chapter.

You may not want to live in the Cape Verde Islands, but you, your spouse and your children under 18 can all obtain citizenship and passports there if you make a single US $35,000 donation to a foundation established by the Cape Verde government. This is one of the rare situations in which you can legally obtain citizenship under a bona fide *economic citizenship program* without years of prior residence. In fact, you don't have to go to Cape Verde at all; everything can be handled by the government's overseas agents. Cape Verde may be suitable for you if:

•   You want a comparatively inexpensive second passport that comes with citizenship for you and the members of your immediate family.

•   You want to avoid the hassle and expense of buying or leasing a home somewhere just to establish pre-citizenship residence.

•   You are not overly concerned that your new passport offers comparatively little visa-free travel.

•   You may be working on obtaining a better passport via residence elsewhere and need an inexpensive "bridge" passport.

WHERE IS CAPE VERDE?

The Republic of Cape Verde is located on a group of ten islands about 400 miles off the coast of Senegal in West Africa. The country's total land area is slightly larger than that of Rhode Island, the smallest US state. Cape Verde was a Portuguese colony until it became independent in 1975. Its nearly 400,000 people, mostly Creole and African, speak Portuguese and a creole dialect. The capital, Praia, has about 60,000 people. South African Airways stops at the Sal Island international airport in Cape Verde on its flights from the US to Johannesburg. You can also fly there from Amsterdam, Lisbon, Cyprus and Paris.

Cape Verde is a member of the UN, the IMF, the World Bank, and various other international organizations. Many Cape Verdeans live abroad. In fact, there are about as many people of Cape Verdean ancestry living in the US as there are in Cape Verde.

OTHER ADVANTAGES

The program is completely legal. The Cape Verde Constitution was amended in 1992 and it now provides that:

- Cape Verdeans may be dual nationals.
- Freedom of travel is guaranteed.
- Discrimination is prohibited against all citizens, including those who are naturalized.
- No citizen can be expelled or extradited to any country.

Your US $35,000 donation is held in escrow pending approval or rejection of your application. If it is rejected, you get all your money back. If it is approved, you get certificates of nationality and passports for yourself, your spouse, and your children under 18.

You are not subject to Cape Verdean income, gift or estate taxes except on any local-source income or local assets. You don't ever have to go to Cape Verde unless you want to. You remain a citizen for life, with full rights except the right to vote or hold public office there.

POSSIBLE DISADVANTAGES

Only some 15 West African countries (that you probably won't want to visit) expressly permit visa-free travel on a Cape Verdean passport. About 40 other countries with liberal entry requirements either require no visa or give you one on arrival. Many other countries, including all EU countries, do require a visa. Although it is supposed to be easy to obtain a visa to visit any other country using a Cape Verdean passport, you will still have the hassle and cost of doing so. If you obtain Cape Verdean citizenship, and that is your only citizenship, you may also want to acquire a passport from a country like Uruguay that is granted without citizenship but offers greater visa-free travel. Incidentally, the Cape Verdean government is trying to get more countries to accept its passport without visas. When and if it succeeds, the cost of acquiring a Cape Verdean passport will undoubtedly increase substantially.

FOR MORE INFORMATION

For a brochure containing full details of the Cape Verde economic citizenship program, contact Marshall Langer, Shutts & Bowen, 43 Upper Grosvenor Street, London W1X 9PG, UK. Telephone: (44 171) 493 4840. Fax: (44 171) 493 4299.

THE BOTTOM LINE

A single US $35,000 donation gets citizenship for life and renewable 5-year passports for yourself and each member of your immediate family.

1997 UPDATE

The new address for obtaining a Cape Verde brochure is Marshall Langer, Shutts & Bowen, 43 Upper Grosvenor Street, London W1X 9PG, UK. The telephone and fax numbers have not been changed.

44. CAYMAN ISLANDS

Cayman is a traditional tax haven with no income tax and no taxes at death. This makes it a good place for your residence and domicile. You can obtain residence without the right to work by purchasing a condominium apartment costing at least US $180,000. This chapter is basically unchanged from last year's edition, but a telephone area code change is noted in the *1997 Update* at the end of the chapter.

The Cayman Islands is much more interested in obtaining new companies and new trusts than it is in obtaining new immigrants. It is difficult, but possible, for you to obtain permanent residence there. You first apply for and obtain *initial residency*. Your application for permanent residence cannot be filed until after you have resided in Cayman for at least six months. *Permanent residency* may be granted to persons with substantial investment in Cayman. This generally requires an investment in a home or in a local enterprise amounting to at least CI $150,000 (about US $180,000). You must also prove that you have sufficient private income to enable you and your family to live in Cayman without having to work.

You can also establish your domicile in Cayman but you can't really become a citizen. Cayman is a UK dependent territory but those persons who "belong" to the islands have *Caymanian status*, a form of local citizenship. It is almost impossible for foreign-born residents to obtain Caymanian status unless they have close family connections to the islands. Only about 12 such applications are approved during any year. Cayman may be suitable for you if:

• You already have a satisfactory citizenship and passport.
• You want a new permanent residence in which you can actually reside as little or as much as you want.
• You like the idea of living on a small Caribbean island.

IMMIGRATION LAW

Cayman enacted a comprehensive new Immigration Law in 1992. It establishes who is entitled to *Caymanian status* and who can obtain permanent residence with or without the right to work. A *permanent residence certificate* does not ordinarily give you the right to work in the islands. However, many long-term work permit holders are now being granted permanent residence with the right to work.

The new law also clarifies that a married woman can adopt her own domicile of choice. However, she must do so affirmatively. Otherwise she is assumed to have retained her husband's domicile as her own.

IMMIGRATION QUOTAS

Cayman has about 28,000 residents, about 60 percent of whom are Caymanians. There are only about 11,000 foreigners in the islands. New residents are apparently subject to a quota system based on where they come from. The government tries to keep a roughly equal balance among these five different categories of immigrants: (1) the UK and Ireland; (2) Jamaica and Honduras; (3) the US and Canada; (4) the rest of the Caribbean; and (5) the rest of the world. Until now it has been possible to obtain temporary permits outside these quotas but that may not continue.

OTHER ADVANTAGES INCLUDE NO TAXES

Cayman is a traditional tax haven with no taxes on income or capital gains and no taxes at death. Cayman is a safe place to establish your new domicile. It has no exchange controls. It has lots of sunshine, fabulous *Seven-Mile Beach* and water sports. There are regular flights from Grand Cayman to several different US cities. It is reasonably close to Florida; flying time to Miami is about one and a half hours. US newspapers are available on the day they are published. US television is available by cable TV.

POSSIBLE DISADVANTAGES

The Cayman dollar has been pegged to the US dollar for many years. One Cayman dollar (CI $1) is worth US $1.20. However, you have to pay a fee to the bank every time you convert from one currency to the other. At the prevailing rate charged by banks, CI $1 costs US $1.22. Prices are quite high because virtually everything you consume in the islands is imported and is subject to high import duties.

FOR MORE INFORMATION

The *Cayman Islands Yearbook & Business Directory*, a book of about 500 pages, is published annually by Cayman Free Press, P.O. Box 1365, Grand Cayman, British West Indies. Telephone: (1 345) 949 5111. Fax: (1 345) 949 7033. It contains a wealth of information, including a brief section on immigration.

THE BOTTOM LINE

A condominium apartment costing at least US $180,000 gets you Cayman residence and a safe domicile with no taxes at death. Forget about citizenship (belonger status) or a passport.

1997 UPDATE

Cayman has changed its telephone area code from 1 809 to 1 345.

45. THE CHANNEL ISLANDS (JERSEY/GUERNSEY/SARK)

Jersey and Guernsey are the largest of the Channel Islands. Each imposes a 20 percent income tax on worldwide income, but no taxes at death. These islands have housing controls that make it expensive for you to live there. Sark has no income tax, but it is very remote. This chapter has not been changed from last year's edition.

The Channel Islands have long been an attractive destination for wealthy British tax exiles. Jersey and Guernsey are each only an hour from London by plane, and their income tax rates are considerably lower than those imposed in the UK. Individuals residing in Jersey or Guernsey pay 20 percent income tax on their worldwide income, plus social security contributions. The more remote island of Sark has no income tax. There is no wealth tax in any of the islands. There are no estate, inheritance or gift taxes in any of the Channel Islands. Jersey or Guernsey may be suitable for you if:

- You are British and you are willing to pay a 20 percent income tax for the privilege of living close to London. If you are a foreigner, you can get a better deal by living in Britain or Ireland as a non-domiciled resident.
- You are trying to escape UK inheritance tax.

JERSEY WANTS ONLY THE VERY RICH

The Channel Islands are small and fairly heavily populated. Housing controls generally permit newcomers to acquire or occupy only the more expensive homes. Jersey is the most restrictive; it now accepts only about ten new immigrants a year, and they must be very wealthy to qualify. Each of them is expected to have an income of over £500,000 a year and liquid assets of at least £8 million. Even at Jersey's low 20 percent rate the annual income tax will be at least £100,000.

GUERNSEY IS MUCH LESS RESTRICTIVE

Guernsey's housing problem is much less severe than that of Jersey so it does not limit the number of people who can settle there. You can move to Guernsey if you can afford to do so. The catch is that there is a two-tier housing market. About 90 percent of the houses are in the *local market*, generally restricted to those born in Guernsey. The other ten percent of homes -- less than 1,800 of them -- are in the *open market*. It should not surprise you therefore that an open market house sells for two to three times its local equivalent. As of 1993, an average open market house in Guernsey would have cost you about £400,000 (down from over £500,000 because of the recession). You are unlikely to find any housing in the open market costing less than £150,000 to £200,000.

OTHER ADVANTAGES

The Channel Islands are part of the UK telephone and postal systems. The islands receive UK television. There is no delay in receiving British newspapers.

POSSIBLE DISADVANTAGES

Some of the laws are quaint, based on Norman French concepts rather than English common law. For several years, the UK continued to apply its death duties (then called capital transfer taxes) permanently to wealthy Britons who moved to the Channel Islands. Today, an individual who changes his domicile from the UK to the Channel Islands (or anywhere else abroad) continues to be *deemed domiciled* in the UK for inheritance tax purposes for three years after he leaves the UK.

POSSIBLE RESIDENCE OR DOMICILE IN SARK

Since there are virtually no taxes on Sark some tax exiles would like to convince their own tax authorities that they live in Sark. Only about 550 people really live on the island which is very remote and has no cars. *Residence* requires some ongoing physical presence. *Domicile* requires some physical presence plus an intention to remain there indefinitely. You cannot establish a domicile by having a mail drop in a place you have only visited once or have never visited at all.

Unlike Jersey and Guernsey, Sark does not have housing controls but property is scarce and expensive. There are only 40 freehold parcels of real estate on the island; each consists of about 30 acres and it cannot be subdivided. It cannot be sold either without the consent of the Seigneur of Sark, Michael Beaumont, and it can only be bought by British citizens. You may be able to lease land there, but you would have to reside on Sark for at least 15 years before you could build a house.

THE BOTTOM LINE

Jersey is outrageously expensive for what it gives you -- an aura of prestige, residence and a safe domicile. Only the wealthiest of Londoners who can't bear to be more than an hour away from home will even consider it unless, of course, Labour wins a UK election. Guernsey offers a reasonable alternative for those who are less snobbish.

46. COSTA RICA

Costa Rica does not tax foreign-source income and it has no taxes at death. Pensioners and retired investors can establish residence there under a favorable program. This chapter has not been changed from last year's edition, but the Costa Rican colon has continued to depreciate against the US dollar as noted in the *1997 Update* at the end of the chapter.

For over 20 years, Costa Rica has had an attractive, popular program to encourage retired persons to become residents. The program is aimed at individuals living on pensions (*pensionados*) and investors who have a guaranteed minimum income from abroad (*rentistas*). It used to be possible for *pensionados* and *rentistas* to obtain Costa Rican passports similar to those issued to Costa Rican citizens. The issuance of passports to non-citizens was stopped in 1983. Costa Rica may be suitable for you if:

- You already have a satisfactory citizenship and passport (you cannot expect to obtain either in Costa Rica for at least seven years).
- You want a new permanent residence and you are prepared to live in Costa Rica for at least four months each year.
- You have an income of at least US $600 per month for at least five years from a foreign pension or an income of at least US $1,000 per month for at least five years from some other source. The latter could, for example, come from a certificate of deposit with a local or foreign bank.

OTHER REQUIREMENTS FOR *PENSIONADO* STATUS

Once a completed application has been filed, you can expect a decision within three months. The grant of residence covers you, your spouse and any children who are still students. A *pensionado* or *rentista* cannot work as an employee in Costa Rica. You can run your own business, however, from which you can receive dividends but not a salary.

NO TAX ON FOREIGN INCOME

Since Costa Rican tax is imposed on a territorial basis, its income tax covers only income from sources within the country. All of your foreign-source income is therefore tax-free. Qualifying income is exempt from Costa Rican income tax even if it comes from a Costa Rican bank. There is no estate or inheritance tax on transfers at death.

Costa Rica is generally considered to be one of the nicest places in which to live in all of Latin America. The plateau area in and around the capital city of San José has a pleasant climate throughout the year. During the rainy season there are brief showers every afternoon. Costa Rica is relatively close to the US; there are several flights each day from

San José to Miami and other US cities. Flying time to Miami is about two and a half hours. Some US newspapers are available late on the day they are published. US television is available by cable TV. The Costa Rican colon has deteriorated in value during the past several years; as of February 1997 there were about 220 colones per US dollar. Prices of many goods and services are lower than those in other retirement havens.

POSSIBLE DISADVANTAGES

You must speak Spanish to survive on a day-to-day basis even though English is widely used and understood by most business and professional people. Import duties are quite high and a *pensionado* or *rentista* is no longer entitled to duty-free importation of his car, furniture and household goods.

FOR MORE INFORMATION

The *Pacheco Coto* law firm has published a brief ten-page paper in English entitled *Memorandum on Rentist and Pensioner Status in Costa Rica*. You can obtain a copy by contacting Licenciado Humberto Pacheco A, Pacheco Coto Law Offices, P.O. Box 6610, 1000 San José, Costa Rica. Telephone: (506) 223 2760. Fax: (506) 255 2783.

THE BOTTOM LINE

Costa Rica offers a good residence and a safe domicile with no death taxes. It was even better when passports were available.

1997 UPDATE

As of February 1997 there were about 220 Costa Rican colones per US dollar.

47. CYPRUS

Cyprus offers you interesting tax benefits if you are a retired investor or an author, musician or inventor. To obtain these tax benefits, you should become resident but not domiciled in Cyprus. This chapter is basically unchanged from last year's edition, but two changes are noted in the *1997 Update* at the end of the chapter.

Cyprus has been a divided island since 1974. The southern portion of the island is Greek-Cypriot; that is the part I am discussing here. Despite UN efforts, Turkish troops still occupy the northern part of the island. Nicosia is a divided city with a wall similar to that which used to divide Berlin. Cyprus may be an attractive destination for you if you are a retired investor or if you receive substantial royalty income. It should be relatively easy for you to obtain a residence permit if you can prove that you have adequate means of support. You will not be allowed to carry on any business there. Cyprus may be suitable for you if:

- You are a retired investor, particularly if you receive dividends or interest from countries with which Cyprus has favorable income tax treaties.
- Or, you are an author, musician or inventor who receives royalty income.
- You already have a satisfactory citizenship and passport.
- You have a suitable domicile and you have no problem retaining it. To obtain the tax benefits discussed here, you must become resident but not domiciled in Cyprus.

LOW INCOME TAX FOR NON-DOMICILED RESIDENTS

As a *non-domiciled resident* you will pay a flat tax of five percent on your *investment income* from abroad that is remitted to Cyprus. The first Cyp£2,000 (about US $4,000) of remitted investment income and all investment income that is not remitted to Cyprus is tax-free. *Royalties* are treated as investment income. You may want to remit the income to Cyprus in order to reduce foreign withholding taxes under one of Cyprus' many tax treaties. If you do, the foreign withholding tax will be creditable against the Cyprus tax; this may wipe out the five percent Cyprus tax. Unfortunately these benefits do not work under either the Cyprus-UK or Cyprus-US treaties, but they seem to work well under most other Cyprus treaties. Similar rules apply to *pension* income and, in that case even the Cyprus-US treaty permits treaty benefits unless you are or were a US citizen.

OTHER ADVANTAGES

Located in the Mediterranean, Cyprus has a pleasant climate throughout most of the year.

POSSIBLE DISADVANTAGES

Although English is widely spoken, the official language is Greek. You will need approval to buy any property in Cyprus but you should have no difficulty if you buy a house or apartment to live in. Cyprus still has exchange controls, but as a new resident you should be able to remain nonresident for exchange control purposes. You can then keep your funds in foreign currencies both in Cyprus and abroad but you will need approval to invest in Cyprus or to borrow money there. Cyprus has death duties but non-domiciled residents pay them only on assets located in Cyprus at the time of death.

THE BOTTOM LINE

Cyprus is useful for residence. It helps if you speak some Greek. You don't want to be domiciled there. Forget about citizenship and passports.

1997 UPDATE

The Cyprus-US income tax treaty cannot be used for pension income derived by a former US long-term resident who is an expatriate covered by the revised US expatriation tax provisions. *Reason:* these provisions override all tax treaties. As of February 1997, Cyp£2,000 was about US $4,000.

48. DOMINICA

You can obtain citizenship in Dominica at a total cost of about US $75,000. You don't have to live there either before or after you acquire citizenship, but you do have to visit there once. Substantial changes in Dominica's *economic citizenship program* have occurred during the past year, and this chapter has been completely revised to reflect these changes.

The Commonwealth of Dominica (pronounced Dom-i-NEE-ka) has a low-key *economic citizenship program* that offers citizenship and a British Commonwealth passport in return for either a direct cash contribution to the government or an approved investment in the island. This program is currently operating under a *white paper* and new policy guidelines issued by the Dominica government in 1996.

English-speaking Dominica should not be confused with *Republica Dominicana* (the Dominican Republic). Dominica has been affiliated with Britain ever since 1805. It was formerly a British colony; it became an independent country within the British Commonwealth in 1978. Dominica is situated in the Eastern Caribbean, between the French-speaking islands of Guadeloupe and Martinique, a few hundred miles south of Puerto Rico. Its 73,000 people all speak English; most are of African descent. Dominica may be suitable for you if:

• You are seeking a British Commonwealth citizenship and a passport that will give you visa-free travel to over 90 countries.
• You are willing to donate US $50,000 to the government, and to pay government registration fees, professional fees and costs totalling another US $25,000, so as to obtain citizenship and good passports for you and your family for a total outlay of US $75,000.

HOW THE CITIZENSHIP PROGRAM WORKS

A 1991 law permits the Immigration Minister to waive the normal residence requirements for citizenship in special circumstances. He may now do so for you if you qualify under one of these programs:

1. You can invest US $75,000 in 15-year Commonwealth of Dominica government bonds paying 2 per cent interest. You must also pay *government* registration fees of US $15,000 for yourself, US $10,000 for your spouse, US $10,000 for each child under 18, and US $15,000 for each child between 18 and 25 years of age. Professional fees are extra. This is an expensive option.
2. You can make a direct cash contribution to the government of Dominica of US $50,000 and pay reduced government registration fees. Under this plan, either an individual or a family of up to four persons (yourself, your spouse, and one or two

children under 18) can be processed for a single cash contribution and all-inclusive other costs of US $25,000 that include all government registration fees and professional fees. Your total outlay is therefore US $75,000. You and each of your family members become citizens for life and each of you receives a passport. This is generally the best and most popular of the existing programs.

3.   You can invest US $35,000 in Dominica's first luxury hotel project, pay the hotel developer an additional fee of US $25,000, and pay professional fees and expenses of US $15,000, for a total outlay of US $75,000. There are some problems with this alternative. Most of the money is held by the hotel developer while the application is pending and there have been some recent disputes and threatened litigation between the government and the hotel developer. Construction on the hotel has stopped twice during the past year.

4.   The government has also made arrangements with other developers in Dominica under which investments in their projects may qualify an applicant for citizenship. These would generally require an investment of at least US $50,000 for yourself and may require an additional investment for *each* family member. You would also have to pay government registration fees and professional fees.

Under the first and second of these programs, your professional adviser can hold your funds in escrow until you receive preliminary approval from the government. At that time the money will be paid over to the government but the government promises to return the funds to you if your application is thereafter rejected for any reason.

Processing time for citizenship applications generally takes about a month. At least one cabinet minister personally interviews a member of each family to satisfy himself that the citizenship candidates are *bona fide*. Thus, the head of each family must go to Dominica at a mutually convenient time. If you remain in Dominica for a couple of days following the meeting, you should be able to leave with your certificate of citizenship and passport. Dominica permits dual citizenship. Documents required include an application for citizenship, birth and marriage certificates, a police certificate showing no criminal record, reference letters and a medical certificate showing a negative HIV test.

Each new citizen receives a 10-year passport (5 years for children) and a certificate of naturalization. As a citizen, each has an absolute right to renew his passport for the rest of his life. A Dominica passport allows you to travel without a visa to over 90 countries, including Canada, Norway, Sweden, Switzerland, the United Kingdom and many British Commonwealth countries. You should not have any trouble getting visas to other countries.

OTHER ADVANTAGES

The US Social Security Administration has ruled that, based on reciprocity, a Dominica citizen who is not a US citizen or resident can continue to receive US social security benefits to which he is entitled despite continued absence from the US. There is no tax liability to Dominica based on citizenship. Moreover, Dominica's Minister of Finance has told me that even those who are resident there do not pay income tax on foreign-source income. Dominica has no gift or estate taxes.

POSSIBLE DISADVANTAGES

Dominica has a tax information exchange agreement (TIEA) with the US but little or no information is actually exchanged. Getting to Dominica is not difficult but it is time consuming. The easiest way from the US mainland is via American Airlines to San Juan, Puerto Rico, with a connecting American Eagle flight to Dominica. It is also possible to get there via nearby islands such as Antigua, Barbados, Guadeloupe, Martinique or St Maarten.

FOR MORE INFORMATION

For a brief update on the Dominica economic citizenship program, contact Marshall Langer or Stephen Gray, Shutts & Bowen, 43 Upper Grosvenor Street, London W1X 9PG, UK. Telephone: (44 171) 493 4840. Fax: (44 171) 493 4299.

THE BOTTOM LINE

For a total outlay of US $75,000 which includes a donation and all fees and costs, you and your family can legally acquire citizenship and good passports in a British Commonwealth country.

49. GIBRALTAR

Gibraltar's residence program for high net worth individuals may be interesting if you already have a suitable domicile elsewhere. You would typically have to pay an annual income tax of £10,000, the minimum required under the program. This chapter has not been changed from last year's edition.

Gibraltar recently enacted new rules designed to attract wealthy retirees. The program has some attractions but its name has been a real turn-off. None of my clients likes the idea of registering under the *Qualifying (High Net Worth) Individuals Rules 1992*. Tax avoidance may be legal but no one wants to join something called the Aggressive Tax Avoiders Association. Despite the name, Gibraltar's new program may be suitable for you if:

- You cannot escape the clutches of your present place of residence without proof that you have established a new residence somewhere.
- You already have a suitable citizenship and passport.
- You have a suitable domicile elsewhere.

HIGH NET WORTH INDIVIDUALS

You must rent or buy *approved residential accommodation* in Gibraltar. In fact, it appears that the program was created to assist developers of a large new real estate project. Your Gibraltar residence must be available for your exclusive use for at least seven months each year. You must actually live in it for at least 30 days a year. You pay a one-time government fee of £500 and receive a certificate qualifying you as a *high net worth individual*. You and your spouse jointly pay Gibraltar income tax at the regular (high) rates, but only on your first £45,000 of taxable income. Presumably, you are not domiciled and are therefore taxable only on income remitted to Gibraltar. In any case, your minimum tax is £10,000; and your maximum tax cannot exceed £20,000. I am told that high net worth individuals are not subject to Gibraltar estate duty but I cannot find that in the rules. I assume, therefore, that exemption from estate duty is due to the fact that you are not considered to be domiciled there.

QUALIFYING INDIVIDUALS

Gibraltar has another category of persons who can legally avoid its high income taxes. The *Qualifying Individuals Rules 1989* permit you to apply for a *qualifying certificate* if you are neither *ordinarily resident* nor *domiciled* in Gibraltar and you have no Gibraltar income other than from exempt or qualifying companies. You pay a one-time fee of £500 and an agreed tax rate (typically two percent) on your worldwide income. Your maximum income tax liability is £20,000 a year. You are not ordinarily resident in Gibraltar for either income tax or estate duty purposes merely because you own property there which is available for your exclusive residential use provided you don't actually reside in Gibraltar for more than seven months a year.

GIBRALTAR PASSPORTS ARE *EU* PASSPORTS

Unlike the Channel Islands and the Isle of Man, Gibraltar is a part of the European Union (EU). Thus, a Gibraltar passport is an EU passport that gives you the right to live and work anywhere in the EU. Eligibility for a Gibraltar passport is similar to that for a UK passport. You must be resident for five years during which you cannot spend more than 450 days (an average of 90 days a year) outside Gibraltar.

OTHER ADVANTAGES

Gibraltar has no capital gains tax, no wealth tax and no gift tax. Although Gibraltar has a unique status as an EU member (because it is a dependent territory of a member country on the European mainland), it is exempt from a few EU requirements. Thus, for example, it does not have a VAT.

POSSIBLE DISADVANTAGES

Gibraltar is tiny; it has an area of only 2.25 square miles. Despite pressure by Spain, Gibraltar remains staunchly British. Although its frontier with Spain was reopened in 1985, there is still considerable animosity between Spain and Gibraltar. At times there are very long delays in crossing the border between Gibraltar and Spain. Because of Spanish opposition to the use of Gibraltar's airport, there are no direct flights from continental Europe to Gibraltar. For flights to most places other than London you have to drive to the airport at Malaga, Spain.

FOR MORE INFORMATION

Read Dr WG Hill's *The Andorra & Gibraltar Report*, available from Scope International.

THE BOTTOM LINE

Gibraltar offers interesting residence possibilities with a relatively modest tax liability if you have a suitable domicile, citizenship and passport elsewhere.

50. IRELAND

You can move to Ireland and live there tax-free by retaining your foreign domicile and living off remittances of capital from abroad. You can obtain Irish citizenship and an Irish (EU) passport by descent if any of your parents or grandparents was born in Ireland. You may also be able to obtain them by making a very substantial investment in Ireland but, as noted in the *1997 Update*, this naturalization by investment program is now effectively on hold until after the next election. This chapter is otherwise basically unchanged from last year's edition.

Sure now, if one of your parents or grandparents was born in Ireland, you are entitled to obtain Irish citizenship and an Irish passport. Once the paperwork is completed and the application is filed with an Irish embassy, processing should take about six months. Today, an Irish passport is a very valuable document. It permits you to live and work anywhere in the European Union (EU). Can you get an Irish passport without the required parentage? Yes, but it's a lot harder and will require a very substantial investment in Ireland. I have worked with several clients on obtaining Irish nationality. Obtaining permission to live in Ireland is much easier. Ireland may be suitable for you if:

- You want a new nationality and an EU passport and you have the good fortune to have had one of your parents or grandparents born in Ireland. Incidentally, Northern Ireland (which is still a part of the UK) counts for this purpose.
- Alternatively, you want an Irish passport and you are willing to expedite the process by making a safe, substantial investment in Ireland for seven years in return for expedited nationality.
- You simply want to take advantage of Ireland as a good place to live. As a non-domiciled resident you will not be taxed on your foreign income unless it is remitted to Ireland. This is essentially the same deal as that used by foreigners who live in Britain.
- You have a suitable foreign domicile and you have no problem retaining it.
- All (or most) of your income is earned abroad.
- You have (or can obtain) foreign capital which you keep abroad and you can live off amounts of capital that you remit to Ireland from time to time.

CITIZENSHIP BY NATURALIZATION

The Republic of Ireland has only about 3.5 million residents. Yet, the US alone has an estimated 44 million Irish-Americans many of whom qualify for Irish citizenship and passports by descent. The procedure is relatively routine if one of your parents or grandparents was born in Ireland. It used to cover great-grandparents too but this practice was discontinued in 1986.

NATURALIZATION BY INVESTMENT

Ireland normally requires five years of residency before processing an application for naturalization. However, the Minister for Justice has the discretion to set aside the normal requirements for naturalization where the applicant is of Irish descent or Irish associations. This may be done, for example, where an individual makes a significant contribution to the development of the Irish economy, such as a very substantial investment that creates jobs. The investment criteria have been tightened several times in the past few years. Under current guidelines, issued in late 1994, you would need to:

- Lend one million Irish punts (about US $1.6 million) for seven years at a very low rate of interest to an Irish company that would use the funds to produce jobs.
- Buy a substantial house or condominium apartment in Ireland.
- Promise to spend at least 60 days in Ireland during the first two years *after* you are naturalized.
- Travel to Dublin at least once, to be naturalized before a judge in court.

There are, of course, forms to fill in. You must have a spotless record. As you may suspect, you will also have to pay some substantial professional fees. You should require appropriate guarantees that the loan will be repaid. The application will cover you; it will not cover your spouse. Under normal Irish rules, taxes will not be a problem unless you actually move to Ireland. Ireland permits you to have dual nationality.

RESIDENCE FOR INCOME TAX PURPOSES

Ireland's 1994 Finance Act added new statutory rules to determine whether an individual is resident for income tax purposes. These new rules came as a surprise because they had not been mentioned in the budget message nor had they been included in the finance bill on which the act was based. The new rules are based exclusively on physical presence in Ireland. There is a red zone and a green zone. If you stay under the magic numbers, you are in the green zone and you are nonresident for income tax purposes. Ireland's tax years, like those of Britain, begin on 6 April and end on the following 5 April. Thus, for example, the 1997/98 tax year begins 6 April 1997 and ends 5 April 1998. You are resident for Irish income tax purposes that year if you are present in Ireland either:

- 183 days or more that year; or
- 280 days or more in that year and the immediately preceding tax year (1996/97).

The 1994 Finance Act repealed prior legislation under which an individual with a home in Ireland could be treated as resident for income tax purposes if he merely set foot in Ireland during a tax year -- sometimes called the *available accommodation rule*. It also repealed a rule under which an individual was deemed resident for tax purposes if he spent an average of over 90 days a year in Ireland over a four-year period.

THE GREEN ZONE

You can now average 139 days a year in Ireland (about 4 and a half months each year) without becoming resident for income tax purposes. When making these calculations, you ignore any tax year in which you were not present in Ireland for at least 31 days. Moreover, you do not count a day unless you are present in Ireland *at the end of the day*. Thus, you can completely ignore a quick business trip in which you fly in and out of Ireland the same day.

Most new Irish citizens and tax exiles using Ireland as one of several bases will like the new rules. A few, who hoped to use favorable Irish tax treaties without spending much time in Ireland, will find that their task is now more difficult.

ORDINARY RESIDENCE AFFECTS CAPITAL GAINS

The 1994 Finance Act has also changed the *ordinary residence* rules that relate primarily to Irish capital gains taxes. You are generally subject to Irish capital gains tax if you are either resident or ordinarily resident during a tax year. You are ordinarily resident if you have been resident under the rules described above for each of the three tax years preceding the current year. Once you become ordinarily resident, you retain that status unless you cease to be resident for three full tax years. Thus, if you are resident in Ireland for years 1, 2 and 3, you will become ordinarily resident in year 4 whether or not you are resident that year. You will remain ordinarily resident for years 5 and 6 even if you left Ireland before the end of year 3 and have not been resident there since. Under this new rule, a former Irish resident remains subject to Irish capital gains tax for three years after he actually leaves unless he can obtain relief under one of Ireland's tax treaties. Unfortunately, many of Ireland's tax treaties are old and do not have beneficial capital gains tax provisions.

DOMICILE RULES ARE UNCHANGED

The 1994 legislation did not change any of the rules concerning domicile. An individual moving to Ireland can generally maintain his prior domicile indefinitely if he wants to. By doing so, he avoids Irish gift and inheritance taxes on transfers of non-Irish property. Even if he becomes resident, he avoids income tax on his non-Irish and non-UK income if he does not remit that income to Ireland.

The tricky question involves a tax exile who comes to Ireland from the US. He can readily avoid Irish domicile if he retains his US domicile. Typically, however, he also wants to abandon his prior US domicile. He must first find a suitable third country in which to establish a new domicile, and he must then take sufficient steps so that he and his heirs can prove that he is really domiciled in that third country. The question of his domicile is not likely to be raised by either the US or Irish revenue authorities until after he has died. Either or both countries may then claim high death taxes on worldwide assets by contending that he was domiciled there at the time he died.

Jerry Jeroboam may try to avoid this problem by first moving from the US to a safe domicile like Bermuda for a few years. He will then move to Ireland, taking care to maintain his Bermuda domicile. He will be even safer, however, if he stays in Bermuda permanently and merely visits Ireland for about four months a year, without ever becoming an Irish tax resident under the new income tax rules.

OTHER ADVANTAGES

If you are a writer, composer or artist you may qualify for an exemption from Irish tax on the income derived from your created works. The Irish Revenue Commissioners must judge your work to be of cultural or artistic merit. They are apparently looking for another George Bernard Shaw. They are less likely to apply the exemption to someone like me who writes books on taxes.

As a result of the Irish-US Treaty of Friendship, Commerce, and Navigation, an Irish citizen who is not a US citizen or resident can continue to receive US social security benefits to which he is entitled despite continued absence from the US.

POSSIBLE DISADVANTAGES

You don't want to change your domicile to Ireland. That would make you subject to full Irish income tax on your worldwide income at high rates. It would also subject your estate to Irish death duty on your non-Irish property. Therefore, you have to keep your present domicile or establish a new one somewhere else. Ireland and the US are currently negotiating a new income tax treaty. It is likely to be less favorable for taxpayers than the one now in force.

FOR MORE INFORMATION

For current information concerning Irish naturalization by investment, contact Marshall Langer, Shutts & Bowen, 43 Upper Grosvenor Street, London W1X 9PG, UK. Telephone: (44 171) 493 4840. Fax: (44 171) 493 4299.

THE BOTTOM LINE

Like the UK, Ireland is a great place to live if you can avoid being domiciled there. If your mother or grandmother was born in Ireland, run to the nearest Irish embassy and apply for an Irish passport. If not, look into the possibility of obtaining Irish citizenship through close ties evidenced by a substantial investment in the country.

1997 UPDATE

The Irish naturalization by investment program has been effectively on hold for the past year or so and it is likely to remain that way until at least after the next general election. Each of the few cases that has been approved recently has required a purchase of shares or an unsecured loan of IR£1 million in an enterprise whose financial position was not sound enough to justify that size or type of investment. It is technically no longer possible to obtain repayment guarantees. The new address for obtaining information concerning Irish naturalization by investment is Marshall Langer, Shutts & Bowen, 43 Upper Grosvenor Street, London W1X 9PG, UK. The telephone and fax numbers have not been changed.

51. THE ISLE OF MAN

The Isle of Man imposes a 20 percent income tax on worldwide income, but no taxes at death. It is suitable for both residence and domicile. Unlike the Channel Islands, it has no housing controls. This chapter has not been changed from last year's edition.

The Isle of Man is in the Irish Sea, halfway between the UK and Ireland. Its tax structure is much like that of the Channel Islands. Like them, it has succeeded in attracting some wealthy British tax exiles. It did so mostly at a time when there was a greater difference between the Manx income tax rate and that now imposed in the UK. Recent reductions in UK taxes have eliminated part of this difference and some of these exiles have begun to return to the UK. Among the advantages of the Isle of Man, there are no death duties, no gift taxes, no wealth taxes and no capital gains taxes. *Domicile* is not a significant factor in determining the liability for any Manx taxes. This makes the Isle of Man a safe place for someone who needs to establish a new domicile. *Residence* is significant in determining liability for Manx income taxes. An individual who spends 183 days or more in the Isle of Man during any tax year is automatically resident for tax purposes. An individual spending less than 183 days a year in the Isle of Man may also be deemed resident if he keeps a house there. The Isle of Man may be suitable for you if:

- You cannot escape the clutches of your present place of residence without proof that you have established a new residence somewhere.
- You already have a suitable citizenship and passport.
- You would like to establish a safe new domicile.

MANX INCOME TAX RATES ARE LOW

After liberal personal allowances, Manx residents now pay 15 percent income tax on their first £9,000 of *worldwide* income and 20 percent on any additional income. By comparison, the highest rate in Britain is now 40 percent. They also pay social security contributions similar to those in the UK.

The Manx tax system has many features that could be attractive to individuals and families from other parts of the world who are seeking a new place of residence and a new domicile. It would be considerably more attractive to them if it modified its present system so as to tax them on a remittance basis with a minimum required remittance so as to insure that they pay some tax. Taxation of worldwide income is a deterrent for these individuals. Some forms of pre-immigration tax planning using trusts may be acceptable to the Manx authorities. These could reduce your tax liability and allow you to take advantage of the Isle of Man as a safe domicile.

OTHER ADVANTAGES

The Isle of Man has about five times as much land area as Jersey and fewer people. Thus, it has no need for housing controls. This makes it much easier to establish residence in the Isle of Man than in Jersey. Flying time to London is a little over one hour. The Isle of Man is part of the UK telephone system. It receives UK television broadcasts and there is no delay in receiving British newspapers.

POSSIBLE DISADVANTAGES

The Isle of Man taxes you on your worldwide income even if you are not domiciled there. An immigrant coming from somewhere other than the UK will probably find it cheaper taxwise to move to the UK or Ireland and live there as a non-domiciled resident.

MANX PASSPORTS ARE NOT *EU* PASSPORTS

From time to time it is suggested that you may be able to shortcut the minimum five-year residency required before you can apply for a British passport if you do so in one of the offshore jurisdictions such as the Isle of Man. You probably cannot since the British Nationality Act applies. Moreover, the passport is not the same as the one you would get in the UK itself. A passport applied for and issued in the Isle of Man would give you the right of abode in the Isle of Man, not in the UK. And, since the Isle of Man is not within the European Union (EU), it would not be an EU passport and you would not have the right to live or work in any of the EU countries.

FOR MORE INFORMATION

Read *The Isle of Man Report*, available from Scope International.

THE BOTTOM LINE

British tax exiles can reduce their income tax and eliminate capital gains tax by moving to the Isle of Man. By changing their domicile, they can avoid UK inheritance tax after three years of residence in the Isle of Man. For others (who are not domiciled in the UK), it may be cheaper to go to the UK or Ireland.

52. ISRAEL

With proper planning, a new immigrant can escape Israel's high income taxes for many years. Since estate duties have also been abolished, Israel can be an attractive place in which to establish your residence and domicile. If you are Jewish, you will also be entitled to instant citizenship and about a year later you can obtain a full Israeli passport. This chapter is unchanged from last year's edition.

Despite its very high income taxes, Israel can be a very attractive destination for wealthy tax exiles who are Jewish. The *Economist* has noted that some wealthy American citizens of the Jewish faith have moved to Israel and expatriated to avoid the US estate tax. As Jews, they have qualified immediately for citizenship under Israel's law of return. Moreover, Israel has abolished its estate duties and the US ten-year anti-expatriation rule for estate tax purposes does not cover foreign property [*Jerusalem the Golden*, in the *Economist*, 24 August 1985, page 44]. Israel may be suitable for you if:

- You are Jewish and are willing to live at least part-time in a Jewish State.
- You have substantial wealth that you would prefer to leave to your heirs than to the tax authorities of your present high-tax country.
- You need another citizenship and passport in order to expatriate from a country that imposes confiscatory death taxes based on your citizenship. If, for example, you come from the US you may be facing a US estate tax of 55 percent or more of the fair market value of your entire worldwide estate.

FAVORABLE TREATMENT FOR NEW IMMIGRANTS

Israel has strict exchange controls and high income taxes. Neither seriously affects most new immigrants who are retired and earn substantial foreign investment income. A new immigrant to Israel enjoys a 30-year holiday from most exchange control restrictions. During those first 30 years, he may keep his assets anywhere and in any currency. This is particularly significant since Israel generally taxes its residents on foreign-source investment income only if it is remitted to Israel. During his first seven years of residence in Israel, a new immigrant may even be exempt from income tax on some or all of the foreign investment income that he remits to Israel. A new immigrant is also exempt from capital gains tax on assets that he owned before coming to Israel and that he sells within seven years after immigrating. Moreover, interest on foreign currency deposits is exempt from Israeli income tax. If all else fails there are numerous tax incentives for which he can try to qualify.

SHIPPING MAGNATE RETURNS TO ISRAEL

Ted Arison, one of the world's richest men, recently retired as chairman of Carnival Cruise Lines and moved permanently from Miami Beach, Florida to Tel Aviv, the city in which he was born, according to the *Miami Herald* [16 February 1991, page 1C]. His son, Micky, succeeded him as Carnival's chairman. Arison was born in Tel Aviv in 1924 and fought in Israel's war of independence in 1948 before moving to the US. The article noted that Forbes Magazine called him "...one of the world's 400 richest men, with a net worth of $2.86 billion."

The article makes it obvious that Arison has taken a number of steps that should result in changing his domicile as well as his residence. It does not indicate whether he had ever became a naturalized American citizen; one must suppose that if he did, he must also have expatriated. Carnival has about 15 huge cruise ships, probably all owned by foreign corporations. Assuming that Arison is able to convert about three-fourths of his assets into foreign property, his estate could save more than $1 billion in US estate taxes. Even if Arison, who is now over 70, does not outlive the ten years covered by US anti-expatriation rules, those rules would not apply to his foreign property. Israel has high income taxes, but no estate or inheritance taxes. Even if he were to pay a 100-percent income tax for the rest of his life, the enormous estate tax saving would more than make this up. Without this move, US estate taxes might make it impossible for him to pass on Carnival intact to his heirs. This is an excellent example of the *ultimate estate plan*.

OTHER ADVANTAGES

Israel permits you to have dual nationality. As a result of the Israeli-US Treaty of Friendship, Commerce, and Navigation, an Israeli citizen who is not a US citizen or resident can continue to receive US social security benefits to which he is entitled despite continued absence from the US.

POSSIBLE DISADVANTAGES

Israel has had several wars since it attained its independence in 1948. In addition to unfriendly neighbors it has huge numbers of Arabs living within its borders. If you are under 55 years old, don't immigrate without first checking your potential liability for military service.

Although a Jewish individual immigrating to Israel under the law of return obtains instant citizenship, he does not immediately receive a full passport. Instead, at the outset, he is generally given a laissez-passer (which requires visas practically everywhere). After about a year, the *laissez-passer* is replaced with a full Israeli passport. An Israel-US income tax treaty took effect in 1995. Most of its provisions do not benefit current or former US citizens.

THE BOTTOM LINE

Israel could be almost perfect if you are Jewish and very wealthy. You get a new residence, a good domicile, instant citizenship and a full passport within a year. Even if you retain some US assets that could be taxable under anti-expatriation rules, your heirs can argue that your motive was religious, not to avoid taxes. As a new immigrant you are exempt from most exchange controls, can keep your investments abroad and you are not taxed on foreign investment income that is not remitted to Israel. Although an Israeli passport is widely accepted in most countries, if you become an Israeli citizen you may feel safer traveling on a second passport from a country such as Cape Verde, Dominica, St. Kitts and Nevis, or Uruguay.

53. MALTA

Malta has an attractive program for a new resident who has only non-Maltese income. You pay only 15 percent income tax, and that only on the income you remit to Malta. There are modest minimums. Malta works best if you are not domiciled there. This chapter is generally unchanged from last year's edition, but a few items are noted in the *1997 Update* at the end of the chapter.

Malta's *1988 Residence Scheme* has been designed to attract wealthy foreign individuals, including retirees and authors, as new permanent residents. The normal income tax imposed on a Maltese resident quickly reaches a top bracket of 35 percent. However, if you become a new permanent resident you will pay a special 15 percent flat-rate income tax on your foreign-source income, and you will pay that only on the part you remit to Malta. What makes this particularly interesting is that Malta has a good network of income tax treaties many of which were developed before this program was begun. You may be able to reduce your tax in the source country and still pay only 15 percent Maltese tax, with a full credit for whatever foreign tax is imposed at source on that income. For some people this is almost too good to be true. Malta may be suitable for you if:

- You already have a satisfactory citizenship and passport (you cannot expect to obtain either in Malta).
- You want a new permanent residence and you are prepared to reside in Malta for at least part of each year.
- You own assets outside Malta worth at least Lm150,000 (about US $397,500; each Maltese lira (Lm) is worth about US $2.65). Alternatively, you can show that you have an annual income of at least Lm10,000 (about US $26,500).
- You are prepared to remit at least Lm6,000 (about US $15,900) per year to Malta and to pay a minimum annual tax of at least Lm1,000 (about US $2,650).
- You are willing to purchase or rent a residence in Malta. The minimum purchase price is Lm30,000 (about US $79,500) for a house or about two-thirds that much for an apartment. If you lease a residence, the minimum rent is Lm1,200 per year (about US $3,180). You can actually find nice places in Malta at or near these minimums.

OTHER REQUIREMENTS FOR NEW RESIDENTS

You will have to increase the amount remitted to Malta by Lm1,000 (about US $2,650) for each dependent that accompanies you. You cannot work in Malta without permission.

Your application for a residence permit should be accompanied by a banker's certificate showing that you have the required capital or income, a police certificate or other evidence that you are not a criminal, your marriage and birth certificates, three passport photos and either a deed or lease covering the Malta residence you plan to occupy. Processing generally takes a few weeks.

OTHER ADVANTAGES

Almost everyone in Malta speaks both English and Maltese; both are official languages. Malta has exchange controls but, as a new permanent resident, you can keep most of your assets abroad. Moreover, if you bring any capital into Malta, you can freely repatriate any part of it that is not spent and any income earned from it while you are resident. You can also repatriate the proceeds from selling your Maltese residence, including any profit.

POSSIBLE DISADVANTAGES

Malta may have overly promoted some of its tax treaty benefits and its use as an offshore tax haven for companies and trusts. As a result, Britain insisted on a new tax treaty with Malta that severely limits UK tax benefits for Maltese residents. The US has gone even further and will terminate the Malta-US income tax treaty as of the end of 1996. Malta has a death duty but, if you are not domiciled in Malta, it will be imposed only on your Maltese assets, such as your house, car and personal effects. You should take professional advice before you consider establishing a new domicile in Malta.

FOR MORE INFORMATION

The accounting firm of *Zammit Tabona Bonello & Co./Coopers & Lybrand* has published a little brochure entitled *Taking up Residence in Malta*. You can obtain a copy by contacting either John Bonello or Albert Castillo, Zammit Tabona Bonello & Co., 167 Merchants Street, P.O. Box 61, Valletta, Malta. Telephone: (356) 23 36 48. Fax: (356) 62 47 68. You can also obtain a guide called *Moving to Malta* from the Ministry of Finance, Floriana, Malta.

THE BOTTOM LINE

Malta offers inexpensive living, some tax treaty benefits, and low taxes for retirees who become new permanent residents. Domicile may be more of a problem; forget about citizenship or passports.

1997 UPDATE

An election held in 1996 resulted in a change of government. The new government is expected to keep Malta out of the EU, but it is not likely to alter the tax benefits given to new residents. Each Maltese lira is now worth about US $2.65. As expected, the Malta-US income tax treaty has been terminated.

54. MONACO

Monaco is a great place in which to establish your residence and domicile if you can afford to live there and you are not a French citizen. This chapter is basically unchanged from last year's edition but, as noted in the *1997 Update* at the end of the chapter, Monaco now has its own telephone country code.

Monégasques and most other residents of Monaco are free of income tax and hope to retain that status indefinitely. Monaco is tiny and always seems crowded with its hordes of visitors. It has about 30,000 permanent residents, of whom only about 5,000 are Monégasques. Nearly half of Monaco's residents are French citizens, and there are also large communities of Italian and British nationals. Most tax exiles moving to Monaco have no need to work and are there to retire and live the good life. The discussion below covers obtaining a residence permit with no right to work. If you expect to work (even as self-employed), you will also need a work permit. Monaco may be suitable for you if:

- You are retired and have a substantial income; you will need lots of money to live decently in frightfully-expensive Monaco.
- You already have a satisfactory citizenship and passport (you probably cannot ever obtain either in Monaco unless you marry a Monégasque).
- You are not a French citizen.
- You want a new permanent residence in which you will actually reside for at least several months each year.
- You are willing to buy or rent a house or condominium unit in a place where real estate prices are astronomical.

ACQUIRING RESIDENCY TAKES TIME AND MONEY

Although Monaco is an associate member of the European Union (EU), citizens of EU countries (other than France) require a French visa to reside in Monaco. Unless you are either French or Monegasque, you must have a French visa in order to live in Monaco. When you apply for the French visa you must give an undertaking that you will purchase or lease a home or apartment in Monaco if your application is approved. It will probably take about three months for you to obtain the French visa. You then present the French visa and various other documents, including proof that you have actually purchased or rented a residence in Monaco, to the Monégasque authorities. They will hold everything, including your passport, for about seven to ten days. If everything is in order they will then give you a renewable one-year residence permit *(carte de séjour)*. After renewing the one-year residence permit twice, you should be able to get three successive three-year permits. After about 12 years of residence you should be able to get a renewable ten-year *privileged residence permit*. Even after many years of residence it will be virtually impossible for you to acquire Monégasque nationality.

OTHER REQUIREMENTS

In addition to a French visa, you will need a bank reference showing that you have sufficient funds on which to live and a police certificate or other evidence that you have no criminal record. Since you must prove that you have acquired a residence and you cannot be sure that the Monégasque authorities will approve your application, you should sign a purchase contract or lease *subject* to the grant of a residence permit.

NOT FOR FRENCH CITIZENS

Over 30 years ago, in 1962, French President Charles de Gaulle declared that Monaco's status as an international tax haven was detrimental to France. A tax treaty was signed in 1963 under which French citizens who have taken up residence in Monaco since 1957 have to pay French income taxes, but all others remain exempt. The French are now claiming that the Monaco-born children and grandchildren of those French citizens who beat the 1957 deadline are subject to French tax since they are French citizens.

OTHER ADVANTAGES

You are living in France with French food and wines, but without French income taxes and death duties. The location is great--in the heart of the magnificent French Riviera. The climate is wonderful. Traveling is easy, especially if you use the six-minute helicopter service to Nice International Airport which has good plane service to many parts of the world.

POSSIBLE DISADVANTAGES

Monaco remains subject to French exchange controls. Since Monaco is a civil-law country, you would be subject to forced heirship rules that would restrict your power to disinherit your heirs. There are death taxes covering your assets within Monaco, such as your residence, car and personal effects. The rate is zero if the heirs are your spouse or children. However, if you leave your Monégasque assets to your girlfriend or some other unrelated party the tax is as high as 16 percent. You may be able to avoid some of these problems by using trusts and offshore companies. Trusts established under Monaco's 1936 trust law work well, but only when they are created by individuals who are nationals of a country that recognizes trusts.

As a resident of Monaco, you are really expected to live there at least three months a year. When you eventually acquire privileged residence, you will be expected to live there over six months a year. In addition to occasional spot checks by the authorities, you will be asked to produce documentation such as electricity and water bills each time you renew your residence permit.

FOR MORE INFORMATION

Read *The Monaco Report,* available from Scope International.

THE BOTTOM LINE

Monaco is a great place for residence and domicile if you can afford to live there and you are not a French citizen. Forget about citizenship and passports.

1997 UPDATE

Monaco no longer uses the French telephone country code 33; it now has its own country code which is 377. Although this has generally been considered to be a good development, it also means that telephone calls to nearby French towns are now expensive international calls.

55. THE NETHERLANDS ANTILLES

The Netherlands Antilles has enacted a law designed to encourage nonresident pensioners and investors, particularly those from the Netherlands, to retire there. However, as noted in the *1997 Update* at the end of the chapter, the Netherlands has taken steps to curtail these benefits for Dutch emigrants. The chapter is otherwise unchanged from last year's edition.

The Netherlands Antilles (NA) recently enacted a law designed to attract nonresident pensioners and investors as new residents. Until then, NA income tax was imposed on the worldwide income of all NA residents at progressive rates up to about 60 percent. The *Retired Persons Incentive Plan Act* offers attractive alternative methods of taxation to qualified retirees. The NA law is particularly attractive to retirees from the Netherlands in Europe. The Netherlands Antilles may be suitable for you if:

- You already have a satisfactory citizenship and passport (you cannot expect to obtain either in the NA for several years).
- You want a new permanent residence and you are prepared to reside in the NA for at least part of each year.
- You have a substantial pension or investment income from sources outside the NA.
- You would enjoy living in either Curacao (where they primarily speak Dutch and Papiamento) or the Dutch part of the Dutch-French island of St. Maarten (where they mostly speak English).
- You are willing to pay either a five percent income tax on your worldwide income or a flat tax of about US $35,000 per year. You can choose each year between two different systems that make such a result possible.
- You are prepared to acquire and own a residence in the NA costing at least US $135,000.
- You are prepared to employ a local servant for at least 30 hours per week.
  The NA guilder or florin (NAf) is different than the Dutch guilder but it is a stable currency. NAf1.78 equals US $1. It has maintained this value against the US dollar for many years.

THE RETIREMENT PROGRAM

To qualify under the new act, you must meet these requirements:

- You must have resided outside the NA for the five years preceding your application.
- You must obtain an NA *permanent residence permit*.
- You must own an NA residence having a value of at least NAf240,000 (about US $135,000).

- You must employ a local resident as a maid, cook or gardener for at least 30 hours a week.
- You cannot generally be employed in the NA.

If you meet all of these requirements you can elect to be taxed in either of two ways:

- You pay NA income tax on your worldwide income at a flat five percent rate; or
- You pay NA income tax at regular rates on a deemed net income of NAf150,000 (about US $85,000), paying a tax as shown in the table below (which is based on 1993 tax rates).

Your Status	Tax Rate	Tax (NAf)	Tax (in US $)
single	41.5 %	NAf62,250	US $35,000
married	38.5 %	NAf57,750	US $32,500

You will become a resident for tax purposes as of the date you arrive even if it is in the middle of a year. You must file timely annual tax returns. You should probably also obtain a tax ruling confirming your status. Nothing in the act appears to exempt you from NA inheritance or gift taxes. These range from two to six percent on transfers to close family members and from eight to 24 percent on transfers to unrelated parties.

ADVANTAGES FOR DUTCH EMIGRANTS

The Netherlands in Europe has anti-avoidance provisions aimed at Dutch residents who emigrate. For example, the Netherlands continues to impose its inheritance and gift taxes on their Dutch assets for ten years. It also taxes Dutch emigrants on capital gains from the sale of substantial holdings in Dutch companies for five years after they leave. A Dutch resident can apparently reduce the impact of these rules by emigrating to the NA and taking advantage of the new program.

POSSIBLE DISADVANTAGES

Beware! If you perform unauthorized work in the NA you will lose your entitlement to the preferential tax treatment and you will pay full NA income tax (now up to 56 percent) on your worldwide income. The new law does not seem to offer tax relief from NA death taxes.

FOR MORE INFORMATION

The *Loyens & Volkmaars* tax law firm has published a brief five-page paper in English entitled *Tax Facilities for Pensioners and/or Rentiers in the Netherlands Antilles.* You should be able to obtain a copy by contacting Damien Leo, Loyens & Volkmaars, 22 Kaya Flamboyan, P.O. Box 507, Willemstad, Curacao, Netherlands Antilles. Telephone: (599 9) 37 25 44. Fax: (599 9) 37 22 90. A 48-page booklet entitled *Fiscal Emigration to the Dutch Caribbean* is available from New Amsterdam Law Books, P.O. Box 53294, 1007 RG Amsterdam, Netherlands. It contains the text of the law and other helpful material.

THE BOTTOM LINE

Curacao and St. Maarten offer attractive possibilities for a tax exile if he buys a home costing at least US $135,000, employs a local servant, and pays an income tax of up to US $35,000 a year. It is particularly attractive to someone who moves there from the Netherlands; typically, he is already Dutch and has a Dutch passport.

1997 UPDATE

The Dutch have taken steps to close a loophole under which Dutch pensioners and retired investors could move to the Netherlands Antilles, qualify under the Netherlands Antilles *Retired Persons Incentive Plan Act* and thereby escape from the tax rules ordinarily applied to Dutch emigrants. A new tax arrangement between the Netherlands and the Netherlands Antilles took effect in January 1997. It denies treaty benefits for five years to new Dutch emigrants who move to the Netherlands Antilles if a special low-tax regime applies to them. The Netherlands Antilles apparently plans to replace the current retirement program with one that is acceptable to the Dutch authorities.

56. NEW ZEALAND

New Zealand imposes moderately high income taxes on its residents, but it offers a quality lifestyle and it no longer imposes death duties. It is a safe place for domicile and you can get citizenship and a passport after three years of residence. This chapter has not been changed from last year's edition, except for a note as to the increased value of the New Zealand dollar in the *1997 Update*.

One of the more popular destinations for tax exiles during recent years has been New Zealand. It has abandoned most of its socialistic policies and has substantially reduced its income tax rates. Like Australia, it welcomes new immigrants, it offers them citizenship and a first-class passport after about three years of residence, and it has abolished all death duties. It prefers to admit young, well-educated people. New Zealand may be suitable for you if:

- You are unhappy with your present citizenship and passport and would like to replace them relatively quickly.
- You prefer an English-speaking country with Anglo-American traditions. You are willing to pay up to a third of your income in taxes in return for a quality lifestyle that you feel you cannot obtain in some exotic tax haven.
- You already have sufficient wealth so that you are more interested in keeping what you have for yourself and your heirs than building up your assets.

QUALIFYING FOR RESIDENCY

In order to move to New Zealand, you must first qualify for residency there under one of four immigration categories. Two of these -- family reunion and a humanitarian category -- are unlikely to benefit readers of this report. The two that may work for you are a general category (based on points) and a business investment category. These are described below.

THE GENERAL CATEGORY (POINTS SYSTEM)

This category applies only if you are under 55 years old. First, obtain a *self-assessment guide* and other booklets from the nearest New Zealand diplomatic or consular office. In the US, you can telephone the New Zealand Embassy in Washington at (1 202) 328 4800; in Britain, you can telephone the New Zealand High Commission at (44 171) 973 0365. If you score at least 28 points (out of a possible 40) you should be automatically approved; if you score less than 20 points you don't stand a chance. If you score close to 28 points you may be provisionally accepted or your application may go into a pool from which successful applicants are drawn periodically. Two examples will give you some idea of how points are counted:

Gary Gamay gets 15 points for his postgraduate degree, six more for 12 years of work experience, six points because he is only 38 years old, and three points because he has an offer of skilled employment in an approved occupation. With a total of 30 points, he should be automatically approved.

Harry Hawke gets 12 points for his college degree, a maximum of 10 points for over 20 years of work experience, and no age points because he is 51 years old, for a total of only 22 points. He can increase this total to a more helpful 27 points by showing that he has at least NZ $100,000 (about US $69,000) of net assets, including his home equity, that he intends to use for settlement in New Zealand (good for two points), and NZ $300,000 (about US $207,000) more that he will invest in New Zealand for at least two years (good for three more points). If Hawke is not accepted, his name will probably go into the pool from which successful applicants are drawn.

BUSINESS INVESTMENT CATEGORY

Try this category if you are over 55 years old or you don't have enough points under the general category. You will still need some points from education or business experience but you are likely to have enough of these. You have to invest between NZ $500,000 and NZ $750,000 (about US $345,000 to US $517,500) in New Zealand. The amount varies depending on the location of the investment. Since late 1995, it is no longer possible for you to qualify by making passive investments. You must now invest in a commercial venture, either by buying into an existing one or starting a new one. You must also be able to show that the business investment funds came directly from your own business or professional skills.

ACQUIRING CITIZENSHIP BY NATURALIZATION

The Minister of Internal Affairs is authorized to grant New Zealand citizenship to an individual who meets the statutory requirements which include three years of residence in the country. Among other things, you must show that:
- you are entitled to be in New Zealand indefinitely under the 1987 Immigration Act;
- you have been ordinarily resident in New Zealand throughout the three years immediately preceding the application; and
- you intend to continue to reside in New Zealand after you are granted citizenship.

New Zealand allows dual citizenship. You will probably have to take an oath of allegiance to Her Majesty Queen Elizabeth II before you are granted citizenship. Once you are granted citizenship, you can obtain a passport without difficulty.

THE BOTTOM LINE

New Zealand offers residence, a safe domicile with no death taxes and citizenship and a passport after about three years.

1997 UPDATE

The New Zealand dollar has increased slightly in value against the US dollar during the past year; it is now worth about US $0.69 (up from about US $0.66).

57. ST. KITTS AND NEVIS

You can obtain St. Kitts and Nevis citizenship and a British Commonwealth passport for yourself and the members of your immediate family by making a substantial investment in local real estate or government bonds and paying government registration fees and professional fees. St Kitts and Nevis has no income tax or death taxes so, from a tax standpoint, it is also an excellent place for your residence and domicile. As noted under *Increased Costs for Obtaining Citizenship* **and** *1997 Update* **at the end of the chapter, there have been several significant developments in St. Kitts and Nevis since last year's edition of this report.**

The Federation of St. Kitts and Nevis (officially called St. Christopher and Nevis) has a low-key *economic citizenship program* that offers nationality and a passport in return for a substantial investment. Formerly a British colony, it became an independent country in 1983. It remains a member of the British Commonwealth, recognizing Queen Elizabeth II as its head of state. St. Kitts and Nevis is located in the Eastern Caribbean, about 200 miles south of Puerto Rico. Its 40,000 people are predominantly of African descent. They all speak English. St. Kitts and Nevis may be suitable for you if:

- You are willing to invest at least US $250,000 in a condominium and pay fees and costs totalling about another US $72,000 in order to obtain citizenship and good passports for yourself and your spouse. You may be able to reduce the investment amount to about US $200,000 by lending that amount directly to the government for ten years.

- You are seeking a small country with no personal income tax and no inheritance or estate taxes in which you could also establish your residence and your domicile.

BASIS FOR THE CITIZENSHIP PROGRAM

Section 3(5) of the 1984 *Saint Christopher and Nevis Citizenship Act* authorizes the Cabinet to register an individual as a *nonvoting citizen* if the Cabinet is satisfied that he or she has *invested substantially* in the country. Condominiums qualifying for citizenship are available on both islands; they range in price from US $150,000 to about US $600,000. The government now requires that you close on the purchase of the condominium before it issues your certificate of citizenship, but you will, of course, know beforehand that your application has been approved. In the past, a number of applicants have been able to obtain citizenship by lending EC $275,000 (approximately US $103,000) directly to the government for ten years. The government paid them four percent interest per year tax-free; the interest was paid semi-annually and the principal is to be returned after ten years. The Eastern Caribbean dollar (EC $) is used in eight Caribbean countries; EC $2.70 equals US $1 and it has remained at that rate for many years.

One investment covers the applicant and his immediate family. Each eligible family member receives a certificate of citizenship and a 10-year passport. As citizens, they have an absolute right to renew the passports for the rest of their lives. Other costs are government registration fees of US $35,000 for the applicant and US $15,000 for the spouse and each dependent child under 18. It may be possible to include young adults under the same investment, but they will each have to pay a US $35,000 government registration fee. Legal fees and costs will probably add another US $16,000 for the applicant and US $6,000 for each included family member.

Processing time for citizenship applications generally takes about two months and it takes another few weeks to obtain passports. Dual nationality is permitted. There is no residency requirement and you do not even need to visit the country. Documents required include an application for citizenship, birth and marriage certificates, a police certificate or affidavit showing no criminal record, evidence of your own assets, and a medical certificate showing a negative HIV test.

A St. Kitts and Nevis passport allows you to travel without a visa to about 90 countries, including Canada, Greece, Switzerland, the United Kingdom and many British Commonwealth countries. You should not have any trouble getting visas to other countries.

OTHER ADVANTAGES

St. Kitts and Nevis has no personal income tax, no capital gains tax and no inheritance or gift taxes. There is, however, a tax on the purchase of real estate. The US Social Security Administration has ruled that based on reciprocity a St. Kitts and Nevis citizen who is not a US citizen or resident can continue to receive US social security benefits to which he is entitled despite continued absence from the US. Nevis has a Four Seasons Resort which the American Automobile Association (AAA) has rated as one of the best in the Caribbean.

POSSIBLE DISADVANTAGES

Getting to either St. Kitts or Nevis is not difficult but it is time consuming. The easiest way from the US mainland is via American Airlines to San Juan, Puerto Rico, with a connecting American Eagle flight to St. Kitts. There are three or four such flights each day. It is also possible to get there via Antigua or St. Maarten.

FOR MORE INFORMATION

For current information concerning the St. Kitts and Nevis economic citizenship program, contact Marshall Langer, Shutts & Bowen, 43 Upper Grosvenor Street, London W1X 9PG, UK. Telephone: (44 171) 493 4840. Fax: (44 171) 493 4299.

THE BOTTOM LINE

By making a substantial investment in the country and paying required fees and costs, you and your family can legally acquire citizenship and passports in a British Commonwealth country that is also a suitable place taxwise for your residence and your domicile.

INCREASED COSTS FOR OBTAINING CITIZENSHIP

St. Kitts and Nevis substantially modified its *citizenship by investment* program in March 1996. You can still choose between investing in local real estate or making a loan to the government, but the amounts required have increased considerably:

*   The minimum amount to be invested in local real estate was increased to US $250,000 (from US $150,000).
*   The required amount for the alternative ten-year loan to the government was increased to US $200,000 (from about US $103,000). New loans do not pay any interest (old loans paid four-percent per year).
*   The government registration fee for the head of household and for each young adult over 17 was increased to US $35,000 (from US $25,000) while the fee for the spouse and each child under 18 was increased to US $15,000 (from US $10,000).
*   Professional fees are generally unchanged.

1997 UPDATE

The Premier of Nevis has announced plans for that island to secede from the Federation of St. Kitts and Nevis, but the steps to do so may take a year or two and it is not yet clear that Nevis will in fact secede. It is also difficult to predict what effect, if any, secession would have on those who have obtained economic citizenship. An investment in the proposed St. Kitts Hyatt Hotel and Casino project is no longer expected to qualify the investor for economic citizenship.

St. Kitts and Nevis has changed its telephone area code from 1 809 to 1 869. The new address for obtaining current information concerning the St. Kitts and Nevis economic citizenship program is Marshall Langer, Shutts & Bowen, 43 Upper Grosvenor Street, London W1X 9PG, UK. The telephone and fax numbers have not been changed.

58. SWITZERLAND

Despite its fairly high taxes, Switzerland is an attractive destination for many tax exiles. You may be able to obtain a residence permit and a lump-sum tax arrangement, especially if you are retired. Obtaining a work permit is more difficult, but not impossible. This chapter has not been materially changed from last year's edition, but two items are noted in the *1997 Update* at the end of the chapter.

Switzerland has long been a favorite haven for rich and famous tax exiles from all over the world. It is not the easiest country in which to acquire residence but it is possible to do so, particularly if you are retired and have sufficient retirement income to live in Switzerland. Permits to live and work in Switzerland are difficult to obtain, but not impossible.

Individuals residing in Switzerland generally pay fairly high taxes on their worldwide income. They pay federal, cantonal and local income taxes on all income, except for income derived from foreign real estate or from a personally-owned foreign business. They also pay cantonal and local wealth taxes on their capital. Despite this, Switzerland is an attractive destination for tax exiles from other countries, primarily because it is one of the world's safest and most stable countries. Switzerland may be suitable for you if:

- You already have a satisfactory citizenship and passport; you cannot hope to obtain either in Switzerland for 12 to 15 years.
- You are a wealthy retiree over 60 years of age who has never worked in Switzerland.
- You want a new permanent residence and you are prepared to reside in Switzerland for at least part of each year.
- You are prepared to pay a prearranged lump-sum tax to the Swiss each year.

RETIRE WITH A LUMP-SUM TAX DEAL

Wealthy foreigners who have reached retirement age can negotiate a lump-sum tax (forfait) arrangement with the tax authorities. These deals are negotiated with the cantonal tax administrators. The amount you have to pay may vary considerably depending on where in Switzerland you choose to live. Appenzell (Inner Rhodes), Switzerland's smallest canton, has offered attractive tax arrangements to some retired individuals. You should expect to pay at least Sfr65,000 (about US $45,000) a year in Swiss taxes in one of the smaller cantons, and considerably more in one of the larger, better-known cantons. Although you can theoretically apply for residency at a Swiss embassy, I urge you to negotiate directly with the authorities in the canton where you want to live. They have the final say as to whether you can live there and how much tax you will have to pay. Employ a competent local professional to work out the best deal.

VISIT AS A *PT* FOR THREE MONTHS A YEAR

Despite recent changes, you can still visit Switzerland for up to three months each year without obtaining any kind of residence permit and without having to pay Swiss taxes. You have to observe the rules faithfully because the Swiss authorities are likely to know exactly how much time you have spent in the country. Under the new tax rules, you are treated as a Swiss resident for tax purposes if you meet either of these tests:

*   You stay in Switzerland without working for more than 90 days in any year.
*   You work in Switzerland for more than 30 days in any year.

In either of these cases, you are deemed to have been resident from the first day of your stay in Switzerland. It doesn't matter whether you stay in one place or in several different ones. Moreover, brief absences from Switzerland do not suspend your residence.

It used to be possible for a *perpetual tourist (PT)* to "visit" Switzerland twice each year for up to three months each time. Under the new rules, that is no longer feasible. *A suggested program* under the new rules: You can visit one of Switzerland's excellent winter resorts for about a month each February or March and one of its equally marvelous summer resorts for about a month each July or August. You can also spend a few days visiting your bankers at the beginning and end of each stay. It's a great life if you can afford it.

YOU CAN GET A WORK PERMIT

You may be able to obtain a *B permit* authorizing you to live and work in Switzerland. About 17,000 renewable B permits are available each year, most of which are obtained from the cantonal authorities. Each of the cantons has a small annual quota of permits allocated to it. There are no quotas for the annual renewals and these are routinely approved. I have had good success in obtaining such permits for clients from the Canton of Neuchatel under its program to attract new business to the canton. Neuchatel offers special tax programs on a case by case basis for these new residents.

OTHER ADVANTAGES

Switzerland is clean, orderly, safe, stable and prosperous. Everything works and most things work well.

POSSIBLE DISADVANTAGES

Everything in Switzerland is expensive. If you become resident in a Swiss canton, you will also be domiciled there for Swiss inheritance and gift tax purposes. These taxes vary considerably from canton to canton; none are imposed by the federal government. Switzerland has recently introduced a value added tax (VAT), but the rate is much less than it is in most European countries.

FOR MORE INFORMATION

Read Marshall Langer's *The Swiss Report*, available from Scope International.

THE BOTTOM LINE

It is relatively easy for wealthy retirees to obtain residence in Switzerland; it is possible for others to do so. Residence comes with domicile and this requires estate planning to reduce cantonal and local inheritance taxes. Forget about citizenship and passports.

1997 UPDATE

A proposed new Swiss-US income tax treaty was signed in 1996, but it requires ratification and it is unlikely to take effect until at least 1998. With the recent drop in value of the Swiss franc to under US $0.70, a lump-sum tax of Sfr65,000 would now be about US $45,000.

59. TURKS AND CAICOS ISLANDS (TCI)

Turks and Caicos is a traditional tax haven with no income tax and no taxes at death. This makes it a suitable place for your residence and domicile. You can obtain residence without the right to work by purchasing a home or investing in a business. This chapter has not been changed from last year's edition but, as noted in the 1997 Update at the end of the chapter, it is apparently now possible to obtain permanent residence by investing as little as US $40,000 in an approved business.

If you really want to get away from it all, try the Turks and Caicos Islands (TCI). The TCI makes Grand Cayman seem like a major metropolitan area. It has a total population of about 14,000 people, most of whom live on Grand Turk, South Caicos, or Providenciales (which is commonly called Provo for short). The TCI is an extension of the Bahamas chain, but unlike the Bahamas, it is still a British dependent territory.

Renewable annual residence and work permits are available to qualified employees and self-employed individuals. *Permanent residence with no right to work* is now available to retirees who invest in a residence or business. The TCI may be suitable for you if:

- You already have a satisfactory citizenship and passport.
- You want a new permanent residence in which you can actually reside as little or as much as you want.
- You like the idea of living on an island with a very small population.
- You are willing to invest a minimum of US $250,000 in a residence or business in Provo, or at least US $125,000 in a home or business in one of the other islands.

NEW PERMANENT RESIDENCE RULES

New *policy statements* were announced by the government in 1994. The government published a 24-page booklet entitled *Doing Business in the Turks & Caicos Islands: Government Policies.* The TCI government is seeking to promote new investment in the islands while giving *belongers* (citizens) a maximum opportunity to participate in and benefit from any development. An outsider can acquire *permanent residence*, with or without the right to work. A retired individual can immediately obtain *permanent residence without the right to work.* To do so, you must invest in a business or residence. The minimum investment is US $250,000 in Providenciales and is now half that in any of the other islands, including Grand Turk. There is no other residency qualification. It is not clear whether a separate investment would be required for your spouse, but it apparently is not.

If you invest in a business, you cannot operate the business. If you want to work for someone or be self-employed, you will first have to obtain a renewable annual work permit. You will normally have to live and work in the islands for five years before you can apply for *permanent residence* with the right to work. You must then show that you have invested at least US $100,000 in a business or residence and that you are capable of supporting yourself and your family.

The government charges a one-time fee of US $10,000 for a *permanent residence certificate*. Professional and business persons and entrepreneurs must also pay US $2,500 a year; investors and retired persons do not have to pay annual fees. Although a permanent residence certificate is normally granted for life it may be revoked if you become resident outside the islands for a continuous period of five years.

NATIONALITY AND BELONGER STATUS

As in Cayman and some other UK dependent territories you cannot really become a citizen. *Nationality* is determined under the British Nationality Act. *Belongership* is the special status granted to those persons who "belong" to the TCI. Belongership is reserved for the native population and it is virtually impossible for an outsider to attain that status.

OTHER ADVANTAGES INCLUDE NO TAXES

The TCI is a traditional tax haven with no taxes on income or capital gains and no taxes at death other than a small probate fee with a maximum of US $500. The TCI is a safe place to establish your new domicile. It uses the US dollar as its currency and it has no exchange controls. It has lots of sunshine, some good beaches and water sports. The TCI is reasonably close to Florida; flying time to Miami is about two hours. There are regular flights from Grand Turk and Provo to Miami.

POSSIBLE DISADVANTAGES

Prices are high because virtually everything you consume in the TCI is imported and is subject to high import duties.

THE BOTTOM LINE

If you are retired, you can acquire permanent residence in the TCI with no right to work by buying a $250,000 home in Provo or a US $125,000 home in Grand Turk. The TCI is a safe domicile with no taxes at death. Forget about citizenship (belonger status) or a passport.

1997 UPDATE

Recent advertisements in the *International Herald Tribune* have claimed that you can obtain permanent residence in the TCI by making an investment of US $40,000 in an approved business. It appears that the TCI government has approved certain much needed business enterprises for this purpose, including a local airline.

60. URUGUAY

You can obtain an Uruguayan passport by investing US $70,000 in forestry bonds or a certificate of deposit. You can also obtain passports for your spouse and minor children by making additional investments of US $10,000 for each of them. These passports are based on residency rather than citizenship and some countries may therefore not recognize them. This chapter has not been changed from last year's edition but, as noted in the *1997 Update* at the end of the chapter, the local currency has continued to depreciate against the US dollar.

Uruguay used to be known as the *Switzerland of the Americas*. When I first visited Montevideo in 1954, practically every block had banks and currency dealers selling gold and foreign currencies. Even then, Uruguay was widely used by South Americans as a base for holding companies. In later years, Uruguay became highly unstable and subject to strikes, terrorism, uncontrolled inflation and the emigration of many of its professionals and skilled workers. More recently, it has managed to solve most of its problems (other than inflation) and it is once again widely used by Argentineans and Brazilians as their base for holding companies and banking.

Several years ago, clients of mine who needed new passports bought a small farm in Uruguay, thereby establishing a form of residency. Although they were actually living in Europe, they managed to travel to Uruguay for brief stays at least once each year during the next several years. After a few years of such *"residency"* they applied for and were granted Uruguayan nationality and passports. Except for the investment in the farm and travel costs, their expenses were minimal. There is bad news and good news concerning Uruguay. The bad news is that this self-help form of establishing residency and obtaining citizenship and a passport may no longer exist there. The good news is that 1990 decrees authorize a passport (without citizenship) to be issued immediately to a foreigner who invests US $70,000 for ten years. Uruguay may be suitable for you if:

• You want another passport now and you are prepared to invest funds to obtain it.
• You already have a suitable nationality and are not concerned that your new passport comes without citizenship.

THE SELF-HELP PROGRAM MAY BE GONE

The Uruguayan constitution provides that a foreign man and woman with a family who possess capital or property in the country or work there have the right to legal citizenship after three years of *habitual residence* in the country. A foreigner without a family needs five years of such *habitual residence* in the country. Much of course depends on what constitutes habitual residence. It now appears that the Uruguayan government may demand proof of actual habitual residence in the country after you have fulfilled the three-year (or five-year) requirement. Thus, the self-help program may no longer be practical for most tax exiles.

THE INVESTOR PROGRAM

You must invest US $70,000 to buy either Central Bank ten-year forestry bonds or a ten-year certificate of deposit with the Bank of the Republic. The forestry bonds bear 6.5 percent interest payable annually; the entire principal is repayable at the end of ten years. The certificate of deposit bears five percent interest compounded annually, but the interest and principal is all payable at the end of ten years. As a form of surety you have to deposit the investment for safekeeping for a term of ten years in the custodial section of the Central Bank endorsed to the order of the Immigration Department. Passports can also be obtained for your spouse and minor children by making an additional investment of US $10,000 for each of them.

To obtain the passport you must first get: (1) a permanent reentry permit; (2) an Uruguayan identity card; and (3) a police certificate. You may have to go to Uruguay twice, once for about two days to file the papers, and then for a few more days about three months later to obtain the passport. It may be possible for you to avoid the first of these two trips by sending the papers through an Uruguayan consulate but this could cause problems and delays. Recheck this situation when you are ready to apply.

It is recommended that you deposit the US $70,000 needed for the investment in an account in your own name in a major bank in Uruguay prior to filing the documents. The bank can then issue its cashier's check to the Uruguayan government when the funds are needed; that way none of the investment funds are ever held by intermediaries.

My colleagues tell me that everything in Uruguay is working smoothly but slowly. There is no hassle and they have not experienced any problems. You do not have to reside in Uruguay either before or after the passport is issued. You apparently will have to renew the deposit to keep the passport after the initial ten years. If you die before the ten years are up the deposit forms part of your estate.

OTHER ADVANTAGES INCLUDE NO INCOME TAX

Uruguay has no personal income or estate taxes. It has one of the highest standards of living in Latin America.

POSSIBLE DISADVANTAGES

The biggest disadvantage is that some countries, including the United Kingdom and the Benelux countries, do not recognize non-citizenship Uruguayan passports. Visa-free travel is generally extended only to nationals of a country and not to passport holders who are not nationals. Uruguay is very far from most of the places from which tax exiles come. There is a high annual wealth tax (up to three percent) on capital in Uruguay owned by individuals domiciled in Uruguay, but government securities and bank deposits held by individuals are exempt. The currency and inflation is maddening; as of February 1997 there were about 8.9 *pesos Uruguayo* (a relatively new currency) per US dollar.

THE BOTTOM LINE

You can obtain a passport without citizenship by investing US $70,000. Uruguay should be a safe place for domicile since there are no major tax consequences.

1997 UPDATE

As of February 1997, there were about 8.9 *pesos Uruguayo* to the US dollar.

STOP PRESS

As this book went to press, we learned that pursuant to a decree published in March 1997, the Uruguayan passport program was terminated. The decree does not affect passports that were already issued.

61. OTHER *EU* COUNTRIES (FRANCE/GREECE/ITALY/PORTUGAL/SPAIN)

Five Southern European countries have attracted millions of *perpetual tourists "PTs")* who unofficially live in these high-tax countries most of the time without paying income tax or most other taxes. They do not register for either immigration or tax purposes and their homes are owned by offshore companies. Potential pitfalls are discussed. This chapter is unchanged from last year's edition.

MILLIONS OF *PTs* LIVE NEAR THE MEDITERRANEAN

During the past several decades, millions of people from Britain, Germany and the Scandinavian countries have retired to live the good life in Southern Europe. There are huge communities of wealthy *"residential tourists"* along the entire Mediterranean coast.

A recent study indicated that Spain alone has about 1.5 million actual foreign residents, only about one-third of whom are officially registered. The others are *perpetual tourists (PTs)* who try to remain invisible for tax purposes. They come and go, entering the country for up to three months at a time as alleged tourists. They are not officially there for either tax or immigration purposes.

HOMES ARE OWNED BY OFFSHORE COMPANIES

Most of these *perpetual tourists (PTs)* set up offshore companies to buy their homes. They rarely transfer any real estate as such. Most homes are bought and sold by transferring the bearer shares of a single-purpose offshore company incorporated in a tax haven such as Gibraltar. In theory this avoids the payment of real estate transfer taxes and capital gains taxes. It is actually more like tax evasion on which some of the countries have begun to crack down. France, for example, charges an annual tax of three percent of the value of real estate owned by an offshore company from a country that does not have a suitable income tax treaty with France. Spain has also cracked down by imposing a five percent tax on the assessed value of the property unless there is full disclosure of the beneficial ownership of the company.

PTs AVOID OFFICIAL RESIDENCE

These Southern European countries -- France, Greece, Italy, Portugal and Spain -- are all high-tax countries. In fact, they are very high-tax countries if you declare everything you have and pay all the taxes you should.

If you are resident for tax purposes in any of these countries, you can expect to pay an income tax of up to about 50 percent on your worldwide income, a capital gains tax on assets sold and, in some of them, a wealth tax of up to two percent a year on your worldwide assets. You will probably also be subject to gift and inheritance taxes.

Typically, you are resident in one of these countries for tax purposes if you spend more than six months a year there. Few foreigners ever admit to doing so. You are also treated as resident if the country is the center of your economic or business interests, if you maintain your habitual family home there, or if you register as a resident. Amazingly few foreigners ever become residents under any of these tests.

FORMER DOMICILES REMAIN UNCHANGED

In most of these countries, residence and domicile are substantially the same. A *perpetual tourist (PT)* cannot claim that he is domiciled there unless he is resident. The good news is that up to now most of these countries have not made a serious effort to regulate and tax PTs. The bad news is that under the domicile rules imposed in countries such as Britain and the US, the *PT* cannot escape his prior domicile without affirmatively changing to a new one. And, under the residency rules imposed in several high-tax countries, including Australia and Canada, you do not escape from your old residence unless you affirmatively establish a new one somewhere. Even the good news may change as these countries begin to comply with European Union (EU) immigration rules, stamp passports of foreigners entering and leaving the country who do not have EU passports and use computers to determine how long these foreigners are in the country each year.

THE BOTTOM LINE

These popular Mediterranean destinations work well if you move to them from a country that does not require you to establish a new residence or a new domicile in order to escape continued taxation in your prior country. They also work well as a second residence for less than half of each year for someone who has a suitable residence and domicile elsewhere but does not want to live there the entire year. These countries are likely to backfire for those seeking to escape from many high-tax countries, including Britain, Canada and the US.

62. COMPARING SUITABLE COUNTRIES

This chapter contains four tables that compare the attributes of countries and territories located in different areas of the world as to their suitability for residency, domicile, and citizenship and a passport. These tables have been updated from last year's edition.

The tables contained in this chapter briefly compare the key attributes of most of the countries discussed in the preceding chapters of this part of the report. These tables are arranged geographically. They cover the countries and territories in and near the British Isles, other places in and near Europe, Africa and the Middle East, those in and near North America and those in the Southern Hemisphere.

TABLE OF SUITABLE COUNTRIES FOR THE TAX EXILE
IN AND NEAR THE BRITISH ISLES

Country	Residency	Domicile	Citizenship / Passport
Britain (the UK)	remittance basis tax if not domiciled	avoid - results in high income and death taxes	5 years residence + a 2-year wait - EU passport
Channel Islands: Jersey	wants only the very rich - 20% tax on all income	safe - no death tax	long wait - UK rules but not EU passport
Channel Islands: Guernsey	less restrictive also 20% tax on all income	safe - no death tax	long wait - UK rules but not EU passport
Channel Islands: Sark	real residence is difficult - no income tax	safe - no death tax	long wait - UK rules but not EU passport
Isle of Man	not difficult - 15% tax on first £9,000 - 20% on excess	safe - no death tax	long wait - UK rules but not EU passport
Ireland	remittance basis tax if not domiciled	avoid - results in high income and death taxes	requires Irish descent or Irish *associations* - EU passport

TABLE OF SUITABLE COUNTRIES FOR THE TAX EXILE
IN AND NEAR THE EUROPEAN CONTINENT,
AFRICA AND THE MIDDLE EAST

Country	Residency	Domicile	Citizenship / Passport
France, Greece, Italy, Portugal, Spain	high taxes if you concede residency - *PTs* avoid doing so	avoid - high taxes would apply	most take at least 5 years of legal residence
Switzerland	depends on canton - good for retirees over 60 - *forfait* possible	residence equals domicile - death taxes in most cantons	no chance for at least 12-15 years
Campione	taxes not collected	avoid - Italian taxes would apply	may eventually qualify in Italy
Gibraltar	high-net worth individuals pay £10,000+ tax	avoid - may result in death tax	long wait - UK rules - EU passport
Monaco	expensive - not for French citizens	safe - no death tax on foreign assets	no chance
Malta	remittance basis tax with low minimum if not domiciled	avoid - may result in high taxes	probably no chance
Cyprus	remittance basis tax if not domiciled - 5% on royalties, investment income	avoid - results in high taxes	probably no chance
Cape Verde	no tax on foreign income	not practical	citizenship and passport for $35,000 donation
Israel	available - no tax on foreign income	safe - no death tax	available to Jews under law of return

TABLE OF SUITABLE COUNTRIES FOR THE TAX EXILE
IN AND NEAR NORTH AMERICA

Country	Residency	Domicile	Citizenship / Passport
America (the US)	high tax on world income - avoid *green card* or over 120 days presence	avoid - results in 55% estate tax on worldwide assets	5 years residence - results in automatic income and death tax
America (via the USVI)	high income tax - same as US	may avoid US estate tax	no estate tax if citizenship solely through USVI
Bahamas	requires $250,000 investment in house or condo - no tax	safe - no death tax	probably no chance
Bermuda	requires purchase of expensive house or condo - no tax	safe - no death tax except on local propertry	probably no chance
Canada	high income tax - departure tax after 5 years or at death	safe - no impact on taxes	3 years residence + up to 1 year wait
Cayman	requires $180,000 investment in house or condo - no tax	safe - no death tax	probably no chance
Costa Rica	must prove income - no tax on foreign income	safe - no death tax	long wait - old passport program closed
Dominica	apparently no tax on foreign income	safe - no death tax	available for US $75,000 total outlay
Netherlands Antilles	retirees pay up $35,000 tax	possible but watch death tax	long wait
St. Kitts and Nevis	safe - no personal income tax	safe - no death tax	available with large investment
Turks and Caicos	requires investment - no tax	safe - no death tax	probably no chance

TABLE OF SUITABLE COUNTRIES FOR THE TAX EXILE
IN THE SOUTHERN HEMISPHERE

Country	Residency	Domicile	Citizenship/ Passport
Australia	business migration program available	safe - no death tax	2 years residence - good passport
New Zealand	based on points or business investment	safe - no death tax	3 years residence - good passport
Uruguay	not difficult - no income or death taxes - high wealth tax on local assets	safe - no major tax consequences	passport (without citizenship) available for $70,000 investment

63. MYTHICAL *PARADISO*

A country could make itself into an attractive base for potential tax exiles by taking the steps discussed in this chapter. By doing so it could earn substantial amounts of income without incurring significant costs. This chapter has not been changed from last year's edition.

Unlike the other countries discussed in this part, *Paradiso* does not (yet) exist, but I hope that it will soon. Some country can make a lot of money for its treasury without much cost or effort if it adopts the proposals made in this chapter. By taking the recommended steps, such a country can make itself very attractive for a wealthy retiree -- a virtual paradise. The ideal candidate is a country with these criteria:

• It should be small enough so that a few million dollars (or pounds) of added revenue a year with little or no corresponding outlay would be meaningful.

• It encourages tourists and other visitors who do not work and thus do not take away jobs from locals.

• It imposes an income tax, preferably at moderate rates. It would help if Paradiso's income tax is territorial or if foreign-source income is taxed only if it is remitted. Many countries either have such a system today or had it until recent years.

• Paradiso may have lost some of its people in the past through emigration. It may now have an opportunity to welcome back some of its more successful former citizens from the high-tax countries to which they emigrated in search of opportunity.

In terms of location, there is room for several Paradisos in the world, one in or near Western Europe, one in the Caribbean or Latin America and one in the Pacific Basin.

HOW THE PLAN WOULD WORK

Here is how the plan would work:

1. Paradiso would seek to attract new *permanent residents* who would not be allowed to work in the country (other than as self-employed). The program would be designed to attract retirees, authors, composers, motion picture producers and directors, athletes, and entertainers. It would be a modified version of similar programs that already exist in Malta, Ireland, Cyprus, Gibraltar and other countries.

2. An individual who has not lived in Paradiso at any time during the past five years and who is self-supporting should be allowed to qualify as a *"permanent resident."* He would be subject to Paradiso income tax under a special new regime:
    • He would be required to remit from abroad a minimum sum each year on which he would be fully taxable. The tax should be imposed on remitted foreign-source income and the minimum remittance should be an amount that will produce a tax of about US $3,000 (or £2,000) per year for a family. No tax should be imposed on remittances of

capital from foreign sources. If further amounts of foreign-source income were remitted they could be subject to tax either at regular rates or at a flat rate. There probably would not be any excess remittances of income unless benefits were available under income tax treaties.

• Local-source income, if any, would be fully taxed at regular rates. It might be desirable, however, to exclude from tax interest income on local bank deposits.

• Foreign-source income could qualify for double taxation relief under any Paradiso income tax treaties but in no case could the actual Paradiso income tax paid be less than US $3,000 (or £2,000) per year.

• The new permanent resident could be fully taxed under ordinary rules at regular rates if he spent more than eight months a year in Paradiso. There would be no requirement that he actually spend any particular amount of time in the country. Most such persons would probably spend some time in Paradiso and they would contribute to the economy while there by paying VAT, sales taxes and import duties on their local purchases.

• The new permanent resident would be allowed to rent or purchase a home or apartment in Paradiso and to maintain it for his own use. He might be permitted to rent it out to others when he is not using it; but if he did so, he would pay regular income tax on the net rental income.

3.   The new permanent resident would be required to furnish evidence that he has adequate private health insurance to cover his entire family and sufficient funds to support himself and his family without working in Paradiso. He would not pay any Paradiso social security tax and he would not be entitled to social security benefits.

4.   There could also be a one-time charge of up to US $3,000 (or £2,000) for registration as a *permanent resident* under this program. These applications could be filed by local professionals who would earn income for preparing them.

5.   There should be a simple short form income tax return stating:

> • I have remitted US $............... (minimum US $3,000) of income from foreign sources to Paradiso during the tax year.
> • My taxable local-source income during the year was US $.....................
> • I did not spend more than 240 days in Paradiso during the tax year.

6.   The program could be limited initially to a maximum of 2,000 new families. This would produce US $6 million in registration fees and at least US $6 million per year in direct taxes with little or no cost for services.

7.   Each applicant would have to be approved. A minimum age requirement would make it unlikely that there would be any children requiring schools. Children could be required to attend private schools unless the parents agree to pay a special tuition or full income tax at regular rates.

8.   It should be possible for a new permanent resident to become domiciled in Paradiso (under Anglo-American concepts of domicile) without thereby incurring any local tax problems.

9.   If Paradiso now imposes taxes such as a wealth tax, an estate or inheritance tax or a gift tax, these should not apply to new permanent residents except on their local assets.

10.   If legally able to do so, Paradiso should also consider offering *economic citizenship* to these new permanent residents, either immediately or after they have been resident under the program for two years. If offered immediately, there could be an additional charge of US $25,000 or so for such immediate naturalization.

THE BOTTOM LINE

A country able to meet the needs of individuals seeking a new place of residence and domicile can generate substantial income for its economy without incurring much in the way of costs. Such a country will also derive many indirect benefits from those who come to live there and those who merely come to check it out.

64. OTHER POSSIBLE DESTINATIONS

There are several other countries that you may wish to consider for your residency, your domicile, or your citizenship and passport. These are discussed briefly in this chapter. Some of them may receive expanded coverage in future editions of this report. This chapter is generally unchanged from last year's edition, but potential new economic citizenship programs in *St. Vincent and the Grenadines* and in *Grenada* are discussed under *Potential New Economic Citizenship Programs* near the end of the chapter.

There are so many potential destinations to which a tax exile might consider moving that it has not been possible to discuss all of them in detail in this report. Not surprisingly, several of the places mentioned below are present or former British colonies that still enjoy the quaint UK rule under which a *non-domiciled* resident is taxed only on local income and remitted foreign-source income. You can safely reside in any of them if you live off remittances of capital and you keep your income abroad. You do not want to be both *resident* and *domiciled* in most of them. Here is a brief snapshot of some of these other possible safe havens:

TINY ANDORRA VOTES FOR INDEPENDENCE

Andorra is a tiny country located in the Pyrenees mountains. In 1993, Andorra's 12,000 citizens voted for independence, severing most of the country's feudal links to France and Spain that had been maintained since the year 1278. Andorra still has no income or capital gains taxes, no estate or inheritance taxes and no sales taxes or customs duties, but this may change someday. An estimated 1,500 UK tax exiles live there. To say it is remote is an understatement. One of the best ways to get there is by bus, taxi or car from Barcelona, Spain, which is about 150 miles away. It is easy to establish residency there by simply moving there; it is much more difficult to obtain any documentation stating that you are really resident. For details, read Dr WG Hill's *The Andorra & Gibraltar Report*, available from Scope International.

ANGUILLA -- ESCAPING FROM CIVILIZATION

Anguilla is a small British dependent territory in the Caribbean that attracts some wealthy tourists during the winter months. You can reach it by plane from San Juan, Puerto Rico, or by boat from the nearby Dutch-French island of St. Maarten. It has no income tax and no inheritance or estate taxes. Anguilla could be suitable for your residency and domicile if you really want to escape from most civilization. You cannot expect to get citizenship or a passport there.

ANTIGUA HAS BEAUTIFUL BEACHES

Antigua, one of the more popular Caribbean islands, is renowned for its beautiful beaches that attract wealthy jet setters each winter. It has good tourist facilities and direct airline service from London, Toronto, New York and Miami. Antigua and Barbuda is now an independent country but it retains its ties to the British Commonwealth. It has no personal income tax (except on local business income) and no death tax so it could be suitable for your residency and domicile. Antigua is seeking to attract retirees from Britain. It charges them a fee for permanent residency and offers them reduced UK tax on their UK-source pension income under the Antigua-UK double tax agreement. Antigua has also considered the possibility of offering passports to qualified foreigners, but it has not yet implemented a formal program. It is not likely to do so.

BARBADOS -- A SOPHISTICATED CARIBBEAN ISLAND

Barbados is one of the nicest and most sophisticated Caribbean islands and it is an extremely popular tourist destination. It is easily reached by direct flights from the UK, US and Canada. It has no death tax. It has a personal income tax which quickly reaches a top rate of about 40 percent on worldwide income. However, you are not resident for income tax purposes unless you spend more than 182 days in Barbados during the calendar year. As in Britain, if you become resident but are not domiciled in Barbados your foreign income will be taxed only on a remittance basis. Thus, Barbados is suitable for a *perpetual tourist (PT)* or for a non-domiciled resident. It may even be okay to be domiciled but not resident there. You don't want to be both domiciled and resident there. There seems to be virtually no chance of obtaining citizenship or a passport there without many years of legal residence.

BELIZE ONCE AGAIN OFFERS PASSPORTS

Belize (formerly British Honduras) attained its independence from Britain in 1981. It would have done so years earlier but for the fear that its big neighbor -- Guatemala -- would march in and take over. Guatemala, with about 40 times as many people, has long claimed Belize as part of its territory in much the same way that Iraq has claimed Kuwait. British troops remained in Belize following its independence to guarantee its security, but they have now been withdrawn.

Belize changed its constitution and laws in 1985 so as to permit economic citizenship and its exclusive marketing agent ran a successful program under which hundreds of people acquired citizenship and passports. Following 1989 elections in which the sale of citizenships became a major issue, the new government "officially" cancelled the program. Although the program was officially closed from 1990 through 1994, hundreds (and perhaps thousands) of passports were sold during those years by corrupt officials and former officials who pocketed the money. Reportedly none of this money ever found its way into the Belize government treasury. Nor is there any reason to believe that there was a serious background check of any of those who bought their passports during this period.

In January 1995, the Belize government reestablished an official economic citizenship program. It published its Policy on Economic Citizenship Investment Programme and granted licenses to a number of approved immigration consultants. It initially required a US $50,000 "investment" in the Belize Economic Citizenship Fund (essentially a donation), a US $25,000 registration fee for the applicant, a US $5,000 registration fee for the applicant's spouse and each child under 18 and a US $15,000 registration fee for each "child" over 17 years old. Fees to licensed immigration consultants were apparently limited to about US $15,000. A report published in late 1995 indicated that the government had substantially reduced the required investment in order to encourage new applications.

THE BVI OFFERS SUPERB SAILING

The British Virgin Islands (BVI) are in the Caribbean, near the US Virgin Islands and only a short flight from Puerto Rico. The BVI has some of the most beautiful sailing waters in the entire world. It is a British dependent territory but it uses the US dollar as its currency. Most of its 11,000 people live on Tortola. The BVI has no estate, inheritance or gift taxes. It has a maximum income tax rate of 20 percent, but you pay it only on local income and remitted foreign income unless you are both resident and domiciled in the BVI. Therefore, it makes sense for you to be resident or domiciled there, but not both. You cannot expect to get citizenship or a passport there until after many years of legal residence.

DOMINICAN REPUBLIC PASSPORTS OFFERED

The Dominican Republic, not to be confused with Dominica, is a Spanish-speaking country that occupies the eastern part of the Caribbean island of Hispaniola which it shares with Haiti. Although it has no formal program for granting economic citizenship to foreigners, its passports have been regularly offered for sale at comparatively low prices, but many of them are probably invalid.

JAMAICA SEEKS BUSINESS MIGRANTS

The *Financial Times* has reported that Jamaica has a program that seeks to attract business migrants, primarily from Hong Kong. Investors are expected to invest at least US $100,000 in a venture creating local jobs, a venture capital fund, or nontransferable ten-year government bonds. If the bonds are denominated in Jamaican dollars they represent a huge currency risk. I remember when the Jamaican dollar was worth more than a US dollar; today you can get about 34 Jamaican dollars for a US dollar. Successful applicants are granted resident status and a passport, and they may apply for Jamaican citizenship. It is not clear whether they are required to live in the country and to become residents for tax purposes.

Jamaica apparently still follows the British system and taxes non-domiciled residents only on Jamaican-source income and foreign-source income that is remitted to Jamaica. Virtually all taxable income now pays a flat 25 percent tax. Gains from local real estate and some securities are taxed when they are sold or when you die.

MAURITIUS -- IN THE INDIAN OCEAN

Mauritius, in the Indian Ocean, has a British-type tax system with a maximum income tax rate of about 35 percent. It has no capital gains tax. If you are neither a citizen of Mauritius nor domiciled there you don't pay Mauritian income tax on your foreign investment income even if it is remitted to Mauritius. It may therefore be suitable for you to be resident but not domiciled there. At one time Mauritius passports were being offered to South Africans who invested in the country, but this program appears to have been discontinued.

MEXICO ATTRACTS RETIRED AMERICANS

Thousands of older Americans have moved to Mexico because their retirement dollars go much further there than they do in the US. Mexican income tax rates are not very different than those in the US for those individuals who concede that they are Mexican residents. The top tax rate is 35 percent and the effective rate for most foreigners living there should be about 30 percent. Mexican residents are taxed on their worldwide income. You are deemed resident in Mexico if you have a permanent home there unless you can prove that you are outside the country for more than half the year and that you are resident for tax purposes in another country. There is no inheritance tax as such but real estate transfers at death are taxed and gifts received from persons who are not close family members may be taxable income. An American tax exile who officially lives in Mexico and pays income tax there could safely claim that he is domiciled in Mexico. A *perpetual tourist (PT)* might be able to live there as a nonresident but he would be unable to claim that he has changed his domicile to Mexico. There are both an income tax treaty and a *tax information exchange agreement (TIEA)* in force between Mexico and the US and they now exchange a great deal of tax information. Mexico is also entering into tax treaties and TIEAs with other countries.

One way to establish legal residence in Mexico has been to purchase a US $100,000 unit in a Mexican *immigrant investor fund*. The investor then applies for immigrant status in Mexico and the processing of his application is expedited. In one example I have seen, the investor was guaranteed that he would get his US $100,000 principal back after ten years. In the interim, he receives the equivalent of a four percent per year return on his investment.

MONTSERRAT -- NORMALLY A PLEASANT CARIBBEAN ISLAND

Once an Irish colony, and now a British dependent territory, Montserrat is normally a pleasant Caribbean island. It can be reached by a short plane ride from nearby Antigua. A long-dormant volcano began erupting in 1995 and it has caused some serious disruptions in the island. Income tax at a maximum rate of about 30 percent is paid by non-domiciled residents only on local income and foreign income that is remitted to Montserrat. There is no capital gains tax and no death tax. It may be suitable as your residence but probably not as your domicile. You cannot expect to get citizenship or a passport there until after many years of legal residence.

NORTHERN MARIANAS -- A PLAN TO SAVE TAXES

The true tax exile will go to the ends of the earth to achieve his or her goals. Would you consider moving to some exotic Pacific island for a couple of years to try to save about $1 million in capital gains tax? It may have been possible for US citizens to do so prior to the 1986 repeal of a section of the US Internal Revenue Code. One family tried it, but they may not have stayed there long enough to succeed.

There may be more remote places in which to live than Saipan, in the Commonwealth of the Northern Mariana Islands (CNMI), but I can't think of many. Yet that is where Debra Preece moved herself and her family in an effort to reduce US capital gains tax on the sale of her shares in the Diet Center, a very successful family-owned business founded by her parents.

Before the second world war, the islands now comprising the CNMI were mandated to the Japanese, and after the war they were administered by the US. In 1975, the people of the islands approved a covenant that established the CNMI as a political union with the US. For several years, US law permitted CNMI residents to file a single income tax return in the CNMI covering both their US and CNMI income. The CNMI gave them a 95 percent rebate of taxes imposed on their local-source income.

In March 1985, shortly after learning of the proposed sale of the Diet Center and receiving tax advice that she could save substantial taxes, Debra, her husband, David, and their young children (all US citizens) moved from the US to Saipan. They rented an apartment, enrolled the children in school, bought a car, opened bank accounts, registered to vote, obtained drivers' licenses and involved themselves in a local church. In April 1985, Debra sold her shares for more than $5 million. A year later, in April 1986, Debra and David filed their 1985 tax return in the CNMI; on it they reported the sale of Diet Center shares as income from CNMI sources which qualified for the local 95 percent income tax rebate. Shortly thereafter, in July 1986, they moved back to the US.

The US Internal Revenue Service (IRS) determined that Debra and David had improperly failed to file US federal income tax returns for that year, presumably on the theory that they were not really CNMI residents. Debra and David argued that as CNMI residents they were relieved of filing federal returns by a law which then permitted US citizens residing in the CNMI to satisfy their US tax liability by filing their returns in the CNMI. They took the matter to court. They contended that they were residents of the CNMI for 1985 as a matter of law because they spent more than 182 days in Saipan that year.

The Chief Judge of the US Tax Court held that they were not automatically residents of the CNMI in 1985 merely because they spent more than half the year there. Whether they were really CNMI residents that year would have to be determined at a trial based on all of the relevant facts and circumstances. For the full text of the decision, see *Preece v. Commissioner*, 95 Tax Court 594 (1990). I have not seen any report showing the outcome of a subsequent trial. It is likely that there wasn't any and that the case was settled.

Even if this plan did work for Debra and David Preece, it will not work for you. In 1986, Congress repealed the section that would have permitted you not to file a US return if you are a resident of the CNMI.

PANAMA AS A PLACE TO RETIRE

Post-Noriega Panama still adheres strictly to a territorial tax system under which only local-source income is taxed. It is easy for you to immigrate to Panama if you are at least 45 years old, don't need to work there and can show that you have a private income of at least $1,000 per month. You can buy most local real estate without problems. Inheritance tax has been abolished, but there is a tax on gifts of Panamanian property. Citizenship and passports are available and the theoretical five-year residency requirement is sometimes waived. Panama could be suitable for your residency, domicile, citizenship and passport if you are prepared to cope with the instability that still remains following the ouster of General Noriega by US military forces.

PERU NEVER IMPLEMENTED ITS CITIZENSHIP PROGRAM

Peru suddenly emerged as a potentially-viable country for economic citizenship as the result of a new program enacted by the Peruvian Congress and announced by President Alberto Fujimori in 1993. Unfortunately, this program has never been implemented. In theory, you should have been able to obtain immediate naturalization without prior residency by making a nonrefundable cash contribution of US $25,000, and up to eight dependents could be covered for an additional US $2,000 each. The "program" was supposed to attract thousands of new immigrants to Peru, mostly from Asia. It was never made clear whether the new citizens would have been expected or required to reside in Peru following their naturalization.

SINGAPORE ATTRACTS HONG KONG CHINESE

Singapore has attracted many professionals from Hong Kong by granting them *provisional permanent residence status*. This has enabled them to remain in Hong Kong for up to five years before actually moving to Singapore. Income tax in Singapore is high but the system is basically territorial. If you are resident in Singapore you are taxed on foreign-source income only if it is received in Singapore. Estate duty is levied on your worldwide assets if you are domiciled there, but only on Singapore property if you are not. Thus, Singapore is suitable for residency but probably not for domicile.

SOUTH AFRICA IS STILL UNSETTLED

South Africa taxes only income from local sources. You are not taxed on foreign-source income whether or not you are resident, domiciled, or a citizen. I visited South Africa several years ago and found the area around Cape Town to be spectacular. It would make an excellent destination for a tax exile were it not for the country's ongoing political problems, rampant crime and strict exchange controls. Even if you could get a South African passport, you might have difficulty using it to travel to some parts of the world.

SRI LANKA IS DISTURBED POLITICALLY

Sri Lanka, formerly known as Ceylon, has tried to establish itself as a retirement haven. Tax concessions are available to approved foreigners who become resident guests or settlers. However, its disturbed political situation makes it a questionable place today for serious consideration as a retirement haven.

TONGA HAS OFFERED PASSPORTS

Author Paul Theroux, in his best-selling book called *The Happy Isles of Oceania*, tells how His Majesty, King Taufa'ahau Tupou IV, the king of Tonga, authorized the sale of Tongan passports to Hong Kong Chinese and others. Initially, each buyer paid US $10,000 and he was called a Tongan Protected Person. He received a Tongan passport on which he could travel anywhere except Tonga; he could not settle there. Because of this restriction, some countries considered these passports invalid. Subsequently, Tonga sold hundreds of regular passports at US $20,000 for an individual, or US $35,000 for a family of four. The program is apparently no longer in operation; Theroux says it produced about US $30 million for the Tongan government.

POTENTIAL NEW ECONOMIC CITIZENSHIP PROGRAMS

Two more member countries of the British Commonwealth in the Eastern Caribbean have taken steps to introduce economic citizenship programs. One of these, **St. Vincent and the Grenadines**, amended its Citizenship Act in 1996 to authorize the Minister in charge of citizenship to grant *"honorary citizenship"* to selected individuals who do not otherwise qualify for citizenship, presumably because of insufficient residency. An honorary citizen receives a passport and enjoys many citizenship rights, but he cannot vote, run for public office or acquire local real estate without paying an alien's land holding license fee. There are too many grounds on which he can be deprived of his honorary citizenship, including fraud in obtaining it, conviction of a crime, becoming an undischarged bankrupt, engaging in activities prejudicial to the country, or conducting himself in a manner that is not conducive to the public good, whatever that means. I have not yet seen any implementing regulations so I don't know how you apply for this honorary citizenship or how much it will cost. The biggest problem, however, is that honorary citizenship is a bit like *honorary pregnancy*; it does not produce the desired result. It is unlikely that most other countries will recognize such citizenship or passports issued to honorary citizens.

The neighboring country of **Grenada** also enacted an economic citizenship program in early 1997. I understand that it may be patterned on the St. Vincent legislation and that it too may offer honorary citizenship.

OTHER POSSIBLE SAFE HAVENS

If you know of other safe havens that you think should be discussed in future editions of this report, please let me know. Write to me in care of Scope International and give me as much information as you can about the place, the ease or difficulty of establishing residence or domicile there, and whether or not it is possible to obtain citizenship and a passport.

We have looked at the problems involved in leaving your present homeland and the advantages and disadvantages of many of the safe havens to which you might consider moving. Now it is time to determine whether you should become a tax exile.

PART VII

SHOULD YOU BECOME A TAX EXILE?

65. YOUR ULTIMATE ESTATE PLAN

Your advisers can give you guidance and advice but you must make the final decision as to whether you should expatriate. The questions and answers contained in this chapter may help you to reach the correct decision. This chapter is basically unchanged from last year's edition, but two legislative changes are noted in the *1997 Update* at the end of the chapter.

Now that you know what is required you must determine whether it makes sense for you to become a tax exile. Only you can decide whether it is worthwhile for you to develop your own *ultimate estate plan.*

Examine your present will and estate plan. How much will you and your spouse have to pay in taxes when you pass on your estate to the next generation? How much of this could be saved if you became a tax exile? Look at your present sources of income and how much of that income now goes to pay taxes. How much of that income could you still earn after taxes if you became a tax exile?

THE DECISION IS YOURS

If you carefully analyze these questions and the answers to them, you are likely to reach one of three conclusions:

1. You enjoyed reading about the possibilities, but you feel that becoming a tax exile would be too disruptive to your present and future lifestyle. You will stay and pay. Your children and grandchildren will have to make do with whatever is left after taxes.

2. You feel that the savings during your lifetime and to your heirs would be great but you can't afford to move now. You will begin to take steps that will make it possible for you to move when you can.

3. You are ready, willing and able to become a tax exile now. The after-tax savings will improve your lifestyle for the rest of your life, and the eventual savings to your family will be substantial.

If you have chosen either 2 or 3, you have further work to do. Sit down with your legal and tax advisers and work out your plan. This is an area where no two plans can ever be the same. You already have a general idea of the steps you must take to leave your present home country.

RESIDENCY QUESTIONS

At a minimum you must terminate your existing *residency.* You will want to determine whether you must sell or lease your home or whether you can keep it for visits.

Must you establish one specific home base or can you be a *perpetual tourist (PT)* with homes in several different places? Which country or countries will be best for you to move to? Have you already visited or lived in them or in similar foreign countries? Have you gathered all the information you possibly can concerning living conditions there? Are you satisfied that your new base has adequate facilities for health care and your other needs?

Should you terminate your present residence at or near the end of a tax year or can you do it when it is most convenient for you? Are you subject to a departure tax if you leave? How many days a year can you spend visiting your friends and family in your present home country after you leave? Must you stay at a hotel or can you rent an apartment or home for your visits? Can you keep a car or should you rent one during your visits? Will it be safe for you to keep any bank accounts or investments in your present home country after you leave?

DOMICILE QUESTIONS

Must you also change your *domicile*? If so, how will you and your heirs be able to prove that you have made the change? What is your domicile of origin? What is your present domicile? What happens if you leave your present domicile without establishing a new one? Do you retain your present domicile? Do you revert to your domicile of origin? Must you change both your residency and your domicile at the same time or can you change your residency now and your domicile later?

CITIZENSHIP QUESTIONS

Can you retain your present *citizenship*? Even if you can, would you feel safer or more comfortable if you had a second nationality and another passport? Does your present passport make it difficult for you to travel to certain parts of the world that you would like to visit? Trace your family history and that of your spouse. Does your ancestry entitle you to obtain citizenship somewhere? Does your present country permit dual nationality? Does it make sense for you to obtain another nationality now so that you can terminate your present nationality when and if you consider it necessary to do so? Do you know where and how you can obtain another suitable nationality? If you keep your present nationality and passport must you use that passport to enter and leave your present country? Do you know how to terminate your present nationality when and if you decide to do so? Are you subject to a departure tax or ongoing taxation if you give up your citizenship?

OTHER KEY QUESTIONS

Are you *married* and, if so, are your assets subject to community property rules? Are those rules consistent with your own wishes? Will your spouse take the same steps you do to become a tax exile? If you are not married, do you have an ongoing relationship with someone to whom you plan to leave part of your estate? Will that person be treated as *unrelated* for gift or inheritance tax purposes in your present or proposed future home country?

How much of your present income comes from *sources* in your present home country? Will you still be taxed on that income if you leave? If so, can you change the source of that income so as to reduce or eliminate such taxes? Can you use your new home country's tax treaties to reduce the tax at source on any of your income?

How much of your assets are *located* in your present home country? Will you still be taxed on gifts or other transfers of those assets after you leave? If so, can you change the location of those assets to reduce or eliminate gift and death taxes?

Do you know *when* to take each of the steps required to achieve the most beneficial results? Will most of your beneficiaries move with you or will some or all of them remain in your present home country? If they remain behind are there special steps you need to take to ensure that they are not pounced on for taxes on your estate after you are gone?

You will find preliminary answers and guidance to many of these questions in this report. However, your own personal circumstances may require you to take steps that are different than those that might be suitable for someone else. Check each step carefully. Develop your own *ultimate estate plan*. If you want to become a tax exile, do it right or don't do it.

ANSWERS FOR THE HYPOTHETICAL FAMILY

To help you get started, let us take another look at *Larry and Laura Latour* whose status we looked at in part II of this report when we first began examining the tax octopus. You may recall that they were American citizens, resident and domiciled in California. Her estimated estate is $25 million and his is about $1 million. Since this is a second marriage for both of them and each of them has grown children from a prior marriage, they signed a premarital agreement under which their existing assets at the time of marriage remain separate property rather than community property. Let us say that their combined income averages about $2 million a year before taxes and that they spend about $400,000 a year to live. If they remain in California, their federal and state income taxes will take at least $900,000 a year. Other taxes, including property taxes, may cost them another $100,000 a year. Thus, by leaving, they could save an extra $1 million a year.

If Laura dies first, she plans to leave Larry enough income to enable him to maintain his present lifestyle, but she expects to leave the bulk of her estate to her grown children from a prior marriage. Little, if any, of her estate would qualify for the estate tax *marital deduction* since she will not leave her estate to Larry outright nor will she give him the absolute power to choose who will receive it when he dies. If she remains a US citizen or retains her California domicile, her $25 million estate will pay a federal estate tax of around $13.75 million when she dies. If she tries to leave substantial sums to her grandchildren rather than her children, a further generation-skipping transfer tax will eat up most of the rest of the estate.

If Larry dies first, he plans to leave his entire estate to his children since Laura has no need for either capital or income from his estate. His estate will get the equivalent of a

$600,000 exemption. Thus, if his taxable estate is $1 million, the estate tax would be $153,000. If his estate increases to $2 million, the estate tax would jump to $587,200. If it increases to $3 million, the estate tax would be $1,098,000.

Laura Latour has decided that she definitely wants to become a tax exile. She is prepared to terminate her residency, domicile and citizenship if that is what it takes. She has selected Bermuda as the best place for them to move to. Larry plans to move with her, and he is willing to change his domicile from California to Bermuda so there is no risk that Laura remains stuck with his California domicile despite her wish to change. He is also willing to obtain a second nationality, but he would prefer to retain his American citizenship even if Laura gives up hers.

They are investigating various ways to acquire another nationality and passports from that country. They plan to acquire a condominium apartment in Bermuda and to establish residency there before the end of the current year. They will also take whatever steps are needed to change their domicile at that time. They realize that it may take them some time to acquire a suitable new nationality. As soon as they can do so, Laura will relinquish her US citizenship. Larry will decide whether to do so later.

Laura Latour and her advisers feel that she can convert a large part of her income into foreign-source income on which she will no longer be subject to US income tax even if she is treated as a tax-motivated expatriate. Her remaining US-source income may still be subject to US federal income tax for ten years. Larry will remain taxable on his separate income from all sources if he remains a US citizen.

Laura had planned to set up a British Virgin Islands (BVI) company shortly after she moved and relinquished her citizenship. She was going to transfer most of her US securities into that company, *Magnum Limited*, in exchange for Magnum's shares. She had received preliminary advice from her advisers some time ago that she would not be taxed on the transfer but that she would be taxable if she sold the Magnum shares or liquidated the company within ten years after her expatriation. She had planned to keep the Magnum shares indefinitely. Magnum, however, was going to sell its US securities and replace them with comparable foreign securities. That would not have resulted in any US tax on either Magnum or Laura Latour since none of these securities was in real estate holding companies. Unfortunately, she did not leave in time to carry out this plan.

Laura and Larry estimate that it will cost them $100,000 a year more to live in Bermuda than it does now in California. This should cover their extra living expenses and the additional cost of travel for their visits to the children and the family's visits to Bermuda. They feel that this will be more than made up by the annual income tax saving.

If Laura dies within ten years after her expatriation owning the shares of Magnum, her estate may be taxable on any US securities or property owned by Magnum at the time of her death, so she plans to keep these to a minimum. Laura would like to make some gifts to her children after she leaves the US, but she will confine these to foreign-situs assets.

Laura is concerned that if Larry does not relinquish his citizenship, she may face residual tax problems to the extent that any of their assets are considered to be community property. She is also concerned that Larry's continued citizenship may require him to file all kinds of information returns with the IRS and the Treasury Department including, for example, forms concerning bank accounts and securities accounts outside the US on which he can sign and information returns concerning her foreign corporations. She has been told that a US citizen married to a nonresident alien must theoretically file detailed information returns concerning foreign corporations owned by the alien spouse even if the citizen spouse doesn't actually own any of the shares of the foreign company. She asked whether Jackie Onassis ever filed such returns concerning all of the companies owned by her husband when Aristotle Onassis was still alive. Her advisers said they didn't know, but that under the law such returns may have been required. Because of these complications, Laura would prefer that Larry joins her in expatriating. He has promised to think about it.

What if someday they decide they have made a mistake and they want to move back to the US? The easiest way would be for one of their adult children (over 21) to sponsor them for green cards. There is no quota and no wait for adult children who obtain green cards for their parents. If that were to present a problem, there are other possibilities such as obtaining a treaty investor visa or qualifying under an investor program.

Laura has made up her mind. She is going to proceed with her *ultimate estate plan*.

1997 UPDATE

Laura Latour's advisers are modifying their plan to take into consideration the impact of the revised expatriation tax provisions discussed in Chapter 21 above. They are also considering whether the amended immigration legislation discussed in that chapter might make it more difficult for the Latours to visit the US or return to America if they ever decided that they had made a mistake.

66. THE PAST, THE PRESENT AND THE FUTURE

By looking back at the introduction of the original US expatriation tax rules in 1966 and the Canadian departure tax rules in 1972, we can better understand more recent developments. This chapter has been rewritten for the 1997 edition.

FLASHBACK TO 1966: THE *US*

The original US expatriation tax rules were not enacted in response to any concern that large numbers of Americans wanted to leave. They were enacted over 30 years ago as part of the *Foreign Investors Tax Act of 1966* in which Congress gave nonresident aliens special incentives designed to encourage them to invest in the United States. There was some concern that those benefits were so substantial that a few Americans might be encouraged to leave in order to be able to enjoy those benefits *with respect to their US investments*. Over the past 30 years, that law generally accomplished what it was intended to do. Meanwhile, many of the special incentives given to encourage foreign investment in the US were repealed.

FLASHBACK TO 1972: CANADA

Canada does not tax gains derived from the sale of a principal residence. It did not begin taxing other capital gains until 1972. As of the date on which it began taxing capital gains (called Valuation Day or V-Day), every Canadian taxpayer was given a new valuation basis for each of his capital assets. He was initially also given a lifetime capital gains exemption of Cdn $500,000; and only half of any gain was taxable as income, so the rate was low. To make the process fair, each new immigrant to Canada since then has been given his own V-Day as of the date on which he arrives in Canada. Each emigrant who has resided in Canada for over five years is treated as having disposed of his property as of the date he leaves. The system is symmetrical and has generally been perceived of as being fair.

In the early days following the 1972 V-Day, few Canadians paid much tax on capital gains. Many Canadians were lulled into remaining in Canada until it was too late for them to leave without having to pay a large departure tax. As their assets grew in value, their unrealized gains became larger and larger. Meanwhile, the taxable portion of a capital gain was increased from half to three-fourths and the lifetime exemption was eliminated except for certain targeted areas like farms.

Most Canadians with very large unrealized capital gains now find that it is too costly for them to try to escape the looming tax liability by moving abroad. Most of them prefer to postpone the inevitable tax on capital gains until they sell the assets or die. Unlike Americans, Canadians are subject to tax on their unrealized capital gains at death which is treated as another form of departure. Offsetting this, however, Canadians are not subject to any estate or inheritance tax when they die.

For wealthy taxpayers generally, a tax of about 40 percent on the difference between an asset's basis and its value at death is less burdensome than a 55 percent estate tax based on the asset's entire value at death. Moreover, when a wealthy Canadian realizes a capital gain and pays tax thereon, the after-tax proceeds are his to keep, enjoy and pass on to his heirs without any further tax. When a wealthy American realizes a capital gain and pays tax thereon, the after-tax proceeds remain in his estate where they are subject to the inevitable estate tax liability. It is entirely possible, therefore, that Americans might react quite differently to a possible US departure tax than Canadians have done to theirs.

There is an old saying that if you throw a frog into a pot of boiling water, it will jump out and may escape. If instead you put the frog into a pot of cool water and gradually heat it, the frog is likely to remain in the pot until it is too late and it is cooked. The Canadian departure tax was introduced in a way in which it affected taxpayers gradually until for many it has become too late to leave. On the other hand, the US departure tax proposed by President Clinton in 1995 was introduced suddenly and without notice. Some shocked taxpayers reacted by seeking ways to "beat the system" anyway they could. Neither version of the new US expatriation tax rules considered by Congress during 1995 and 1996 was foolproof and some well-advised taxpayers will almost certainly escape some or all of the intended tax liability.

FLASHBACK TO 1995 AND 1996: THE *US*

The technical aspects of the revised US expatriation tax rules have already been discussed in Chapter 21 above. How they were developed is also interesting and that is discussed here. The saga began with a *Forbes* cover story published in November 1994. It named a few American billionaires who had already escaped the US capital gains tax and the inevitable 55 percent estate tax by giving up their US citizenship. It suggested that others were planning to do so. The Treasury Department and the IRS began developing a plan to impose an expatriation tax without warning in order to trap as many as possible of those wealthy Americans who were considering leaving but had not yet done so.

The trap was sprung by President Clinton's February 1995 budget proposal. As subsequently modified, it would have required wealthy US tax exiles leaving after 5 February 1995 to pay an *expatriation tax* on their *unrealized* capital gains. The exit tax would have applied to any US citizen who expatriated and to any resident alien who gave up his green card after holding it for over eight years. Aimed principally at the wealthy, the proposal would have exempted your qualified retirement plans, your US real estate (since it would be taxed anyway when you sell it), and the first $600,000 of your unrealized gains on other assets. Because of this, Treasury claimed that the proposal would rarely apply to anyone whose gross assets were less than $5 million.

The President's proposal generated a great deal of controversy. There was general agreement in Congress that something should be done, but the Republican majority felt that a different approach was warranted. Three hearings were conducted on the subject of the proposed expatriation tax, two by the Senate Finance Committee and one by the House Ways and Means Committee. I testified by invitation at the first Senate Finance Committee hearing. The second Senate Finance Committee hearing was nationally televised on C-Span. At one point during that hearing, Senator Moynihan held up an earlier edition of this report and said *"All you need is the manual."* He also said *"*** it is a pretty good book. It tells you how to avoid all this."*

The staff of the Joint Committee on Taxation prepared a 500-page report on the expatriation tax proposals. Based on the staff's findings, Chairman Archer of the Ways and Means Committee introduced his bill which took an entirely different approach. It left the existing rules in place and tightened them so that they would work. That is the approach that was adopted in the 1995 bill that was subsequently approved by Congress but vetoed by the President. It was adopted again in 1996 as part of the Health Insurance Portability and Accountability Act and this time it was signed into law by President Clinton.

The modifications to the President's proposal made by Congress target departing taxpayers with much less than $5 million in assets. The Archer bill, as enacted, covers a departing citizen or resident who meets *either* of two tests. Only wealthy taxpayers are likely to meet the first test, paying an average income tax of more than $100,000 per year. Many less affluent taxpayers will, however, meet the second test, having net assets of over $500,000. Many middle-class Americans have an equity of more than $500,000 in their homes. I suspect that Chairman Archer and those who helped him draft his bill originally planned to include a much higher figure in the second test, probably $5 million. Then, they probably found that they had to reduce that amount considerably in order to generate a revenue estimate higher than that shown for the President's proposal.

While the proposed expatriation tax proposals were working their way through the tax-writing committees of Congress, another House committee was working on a massive immigration reform bill. Congressman Jack Reed, a Rhode Island Democrat who has since been elected to the Senate, introduced an amendment that would authorize the US Attorney General to classify an alien who had renounced citizenship to avoid taxes as *excludable*. No one on the committee seemed to have the guts to point out what a horrible piece of legislation this was and the committee approved it by a large margin. It was included in the bill that finally passed the House of Representatives. There was no comparable provision in the Senate version of the immigration reform legislation and everyone thought the provision would disappear, especially after the Deputy US Attorney General wrote a letter stating that the Administration was opposed to this provision. Unfortunately, she also wrote a second letter a few weeks later that seemingly reversed that position although it was much less precise than her earlier letter. We may never know whether the second letter was really intended to reverse the first one or whether it simply contained an erroneous section reference. In any case, a conference committee included the provision in its final bill which became law in September 1996. The only change made by the conference committee was to clarify that the provision could only affect those who renounced citizenship on or after the date of enactment, 30 September 1996. A few days later, Senator Moynihan made a statement on the floor of the Senate in which he denounced the provision and called for it to be repealed. He correctly indicated that expatriation to avoid taxes is a tax matter that should be dealt with in tax legislation, not in an immigration reform law. Incidentally, that is also the position that was taken by the Deputy US Attorney General in her original letter. It remains to be seen how this provision will be applied and whether there will be any serious attempt to repeal it. The provision certainly sends the wrong message to prospective citizens. It tells them that citizenship is a one-way street; once you acquire it you may be locked in permanently. That is precisely the message that the former USSR and its satellites sent to their citizens when they erected the Berlin Wall.

THE PRESENT SITUATION

President Clinton's February 1997 budget message did not request any further legislation concerning expatriates. The President, the Treasury Department and the IRS have apparently decided instead to try to make the revised expatriation tax rules work. Senator Moynihan will probably reintroduce his bill but, without the support of the President and the Treasury, it is not likely to be enacted by the 1997-98 Congress.

As this edition goes to press, the IRS is working on the implementation of the expatriation tax rules as they were revised in 1996. On 24 February 1997, the IRS issued *Notice 97-19*, a 16,000-word notice containing guidance for expatriates under the revised expatriation tax legislation. Because of its importance, I have included the entire text of this notice in an appendix to this report. Any US citizen or long-term resident who has expatriated since 6 February 1995 must file a statement containing detailed financial information required by the notice.

The name of each citizen who expatriates is now furnished by the State Department to the Treasury Department. These names are now published quarterly in the Federal Register. The first such list, covering those who received certificates of loss of nationality during the last quarter of 1996, has already been published. It contained 90 names. As in earlier lists published by the Joint Committee on Taxation, many of these were apparently Koreans who had returned to South Korea and were required by that country to give up US citizenship in order to reacquire their Korean citizenship.

SOME THOUGHTS ABOUT THE FUTURE

Many non-American readers have asked why so much of this report has been devoted to the US rules. The answer is that most of the recent attacks on tax exiles have been made by the US government. That was not true in the past, nor will it necessarily be true in the future. Many Americans are kicking themselves for not having paid more attention to the Canadian departure tax rules in recent years. These would have given them a better indication of what to expect and how to plan for it.

Britain could be next. A general election must be held by May 1997. Many predict that "New Labour" will be elected and that Tony Blair will become the next Prime Minister. Blair and his Shadow Chancellor, Gordon Brown, have said relatively little thus far about what they will do about taxes. They have recently stated that they will not increase the current 40 percent maximum income tax rate but they could certainly raise more taxes from wealthy taxpayers without raising the tax rate. They have also said that no one should fear New Labour's tax policies except the *"undeserving rich"*. Does that category include you? Will Labour increase actual income taxes and inheritance taxes? Will they impose a gift tax and an annual net wealth tax? Will Labour tax *non-domiciled residents* on their worldwide income? Might they impose an *exit tax* on residents who leave Britain?

Some of these possibilities concern me more than others. If you are a British resident, they should concern you too. Labour leaders have a close rapport with President Clinton and leaders of the Democratic Party in the US. The Democrats have been experts at squeezing rich taxpayers without raising tax rates excessively. They have learned how to use an alternative minimum tax and other devices to impose a high-rate flat tax on wealthy individuals. The last time Labour governed Britain, tax rates reached 83 percent on earned income and 98 percent on passive income such as interest. That, of course, was under "Old Labour." No one seriously expects such rates again. But, there is a general expectation that a Labour government would increase taxes even if they do not increase tax rates. Many people expect a phaseout of deductions such as that now commonly used in the US. The effect would be to require top-rate taxpayers to pay the maximum rate on substantially all of their income. Under that diabolical system, aggressively used in the US since 1986, a top-rate taxpayer pays a flat rate of about 40 percent on virtually all of his income. Applying these principles, a Labour government could keep maximum tax rates at or near 40 percent and still generate as much tax revenue as they would have been able to raise with a much higher tax rate under the old rules.

The current British inheritance tax is full of interesting loopholes many of which could disappear under a money-hungry Labour government. Will Labour follow the lead of the US and impose a foolproof unified gift and estate tax at a flat rate of 55 percent or more on large estates, *with no exceptions?* They could easily eliminate most of the present loopholes. They could, for example, change the rules that permit non-domiciled residents to escape that tax. Alternatively, they could simply say that a resident is deemed to be domiciled for inheritance tax purposes after five years of residence, instead of the present 17 out of 20 years test. They could also make it more difficult to escape the inheritance tax net by requiring a much longer period of domicile abroad before permitting you to escape the inheritance tax.

Although many of my British colleagues disagree with me, I think non-domiciled residents are at risk if Labour is elected. The civil servants at Inland Revenue have wanted to change these rules for many years. They devoted a great deal of effort to a 60-page *green paper* that was published in 1988, discussed in Chapter 40 above. That paper would have imposed worldwide taxation on all British residents. The rules proposed were virtually identical to the *substantial presence test* rules discussed in Chapter 15 that were enacted by the US Congress in 1984. From all indications, the British proposal was personally vetoed by then Prime Minister Margaret Thatcher (now Lady Thatcher). She had both economic and political reasons for doing so. She wanted to keep wealthy Greek shipowners and others from leaving London where they employ large numbers of people; no government would want to drive out those who employ lots of local people. Many of those same Greek shipowners were, however, reputed to have been big contributors to the Tory Party; Labour would obviously not have the same political incentive to keep these people happy.

France, Germany and several other EU countries impose an annual wealth tax on worldwide assets; it raises a lot of money. As of a recent date, for example, the French wealth tax exempts an individual's net wealth under about FF4.6 million (about £500,000). The tax then begins at a rate of 0.5 percent and increases to 1.5 percent on net wealth exceeding about FF45 million (about £4.8 million). Beginning in 1995, a "temporary" additional 10 percent surtax is being levied on the wealth tax liability. Few British taxpayers with that kind of wealth are likely to be Labour voters so such a tax would be politically expedient for a Labour government.

Suppose these kinds of tax increases are announced. Many might then consider leaving Britain, just as their parents and grandparents did the last time Labour was in office. It might be too late to do so then. A budget message announcing these kinds of taxes might also impose an exit tax, effective for anyone seeking to abandon British residence or domicile after 6pm that day. That is the way it was done in the US. When President Clinton proposed his exit tax in February 1995, he announced that it would be effective for American citizens or residents leaving that day or at any time thereafter. Although it changed the nature of the legislation, the US Congress retained that effective date. A few days after the President's 1995 budget proposal, Treasury Assistant Secretary Leslie Samuels told a national television audience:

> "If we didn't make the proposal effective the day we'd announced it, there would be a lot of people who would beat our rule."

I would certainly expect any exit tax proposal in Britain to take effect in a similar way.

British readers of this report should consider their options now. They should look at what has happened in the US and other countries that have imposed an exit tax. If they wait too long, it may be too late to take steps to avoid confiscatory new taxes.

67. RESOURCE LIST

This resource list tells you how you can arrange for a private consultation with the author and how you can obtain copies of other publications written by him. It also contains references to other useful publications, including recommended newsletters. This chapter has been revised for this edition.

CONSULTING SERVICES

The author is available for consultations on various subjects related to this report, including: international tax and estate planning; tax and other planning for immigration, emigration and expatriation; residency, domicile, citizenship and second passports; the use of tax havens, offshore companies and offshore trusts; selecting a suitable country to which to move; coping with anti-expatriation rules and departure taxes; tax treaties; and tax information exchange agreements.

Fees (subject to change): for an initial conference of up to two hours at a mutually convenient location in Switzerland, the UK, North America or the Caribbean, £750 (or the equivalent in US dollars or Swiss francs), plus travel expenses, if any. Please arrange to make payment at or before the initial conference. A retainer for any further services can be arranged at the initial conference. No questions by mail, please. To arrange for an appointment for an initial conference contact any one of the following:

- Ms Patricia Robinson, Shutts & Bowen, 43 Upper Grosvenor Street, London W1X 9PG, UK. Telephone: (44 171) 493 4840. Fax: (44 171) 493 4299.
- Mrs Anne Dubois, Marshall J Langer SARL, Rue des Chansons 27, CH-2034 Peseux/Neuchatel, Switzerland. Telephone: (41 32) 731 7017. Fax: (41 32) 724 5194.
- Ms Odalys Gonzalez, Marshall J Langer PA, Shutts & Bowen, 1600 Miami Center, 201 South Biscayne Boulevard, Miami, Florida 33131, USA. Telephone: (1 305) 379 9130. Fax: (1 305) 381 9982.

OTHER BOOKS BY MARSHALL LANGER

The Swiss Report (third edition 1994). Intended for the general reader who wants a rundown on Swiss citizenship and residence, information on Swiss banks, bank secrecy, real estate, corporations, taxes and tax incentives, lump-sum tax agreements, and how to obtain residence and work permits in Neuchatel under that canton's special incentive program. It is available for £60 (US $100) from the publisher, Scope International Limited, Forestside House, Forestside, Rowlands Castle, Hampshire PO9 6EE, UK. Telephone: (44 1705) 63 17 51. Fax: (44 1705) 63 13 22.

Practical International Tax Planning, (third edition, looseleaf, published in 1985 and updated each year). A basic guide to foreign tax havens and how they are used, intended for either professionals or their clients. The book is available for US $195 from the publisher, Practising Law Institute, 810 Seventh Avenue, New York, NY 10019, USA. Telephone: (1 212) 824 5710. Fax: (1 212) 293 3053. For expedited delivery in the rest of the world, you can order the book from Scope International at the address shown in the preceding paragraph.

Rhoades & Langer, US International Taxation and Tax Treaties, with co-author Rufus Rhoades, (six looseleaf volumes, first published in 1970, revised in 1996, and supplemented four times a year). Contains a detailed analysis of US tax rules affecting international transactions and investments and full coverage of US tax treaties and tax information exchange agreements. This set is intended primarily for tax professionals. The set is available from the publisher, Matthew Bender, 1275 Broadway, Albany, NY 12204, USA. Telephone: (1 518) 487 3000. Fax: (1 518) 462 3788.

OTHER USEFUL PUBLICATIONS

REPORTS BY DR WG HILL

Dr WG Hill has written several reports that are *must reading* for anyone who contemplates migration or becoming a tax exile. These are:

The Passport Report
PT
The Andorra & Gibraltar Report
The Campione Report

These reports are available for £60 (US $100) each from the publisher, Scope International.

RECOMMENDED NEWSLETTERS

International Harry Schultz Letter, published about ten times each year, annual subscription is US $285. An outstanding newsletter written and published by Dr Harry Schultz, with investment advice and insights into significant developments throughout the world. Contains periodic forecasts and information concerning key developments in many of the countries to which you might consider moving. HSL, Box 622, CH-1001 Lausanne, Switzerland. (Telephone and Fax in Belgium): Telephone: (32 16) 53 36 84. Fax: (32 16) 53 57 77.

Adrian Day's Investment Analyst, a monthly newsletter edited by Adrian Day, contains helpful insights into investment possibilities in various parts of the world. Available for US$129 per year from Agora Inc., 1217 St. Paul Street, Baltimore, MD 21202, USA. Telephone: (1 410) 234 0691 or (1 410) 783 8440.

Mark Skousen's Newsletter, written by privacy guru, Mark Skousen. It is widely read and helps you to keep up with what is really going on in the world. Available for $137 a year. To subscribe, contact Mark Skousen, Editor, Forecasts & Strategies, 7811 Montrose Road, Potomac, MD 20854, USA. Telephone: (1 301) 424 3700.

John Pugsley's Journal, a monthly newsletter written by John Pugsley who now lives in the British Virgin Islands. Available for $125 a year. To subscribe, contact Marketing & Publishing Associates Ltd., 23-00 Route 208, Fair Lawn, NJ 07410, USA. Telephone: (1 201) 794 1879.

APPENDIX

APPENDIX

In February 1997, the US Internal Revenue Service (IRS) issued Notice 97-19 which explains how the IRS will apply the revised expatriation tax rules enacted in 1996 discussed in Chapter 21 above. The notice is divided into 11 sections. It requires taxpayers to comply with the guidance set forth in the notice until regulations are issued. Because of its importance, the full text of Notice 97-19 is set forth in this appendix.

PART III — ADMINISTRATIVE, PROCEDURAL AND MISCELLANEOUS GUIDANCE FOR EXPATRIATES UNDER SECTIONS 877, 2107 AND 6039F

NOTICE 97-19

PURPOSE

The Health Insurance Portability and Accountability Act of 1996 (the "Act") recently amended sections 877, 2107 and 2501 of the Internal Revenue Code ("Code") and added new information reporting requirements under section 6039F. [1] This notice provides guidance regarding certain federal tax consequences under these sections and section 7701(b)(10) for certain individuals who lose U.S. citizenship, cease to be taxed as U.S. lawful permanent residents, or are otherwise subject to tax in the manner provided by section 877.

This notice has eleven sections. Section I provides background regarding the general application of sections 877, 2107 and 2501. Section II explains how to compute tax under section 877. Section III explains how an individual must determine his or her tax liability and net worth for purposes of sections 877, 2107 and 2501. Section IV explains the procedures that an individual must use to request a private letter ruling that the individual's loss of U.S. citizenship did not have for one of its principal purposes the avoidance of U.S. taxes. Section IV also provides that certain former long-term U.S. residents may use this ruling procedure to request a ruling that cessation of long-term U.S. residency did not have for one of its principal purposes the avoidance of U.S. taxes. Section V provides that certain transactions are treated as exchanges of property under section 877 and explains how to enter into a gain recognition agreement to avoid the immediate recognition of gain on exchanges of property. Section VI provides anti-abuse rules that apply to contributions made to certain foreign corporations. Section VII sets forth annual filing requirements for certain

---

[1 There are currently two provisions of the Internal Revenue Code designated as section 6039F. Treasury intends to seek a technical correction to the Act to redesignate section 6039F, as added by the Act, as section 6039G. All subsequent references to section 6039F in this notice relate to section 6039F as contained in the Act.]

individuals subject to section 877. Section VIII explains how new section 877 interacts with certain U.S. income tax treaties. Section IX explains how to file information statements in accordance with section 6039F and describes the information that must be included on such statements. Section X explains how the transition provision of the Act affects certain individuals who performed an expatriating act prior to February 6, 1995. Section XI explains the application of section 7701(b)(10) and how that section interacts with section 877, as amended by the Act.

Treasury and the Service expect to issue regulations under sections 877 and 6039F, and amend regulations under sections 2107 and 2501, to incorporate the guidance set forth in this notice. Until regulations are issued, taxpayers must comply with the guidance set forth in this notice.

SECTION I. GENERAL APPLICATION OF SECTIONS 877, 2107 AND 2501

Section 877 generally provides that a citizen who loses U.S. citizenship or a long-term resident who ceases to be taxed as a U.S. resident (collectively, "individuals who expatriate") within the 10-year period immediately preceding the close of the taxable year will be taxed on all of his or her U.S. source income (as modified by section 877(d)) for such taxable year, unless such loss or cessation did not have for one of its principal purposes the avoidance of U.S. taxes.

Section 877(a)(2) provides that a former citizen is considered to have lost U.S. citizenship with a principal purpose to avoid U.S. taxes if the former citizen's tax liability or net worth exceeded certain amounts on the date of expatriation. However, a former citizen will not be considered to have expatriated with a principal purpose to avoid U.S. taxes as a result of the individual's tax liability or net worth if he or she qualifies for an exception under section 877(c). To qualify for an exception, a former citizen must be described in certain statutory categories and submit a ruling request for a determination by the Secretary as to whether the individual's expatriation had for one of its principal purposes the avoidance of U.S. taxes. *Section 877(c).*

Section 2107(a)(1) generally provides that U.S. estate tax will be imposed on the transfer of the taxable estate of every nonresident decedent if, within the 10 year period ending with the date of death, the decedent loses U.S. citizenship, unless such loss did not have for one of its principal purposes the avoidance of U.S. taxes. Unless a former citizen qualifies for an exception as provided by section 877(c), such individual will be considered to have expatriated with a principal purpose to avoid U.S. taxes for purposes of section 2107 if the individual's tax liability or net worth exceeded certain amounts on the date of expatriation. *Sections 2107(a)(2)(A) and (a)(2)(B).*

Section 2501(a)(1) generally provides that a tax will be imposed for each calendar year on the transfer of property by gift during such calendar year by any individual, resident or nonresident. Section 2501(a)(2) provides that section 2501(a)(1) will not apply to the transfer of intangible property made by a nonresident not a citizen of the United States. Section 2501(a)(3)(A) provides that this exception does not apply in the case of a donor who, within the 10-year-period ending with the date of a transfer, lost U.S. citizenship, unless such loss did not have for one of its principal purposes the avoidance of U.S. taxes. Unless a former citizen qualifies for an exception as provided by section 877(c), such individual shall be treated as having a principal purpose to avoid U.S. taxes for purposes of section 2501 if the individual's tax liability or net worth exceeded certain amounts on the date of expatriation. *Sections 2501(a)(3)(B) and (a)(3)(C).*

Section 877(e) provides comparable treatment for long-term residents. A long-term resident of the United States will be treated as if such resident lost U.S. citizenship for purposes of sections 877, 2107, 2501 and 6039F if the resident (i) ceases to be a lawful permanent resident of the United States, or (ii) commences to be treated as a foreign resident under the provisions of an income tax treaty between the United States and a foreign country and does not waive the benefits of such treaty applicable to residents of the foreign country.

Section 877(e)(1) defines a long-term resident as a non-U.S. citizen who was a lawful permanent resident of the United States in at least 8 taxable years during the period of 15 taxable years, ending with the taxable year in which such individual ceases to be a lawful permanent resident of the United States or commences to be treated as a resident of another country under an income tax treaty and does not waive the benefits of such treaty applicable to residents of the foreign country. For purposes of section 877, an individual is considered a lawful permanent resident in a taxable year if he or she is a lawful permanent resident during any portion of that year.

Section 877(e)(3)(B) provides that property held by a long-term resident on the date that such individual first became a resident of the United States (whether or not a lawful permanent resident) shall be treated for purposes of section 877 as having a basis of not less than the fair market value of the property on such date. A long-term resident may elect not to have this treatment apply. Such an election, once made, is irrevocable.

Sections 877, 2107 and 2501, as amended by the Act, apply to individuals who expatriate after February 5, 1995, and to individuals subject to section 511(g)(3)(A) of the Act (see section X of this notice).

SECTION II. COMPUTING TAX UNDER SECTION 877

Individuals who expatriate with a principal purpose to avoid U.S. taxes will be subject to tax on U.S. source income (as modified by section 877(d)) under sections 1, 55 or 402(d)(1) [2] of the Code (the "alternative tax"), or under section 871 of the Code, depending on which method results in the highest total tax. *Sections 877(a)(1) and (b).*

The Tax Exile Report

An expatriate is subject to the alternative tax under section 877 only if the total tax imposed thereunder on all items of income for the taxable year exceeds the total tax under section 871 for those same items of income. The following example illustrates how to compute tax under section 877.

Example 1. A, a former U.S. citizen, expatriated with a principal purpose to avoid U.S. taxes on December 31, 1996. In 1997, A earns $100,000 of U.S. source dividend income and $50,000 of U.S. source interest income that qualifies as portfolio interest under section 871(h). After taking into account the deductions and credits allowed under section 877(b)(2), A's net tax liability under section 1 on the dividend and portfolio interest income is $40,000.

The tax imposed under section 871 on A's dividend income is $30,000 (30 percent of $100,000). *Section 871(a)(1)(A).* No tax is imposed on A's portfolio interest under section 871 because section 871(h)(1) exempts portfolio interest received by a nonresident alien from U.S. tax. Thus, A's tax liability under section 871 is $30,000.

Since A's total tax liability computed under section 1 exceeds A's total tax liability computed under section 871, A must pay the higher tax. Thus, A must report $40,000 of U.S. tax on his 1997 U.S. income tax return (Form 1040NR) as a result of section 877.

SECTION III. TAX LIABILITY AND NET WORTH TESTS

Background. Section 877(a)(2) provides that a former citizen is considered to have expatriated with a principal purpose to avoid U.S. taxes if (i) the individual's average annual net U.S. income tax (as defined in section 38(c)(1)) for the five taxable years prior to expatriation is greater than $100,000 (the "tax liability test"), or (ii) the individual's net worth on the date of expatriation is $500,000 or more (the "net worth test"). The $100,000 and $500,000 amounts are subject to cost-of-living adjustments determined under section 1(f)(3) for calendar years after 1996. An individual who does not satisfy the tax liability or net worth test, but expatriates with a principal purpose to avoid U.S. taxes, is also subject to section 877.

Section 2107(a)(2)(A) provides that an individual shall be treated as having a principal purpose to avoid U.S. taxes for purposes of section 2107 if such individual satisfies either the tax liability test or the net worth test under section 877(a)(2). Likewise, section

[2 Section 402(d)(1) of the Code generally provides for 5-year income averaging with respect to certain lump-sum distributions from qualified retirement plans. Section 1401(b)(1) of the Small Business Job Protection Act of 1996 amended section 877(b) by striking "section 1, 55, and section 402(d)(1)" and inserting "section 1 or 55." This amendment applies to taxable years beginning after December 31, 1999.]

2501(a)(3)(B) provides that an individual shall be treated as having a principal purpose to avoid U.S. taxes for purposes of section 2501 if such individual satisfies either the tax liability test or the net worth test under section 877(a)(2). The tax liability and net worth tests also apply for purposes of determining whether a former long-term resident is subject to sections 877, 2107, and 2501. *Section 877(e)(1).*

Determination of tax liability. For purposes of the tax liability test, an individual's net U.S. income tax is determined under Section 38(c)(1). An individual who files a joint income tax return must take into account the net income tax that is reflected on the joint income tax return for purposes of the tax liability test.

Determination of net worth. For purposes of the net worth test, an individual is considered to own any interest in property that would be taxable as a gift under Chapter 12 of Subtitle B of the Code if the individual were a citizen or resident of the United States who transferred the interest immediately prior to expatriation. For this purpose, the determination of whether a transfer by gift would be taxable under Chapter 12 of Subtitle B of the Code must be determined without regard to sections 2503(b) through (g), 2513, 2522, 2523, and 2524.

An interest in property includes money or other property, regardless of whether it produces any income or gain. In addition, an interest in the right to use property will be treated as an interest in such property. Thus, a nonexclusive license to use property is treated as an interest in the underlying property attributable to the value of the use of such property.

Valuation of interests in property. In determining the values of interests in property for purposes of the net worth test, individuals must use the valuation principles of section 2512 and the regulations thereunder without regard to any prohibitions or restrictions on such interest. Although individuals must use good faith estimates of values, formal appraisals are not required.

Special rules for determining beneficial interests in trusts. An individual's beneficial interest in a trust must be included in the calculation of that individual's net worth. For this purpose, the value of an individual's beneficial interest in a trust will be determined using a two-step process. First, all interests in property held by the trust must be allocated to beneficiaries (or potential beneficiaries) of the trust based on all relevant facts and circumstances, including the terms of the trust instrument, letter of wishes (and any similar document), historical patterns of trust distributions, and any functions performed by a trust protector or similar advisor. Interests in property held by the trust that cannot be allocated based on the factors described in the previous sentence shall be allocated to the beneficiaries of the trust under the principles of intestate succession (determined by reference to the settlor's intestacy) as contained in the Uniform Probate Code, as amended. Second, interests in property held by a trust that are allocated to the expatriate must be valued under the principles of section 2512 and the regulations thereunder without regard to any prohibitions or restrictions on such interest. The following example illustrates this special rule.

Example 2. B, a former long-term resident, expatriated on December 31, 1996. B is a potential beneficiary of two trusts during his lifetime. Trust 1's sole asset is an apartment building. Under the terms of Trust 1, B is entitled to receive 100 percent of the income generated by the apartment building during B's life. B's brother, C, is the remainderman. For purposes of computing B's net worth, Trust 1's interest in the apartment building is allocated between B and C. B is treated as owning a life interest in the apartment building. The value of the life interest must be determined under the principles of section 2512 and the regulations thereunder.

Trust 2 was established by B's father for the benefit of B and C. Under the terms of Trust 2, the trust income and corpus may be distributed at the trustee's discretion to either B or C. For purposes of determining B's net worth, all of the interests in property owned by Trust 2 must first be allocated to either B or C based on all relevant facts and circumstances. If the facts and circumstances do not indicate how the interest in the trust's property should be allocated between B and C, the trust property will be allocated under the rules of intestate succession (determined by reference to B's father's intestacy) as contained in the Uniform Probate Code. If B's father had died intestate, the Uniform Probate Code would have allocated his property equally between B and C. Thus, for purposes of determining B's net worth, B will be treated as owning half of the interests in property owned by Trust 2. The value of these interests in property will be determined under the principles of section 2512.

SECTION IV. RULING REQUESTS

Background. Section 877(c) provides that a former U.S. citizen who satisfies either the tax liability test or the net worth test will not be considered to have a principal purpose of tax avoidance as a result of one of those tests if that former citizen submits a request for a ruling within one year of the date of loss of U.S. citizenship for the Secretary's determination as to whether such loss had for one of its principal purposes the avoidance of U.S. taxes. To be eligible to request a ruling, an individual must be within one of the following categories: (1) the individual became at birth a citizen of the United States and a citizen of another country and continues to be a citizen of such other country, (2) the individual becomes (not later than the close of a reasonable period after loss of U.S. citizenship) a citizen of the country in which the individual, the individual's spouse or one of the individual's parents was born, (3) the individual was present in the United States for no more than 30 days during each year of the 10-year period ending on the date of expatriation, (4) the individual lost U.S. citizenship before reaching age 18 1/2, or (5) the individual is described in a category prescribed by regulation. For purposes of sections 2107 and 2501, a former citizen who meets the requirements of section 877(c)(1) will not be considered to have expatriated with a principal purpose to avoid U.S. taxes. *Sections 2107(a)(2)(B) and 2501(a)(3)(C).*

Section 877(e)(3)(A) provides that the exception set forth in section 877(c) with respect to U.S. citizens shall not apply to former long-term residents. However, section 877(e)(4) gives the Secretary the authority to exempt categories of former long-term residents from section 877. In addition, section 877(e)(5) authorizes the Secretary to prescribe appropriate regulations to carry out the purposes of section 877(e).

Additional categories of individuals eligible to submit ruling requests. Treasury and the Service expect to issue regulations that will permit a former long-term resident who is within certain categories to request a ruling under sections 877, 2107 and 2501 as to whether the individual's expatriation had for one of its principal purposes the avoidance of U.S. taxes. Until such regulations are issued, a former long-term resident may request a ruling if:

(1) On the date of expatriation, the individual is a citizen of:
(a) the country in which the individual was born,
(b) the country in which the individual's spouse was born, or
(c) the country where either of the individual's parents were born, *and*
the individual becomes (not later than the close of a reasonable period after the individual's expatriation) fully liable to tax in such country by reason of the individual's residence.

(2) the individual was present in the United States for no more than 30 days during each year of the 10-year period prior to expatriation; or

(3) the individual ceases to be taxed as a lawful permanent resident, or commences to be treated as a resident of another country under an income tax treaty and does not waive the benefits of such treaty applicable to residents of the foreign country, before the individual reaches age 18 1/2.

In addition, former long-term residents and former citizens who narrowly fail to satisfy the criteria of an enumerated category may also submit ruling requests. The Secretary, in his or her sole discretion, may decline to rule on any request if the Secretary determines that the individual does not narrowly fail to satisfy the criteria of one of those categories. If the Secretary declines to rule on an individual's ruling request for this reason, the individual will not be considered to have "submitted" a ruling request within the meaning of section 877(c)(1)(B). Accordingly, if that individual satisfies either the tax liability or net worth test, the individual will be considered to have expatriated with a principal purpose to avoid U.S. taxes under section 877(a)(2).

Examples. The following examples illustrate circumstances in which an individual narrowly fails to satisfy the criteria of an enumerated category, and thus eligible to request a ruling.

Example 3. D, a former citizen of the United States by birth, expatriated on February 15, 1997. D satisfied the tax liability test on the date of her expatriation and thus, will be considered to have expatriated with a principal purpose to avoid U.S. taxes unless she qualifies for an exception under section 877(c). D has resided in the United Kingdom since 1985. D is not a citizen by birth of another country and does not plan to become a citizen of a country in which one of her parents or her spouse were born. D did not spend any time in the United States during the 10-year period prior to her expatriation, except for one year when she vacationed in Hawaii for 35 days. D narrowly fails to satisfy the criteria of section 877(c)(2)(B) because she spent only 35 days in the United States during one year of the 10-year period ending on the date of her expatriation. Thus, D is eligible to submit a ruling request.

Example 4. E is a citizen of France and a long-term resident of the United States. E's parents emigrated from Africa to France in 1950 and acquired French citizenship in 1960. E's parents were employed by the French government and often travelled outside of France. In 1965, E was born while E's parents were stationed outside of France on a short-term assignment. By virtue of his parents' French citizenship, E became a citizen of France at birth. E resided in France from age 1 until age 21. E became a lawful permanent resident of the United States at age 21. E is now 31 years old and wishes to relinquish his green card and return to France. E will satisfy the net worth test on the date of his expatriation.

Although E is not a citizen of France by virtue of being born in France, E narrowly fails to satisfy the criteria of an enumerated category because he was born outside of France only because his parents were temporarily absent from France during an overseas assignment for the French government. E is a citizen of France by birth, became a resident of France at age 1, and plans to become a resident of France after terminating his U.S. residency. Thus, E is eligible to submit a ruling request.

Effect of rulings and pending ruling requests. An expatriate who satisfies the tax liability or net worth test will be subject to new sections 877, 2107 or 2501, unless such individual obtains a favorable ruling, rather than merely submits a request, that the individual did not expatriate with a principal purpose to avoid U.S. taxes. If an individual's ruling request is pending before the Service at the time prescribed for filing the individual's income tax return for a particular year, the individual must report income on his or her U.S. income tax return for that year as if section 877 applied to him or her. If the individual obtains a favorable ruling at a later date, the individual may then amend that previous year's U.S. income tax return accordingly.

Challenging an adverse ruling. An individual who obtains an adverse ruling may challenge the ruling by initiating a refund suit to recover any taxes paid by reason of section 877. *See H.R. Conf. Rep. No. 104, 104th Cong., 2d Sess. 325 (1996).*

Time for submitting ruling requests. Ruling requests must be submitted no later than one year following the date of expatriation. If an individual does not submit a ruling request within this prescribed period and satisfies either the tax liability test or the net worth test, such individual will be treated as having a principal purpose to avoid U.S. taxes. However, an individual subject to new section 877 who expatriated after February 5, 1994, but on or before July 8, 1996, and who wishes to submit a ruling request as to whether such expatriation had for one of its principal purposes the avoidance of U.S. taxes must do so by July 8, 1997.

Ruling requests may be submitted prior to the expected date of expatriation, provided that the individual submitting the request has formed a definite intention to expatriate. The Service will not rule on requests involving alternative plans of proposed transactions or hypothetical situations. *See section 7.02 of Rev. Proc. 97-1, 1997-1 I.R.B. 11, 24.*

Procedures for submitting ruling requests. Individuals should refer to section 8 of Rev. Proc. 97-1, 1997-1 I.R.B. 11, 25, for general instructions on the proper procedures to follow when submitting ruling requests. Individuals should also consult section 15 of Rev. Proc. 97-1, 1997-1 I.R.B. 11, 46, for information on user fees.

Information that must be included in ruling requests. The burden of proof is on the individual requesting the ruling to establish to the satisfaction of the Secretary that the individual's expatriation did not (or will not) have for one of its principal purposes the avoidance of U.S. taxes under Subtitle A or Subtitle B of the Code. Therefore, individuals should submit any relevant information that will help the Secretary make a determination as to whether the individual's expatriation (or planned expatriation) had (or will have) for one of its principal purposes the avoidance of U.S. taxes. The ruling request must include the following information:

(1) the date (or expected date) of expatriation;

(2) a full explanation of the individual's reasons for expatriating;

(3) the individual's date of birth;

(4) all foreign countries where the individual is a resident for tax purposes and/or intends to obtain residence for tax purposes;

(5) all foreign countries of which the individual is a citizen and/or intends to acquire citizenship after expatriation;

(6) the countries where the individual's spouse (if any) and parents were born;

(7) a description of the individual's ties to the United States and the individual's ties to the foreign country where the individual resides (or intends to reside) for the period that begins five years prior to expatriation and ends on the date that the ruling request is submitted, including the location of the individual's permanent home, tax home (within the meaning of section 911(d)(3)), family and social relations, occupation(s), political, cultural, or other activities, business activities, personal belongings, the place from which the individual administers property, the jurisdiction in which the individual holds a driver's license, the location where the individual conducts routine personal banking activities, the location of the individual's cemetery plot (if any), and any other similar information;

(8) a balance sheet, at fair market value, that sets forth by category (e.g. cash, marketable securities, closely-held stock, business assets, qualified and non-qualified deferred compensation arrangements, individual retirement accounts, installment obligations, U.S. real property, foreign real property, etc.) the individual's assets and liabilities immediately prior to expatriation. The balance sheet must also set forth the following:

(i) the source of income and gain, without applying the source provisions of section 877, that such property would have generated during the 5-year period prior to expatriation and immediately after expatriation,

(ii) the source of income and gain, assuming that the source provisions of section 877 applied (as modified by section V of this notice), that such property would have generated during the 5-year period prior to expatriation and immediately after expatriation, and

(iii) the gain or loss that would be realized if the assets were sold for their fair market values on the date of expatriation.

The individual must separately list (not by category) each partnership in which the individual holds an interest, each trust that the individual is considered to own under sections 671 through 679, each trust that the individual is considered to own under Chapter 12 of Subtitle B of the Code, and each trust in which the individual holds a beneficial interest (as determined under the procedures described in section III of this notice). The individual must also describe the types of assets held by each partnership or trust, and indicate the methodology (as described in section III of this notice) used to determine the individual's beneficial interest in each trust. In addition, the individual should indicate whether there have been (or are expected to be) significant changes in the individual's assets and liabilities for the period that began five years prior to expatriation and ends ten years following the date of expatriation. If so, the individual should attach a statement explaining the changes in the individual's assets and liabilities during such period;

(9) a description of all exchanges described in section 877(d)(2)(B) and all removals of appreciated tangible personal property from the United States (as described in section V of this notice), that:

(i) occurred at any time beginning 5 years prior to expatriation (but not including exchanges that took place prior to February 6, 1995) and ending on the date that the ruling request is submitted, or

(ii) occurred, or is expected to occur, during the 10-year period following expatriation.

If the individual is subject to new section 877 because of section 511(g)(3)(A) of the Act (see section X of this notice), the individual must also include a description of all exchanges described under section 877(d)(2)(B) that occurred on or after the date of the individual's expatriating act (see section X of this notice) and before February 6, 1995;

(10) a description of all occurrences under section 877(d)(2)(E)(ii) that are treated as exchanges under section 877(d)(2) (as described in section V of this notice) that:
(i) occurred at any time beginning 5 years prior to expatriation (but not including occurrences that took place prior to February 24, 1997) and ending on the date that the ruling request is submitted, or
(ii) occurred, or is expected to occur, during the 10-year period following expatriation;

(11) a statement describing the nature and status of any ongoing audits, disputes or other matters pending before the Internal Revenue Service;

(12) a statement as to whether the individual satisfied his or her U.S. tax liability during the period that he or she was a U.S. citizen or lawful permanent resident of the United States;

(13) copies of the individual's U.S. tax returns for each of the three years prior to expatriation;

(14) a copy of the information statement filed in accordance with section 6039F, as described in section IX of this notice (if such statement has not yet been filed, provide a draft copy of such statement);

(15) in the case of an individual with gross assets that have an aggregate fair market value in excess of $10,000,000, a calculation of the individual's projected U.S. and foreign income tax liability for the taxable year of expatriation (or expected expatriation) and the two taxable years following expatriation under each of the following circumstances:
(i) if it is determined that the individual expatriated with a principal purpose to avoid U.S. taxes under section 877,
(ii) if it is determined that the individual did not expatriate with a principal purpose to avoid U.S. taxes under section 877, and
(iii) if the individual had remained a U.S. citizen or U.S. lawful permanent resident.

The individual must also indicate whether the individual expects a substantial change in the individual's projected U.S. and foreign income tax liability as a result of a change in income for the remainder of the 10-year period following expatriation;

(16) in the case of an individual with gross assets that have an aggregate fair market value in excess of $10,000,000, an actuarial estimate of U.S. and foreign estate and other death

taxes that would be owed on the individual's property, calculated based on the assumption that the individual owns the same property on the date of death that the individual owned (or expects to own) on the date of expatriation, under each of the following circumstances: (i) if it is determined that thc individual expatriated with a principal purpose to avoid U.S. taxes under section 2107,

(ii) if it is determined that the individual did not expatriate with a principal purpose to avoid U.S. taxes under section 2107, and

(iii) if the individual had remained a U.S. citizen or U.S. lawful permanent resident domiciled in the United States; and

(17) in the case of an individual with gross assets that have an aggregate fair market value in excess of $10,000,000, a statement as to whether the individual expects to make a gift during any year of the 10-year period following expatriation that would be subject to tax under section 2501 if the individual is determined to have expatriated with a principal purpose to avoid U.S. taxes. If so, the individual should describe the gift, provide an estimate of its fair market value, and indicate when and to whom the individual expects to make the gift.

The foregoing list of information must be provided with ruling requests submitted after March 10, 1997. Although individuals must provide good faith estimates of fair market values, formal appraisals are not required. In processing ruling requests, the Service may ask individuals with gross assets that have an aggregate fair market value of $10,000,000 or less to supply the information described in (15), (16) and (17) above. If an individual fails to provide the aforementioned information or any other information that may be reasonably required, the individual's ruling request may be closed pursuant to section 10.06(3) of Rev. Proc. 97-1, 1997-1 I.R.B. 11, 39. If an individual's ruling request is closed, that individual will not be considered to have "submitted" a ruling request within the meaning of section 877(c)(1)(B). Accordingly, if that individual satisfies either the tax liability test or the net worth test, the individual will be considered to have expatriated with a principal purpose to avoid U.S. taxes under section 877(a)(2).

Finally, an individual must attach his or her ruling to the individual's U.S. income tax return for the year in which the individual expatriates. See section 8.05 of Rev. Proc. 97-1, 1997-1 I.R.B. 11, 33. If the individual has already filed a U.S. income tax return for such year, the individual must attach the ruling to the individual's U.S. income tax return for the year in which he or she obtains the ruling.

SECTION V. EXCHANGES AND GAIN RECOGNITION AGREEMENTS

Background. Section 877(c)(1)(A) provides that gains on the sale or exchange of property (other than stock or debt obligations) located in the United States shall be treated as from sources within the United States. Section 877(d)(1)(B) provides that gains on the sale or exchange of stock issued by a domestic corporation or debt obligations of United

States persons, or of the United States, a State, a political subdivision thereof, or the District of Columbia, shall be treated as from sources within the United States. Section 877(d)(1)(C) provides that income or gain derived from a foreign corporation will be from sources within the United States if an expatriate owned or is considered to own (under the principles of sections 958(a) and (b)), at any time during the 2-year period ending on the date of expatriation, more than 50 percent of (i) the total combined voting power of all classes of stock entitled to vote of such corporation, or (ii) the total value of the stock of such corporation. The amount of income or gain that is considered U.S. source is limited, however, to the amount that does not exceed the earnings and profits attributable to such stock earned before the date of the individual's expatriation and during periods that the ownership requirements are met.

Section 877(d)(2) generally provides that certain property transferred in non-recognition exchanges by an individual subject to section 877 during the 10-year period referred to in section 877(a) will be treated as sold for its fair market value on the date of the exchange. Thus, any gain must be recognized by the individual in the taxable year of the exchange. Section 877(d)(2) applies to exchanges that, without regard to section 877, are non-taxable under subtitle A of the Code and involve the exchange of property that would produce U.S. source income or gain for property that would produce foreign source income or gain.

Under section 877(d)(2)(C), however, an individual is not required to immediately recognize gain if the individual enters into an agreement with the Secretary specifying that any income or gain derived from the property acquired in the exchange (or any other property that has a basis determined in whole or in part by reference to such property) during the 10-year period referred to in section 877(a) shall be treated as U.S. source income. In addition, if the transferred property is disposed of by the acquiror, the gain recognition agreement will terminate and any gain not recognized by reason of the agreement must be recognized by the individual as of the date of such disposition.

Section 877(d)(2)(D) provides the Secretary with regulatory authority to substitute the 15-year period beginning five years prior to expatriation for the 10-year period referred to in section 877(a), and to apply section 877(d)(2) to all exchanges that occur during such 15-year period. Section 877(d)(2)(E) also authorizes the Secretary to issue regulations to treat as a taxable exchange the removal of appreciated tangible personal property from the United States, and any other occurrence that results in a change in the source of income or gain from property from U.S. source to foreign source without recognition of gain.

Fifteen-year period and expanded definition of "exchanges". Treasury and the Service expect to issue regulations under sections 877(d)(2)(D) and (E) that extend the 10-year period referred to in section 871(a) and provide an expanded definition of exchanges. The regulations will apply to individuals who expatriate after February 5, 1995, and to individuals subject to section 511(g)(3)(A) of the Act (see section X of this notice). Until regulations are issued, taxpayers must comply with the rules set forth below.

Section 877(d)(2) must be applied by substituting the 15-year period beginning five years prior to expatriation for the 10-year period referred to in section 877(a). In addition, removal of appreciated tangible personal property from the United States with an aggregate fair market value in excess of $250,000 within this 15-year period must be treated as an exchange to which section 877(d)(2) applies. Accordingly, any gain derived from removal of property with an aggregate fair market value of $250,000 or less during this 15-year period will not be taxable under section 877. If an individual removes property with an aggregate fair market value in excess of $250,000 during this 15-year period, the individual must recognize a pro rata portion of the gain attributable to the value in excess of $250,000, unless he or she enters into a gain recognition agreement. A pro rata portion of the gain must be calculated by multiplying the total gain on the removed property by a fraction, the numerator of which is the excess of the aggregate fair market values of all removed property over $250,000 and the denominator of which is the aggregate fair market values of all removed property. Removal of appreciated tangible personal property during the 5-year period prior to expatriation (whether or not the fair market values exceed $250,000) will not be treated as an exchange if the removal occurred prior to February 6, 1995.

Any other occurrence (within the meaning of section 877(d)(2)(E)(ii)) within the 15-year period that results in a change of the source of income or gain from U.S. source to foreign source must also be treated as an exchange to which section 877(d)(2) applies. However, an occurrence during the 5-year period prior to expatriation will not be treated as an exchange if the occurrence took place prior to February 24, 1997.

Determination of source of certain gains. The principles of section 877(d)(1) generally apply for purposes of determining whether any exchange of property changes the source of income or gain from U.S. source to foreign source during the 15-year period beginning five years prior to expatriation. Thus, solely for purposes of determining the source of the expatriate's income or gain with respect to any exchange within this 15-year period, (i) the source of any gain on the sale or exchange of tangible personal property will be based on the physical location of the property, (ii) the source of gain from the sale or exchange of stock will be based on the corporation's place of incorporation (except as otherwise provided in section 877(d)(1)(C)), and (iii) the source of gain from the sale or exchange of debt obligations will be based on the residence of the issuer of such obligations. The source of gain on the sale or exchange of an interest in a partnership during the 15-year period will be determined as if the partner directly disposed of his or her share of the partnership's assets. In determining the partner's share of gain recognized from each partnership asset, the gain on the sale or exchange of the partnership interest shall be allocated among the assets of the partnership in proportion to the gain that the partner would have recognized had the partnership sold each asset for its fair market value. In all other cases, the source of an expatriate's income or gain with respect to any other transaction will be determined under the general source provisions of the Code (e.g. sections 861 through 865).

Recognition of gain. Except as otherwise indicated below, an individual must recognize all realized or unrealized gains, but not losses, as a result of any "exchange" described in section 877(d)(2)(B), (d)(2)(E)(i), or (d)(2)(E)(ii), in the year of the exchange unless that individual enters into a gain recognition agreement. If an exchange occurs during the 5-year period prior to expatriation, the individual must recognize any gain from the exchange in the taxable year of the individual's expatriation unless the individual enters into a gain recognition agreement.

Examples. The following examples illustrate transactions that are treated as exchanges under section 877(d)(2) and when gain from such transactions must be recognized.

Example 5. F, a U.S. citizen by birth, enters into a notional principal contract in March 1997. Under the terms of that contract, F is obligated to make specified annual payments to an unrelated party in exchange for specified annual payments from the unrelated party for a period of five years. F is a calendar year taxpayer who uses the cash method of accounting. F moves her tax home to a foreign country in May 1997. F renounces her U.S. citizenship in 1998 with a principal purpose to avoid U.S. taxes.

The source of income from a notional principal contract is generally determined by reference to the residence of the taxpayer. For this purpose, the residence of an individual is the country in which the individual's tax home is located. *See Treas. Reg. Section 1.863-7(a)(1).*

Before F changed her tax home in May 1997, F's income earned under the contract was treated as U.S. source income. After F changed her tax home, the source of this income became foreign source. Because F's change in tax home changed the source of her income from U.S. source to foreign source, it is an occurrence that is treated as an exchange to which section 877(d)(2) applies. Since this occurrence occurred in the 5-year period prior to her expatriation, F must recognize any gain from the contract in 1998 (the taxable year of her expatriation), unless she enters into a gain recognition agreement.

However, if F also owned stock in a foreign corporation, her change in tax home coupled with her expatriation would not be an occurrence that is treated as an exchange to which section 877(d)(2) applies with respect to such stock. Pursuant to the special source rules described in this notice, the source of gain on the sale or exchange of stock is based on the corporation's place of incorporation. Thus, the gain on the sale or exchange of foreign stock would be foreign source for the entire 15-year period beginning five years prior to expatriation. Accordingly, there would not be an occurrence during this period that would change the source of such gain from U.S. source to foreign source.

Example 6. G is a U.S. citizen by birth. G owns a home in the United States that he uses as his principal residence. In April 1997, G sells his principal residence in the United States at a gain of $1,000,000. In June 1997, G purchases a new principal residence located abroad. G's purchase of the new residence satisfies the requirements of section 1034, and thus G does not recognize the $1,000,000 gain on the sale of his old residence. G expatriates in 1999 with a principal purpose to avoid U.S. taxes.

Under section 861(a)(5), gain from the disposition of a United States real property interest is treated as U.S. source income. A United States real property interest includes real property that is located in the United States. *Section 897(c).* Gain from the sale or exchange of real property located outside the United States is considered foreign source income. *Section 862(a)(5).*

Since G is not required to recognize the gain on the sale of his old residence by reason of section 1034, and the source of this gain would change from U.S. to foreign if G sold his new residence, it is an occurrence that is treated as an exchange to which section 877(d)(2) applies. Accordingly, G must recognize the gain from the sale of his old residence in 1999 (the taxable year of his expatriation), unless he enters into a gain recognition agreement.

Example 7. H is a former long-term resident of the United States. H owns a valuable painting that she purchased in 1965 for $500,000. H became a resident of the United States and brought the painting to the United States in 1975. The fair market value of the painting in 1975 was $2,000,000. H became a lawful permanent resident of the United States in 1980. On January 1, 1996, H expatriates with a principal purpose to avoid U.S. taxes. On January 1, 1997, H removes the painting from the United States. On that date, the fair market value of the painting is $5,000,000.

Under section 877(d)(1)(A), H's unrealized gain in the painting is U.S. source so long as the painting is located in the United States. Since the removal of H's appreciated painting from the United States changed the source of the unrealized gain thereon from U.S. source to foreign source, it is considered an exchange to which section 877(d)(2) applies. For purposes of section 877, H's basis in the painting is the painting's fair market value on the date that H first became a U.S. resident (i.e. $2,000,000). *Section 877(e)(3)(B).* Thus, H's unrealized gain on the painting on the date of removal is $3,000,000 ($5,000,000 - $2,000,000).

Because the value of H's painting on the date of removal exceeds $250,000, H must recognize a pro rata portion of the gain attributable to the value in excess of $250,000, unless she enters into a gain recognition agreement.

The pro rata portion of such gain is $2,850,000, determined by multiplying the total gain ($3,000,000) by a fraction, the numerator of which is the excess of the fair market value of the painting over $250,000 ($4,750,000) and the denominator of which is the fair market value of the painting ($5,000,000). Thus, H must recognize $2,850,000 in 1997 (the taxable year of the removal) unless she enters into a gain recognition agreement.

Example 8. J, a U.S. citizen by birth, expatriates on January 1, 1999, with a principal purpose to avoid U.S. taxes. On the date of J's expatriation, J owns appreciated stock in a domestic corporation. On January 1, 2000, J creates a foreign trust, FT, and contributes the stock to FT. Under the terms of the trust instrument, the income and corpus from FT may be distributed at the discretion of the trustee to J, J's spouse, or J's children.

If J had directly disposed of the domestic stock instead of contributing it to FT, the gain realized thereon would be treated as U.S. source income. *Section 877(d)(1)(B).* However, if FT disposed of the stock, the gain realized would be foreign source because FT is not a resident of the United States. *See sections 865(a)(2) and (g)(1)(B).* If FT then distributed the proceeds to J, his gain would also be foreign source.

Since J's contribution of the domestic stock to FT is non-taxable under subtitle A of the Code and changed the source of gain on the stock from U.S. to foreign, it is an occurrence that is treated as an exchange to which section 877(d)(2) applies. For this purpose, J's beneficial interest in FT is treated as property acquired in the exchange, and the stock contributed to FT is treated as property transferred in the exchange. Therefore, J must recognize the pre-contribution gain on the appreciated stock in 2000 (the taxable year of the exchange), unless he enters into a gain recognition agreement.

Guidance on gain recognition agreements. An individual who wishes to enter into a gain recognition agreement with the Secretary with respect to any exchange described in section 877(d)(2) must submit the agreement with the individual's U.S. income tax return (normally Form 1040NR) for the taxable year of the exchange. If an exchange occurred during the 5-year period prior to expatriation, the individual must submit a gain recognition agreement with his or her U.S. income tax return for the taxable year of the individual's expatriation. If an exchange occurred before the individual's 1996 taxable year the individual must submit a gain recognition agreement with his or her 1996 Form 1040NR to avoid the recognition of gain.

The gain recognition agreement will be triggered if the individual disposes of the property to which the gain recognition agreement applies. In addition any disposition of the transferred property by the acquiror of such property will also trigger gain, even if the disposition is otherwise part of a non-recognition transaction. For purposes of the gain recognition agreement, property removed from the United States and property the source of income or gain from which changed from U.S. to foreign will be treated as property acquired in an exchange.

All gain recognition agreements must be signed under penalties of perjury and set forth the following information:

(1) a description of all property subject to the agreement, (i.e. a description of property both transferred and acquired in an exchange, a description of any appreciated tangible personal property that was removed from the United States, and/or a description of all property affected by an occurrence that changed the source of income or gain from the property from U.S. source to foreign source);

(2) a good faith estimate of the relevant fair market values of the property transferred and acquired in the exchange (formal appraisals are not required), their adjusted basis for U.S. tax purposes, and a calculation of the gain not recognized by reason of the gain recognition agreement (the "deferred gain") on a property-by-property basis;

(3) a statement that the individual agrees to recognize, under section 877, any income or gain during the 15-year period that begins five years prior to expatriation as U.S. source income if it is derived from property that was acquired in an exchange (as described in this notice);

(4) a statement that the individual agrees to recognize, under section 877, a proportionate amount of the deferred gain as U.S. source income as of the date of disposition if the acquiror of the transferred property disposes of all or a portion of the property in any manner during the 15-year period beginning five years prior to expatriation;

(5) a statement that the individual agrees to file a U.S. income tax return (normally Form 1040NR) for each year of the 10-year period following expatriation (whether or not such individual is otherwise required to file a return) that includes an annual certification each year describing any income or gain that is taxable pursuant to the gain recognition agreement. If the individual did not derive any income or gain that is taxable pursuant to the gain recognition agreement, the certification must provide a statement to that effect;

(6) if an exchange to which the gain recognition agreement applies occurred during the 5 year period prior to expatriation, a certification describing any income or gain during this 5-year period that is taxable pursuant to the gain recognition agreement. If the individual did not derive any income or gain that is taxable pursuant to the gain recognition agreement during this period, the certification must provide a statement to that effect;

(7) a representation that all records relating to the property to which the gain recognition agreement applies, including those of the acquiror (if any) will be made available for inspection by the Service during the period that ends 3 years from the date on which a U.S.

income tax return is filed for the year in which any income or gain that is taxable pursuant to the gain recognition agreement is recognized;

(8) a statement that the individual agrees to furnish a bond or other security that satisfies the requirements of Treas. Reg. Section 301.7701-1 if the District Director determines that such security is necessary to ensure the payment of tax upon the deferred gain and any other income or gain that is taxable pursuant to the gain recognition agreement; and

(9) if applicable, the name, address, and U.S. taxpayer identification number (if any) of the acquiror of any property subject to the agreement.

If, during the period that the agreement is in force, the individual disposes of the property acquired in the exchange in a transaction in which gain or loss is not recognized under U.S. income tax principles, then the individual shall not be required to recognize gain, provided that the individual notifies the Secretary of the transfer with his or her next annual certification and modifies the gain recognition agreement accordingly.

Example. The following example illustrates how to enter into a gain recognition agreement.

> *Example 9.* Assume the same facts as in example 8 above. To avoid the immediate recognition of gain on the contribution of stock to FT, J must attach a gain recognition agreement to his U.S. tax return for the year 2000 (the taxable year of the exchange). As part of such agreement, J must agree to recognize any income or gain that J derives from his beneficial interest in FT as U.S. source income during the remainder of the 10-year period following expatriation. J must also agree to recognize the pre-contribution gain on the transferred stock as U.S. source income if FT directly or indirectly disposes of the stock. In addition, J must agree to file an annual certification for each year of the remaining 10-year period following expatriation that indicates whether J derived any income or gain from his beneficial interest in FT and whether FT disposed of the stock. J must represent that all records relating to the transferred stock, including the trust's records, will be made available for inspection by the Service for the period ending 3 years from the date on which J files a U.S. income tax return for the year in which he recognizes the deferred gain as a result of a direct or indirect disposition of the stock by FT. J must also represent that all records relating to his beneficial interest in FT will be made available for inspection by the Service for the period ending 3 years from the date(s) on which J files a U.S. income tax return for the year(s) in which he recognizes any income or gain from his beneficial interest in FT.

SECTION VI. CONTRIBUTIONS TO CONTROLLED FOREIGN CORPORATIONS

Background. Section 877(d)(4) generally provides that when an expatriate contributes U.S. source property ("contributed property") to a corporation that would be a controlled foreign corporation (as defined in section 957) and the individual would be a United States shareholder (as defined in section 951(b)) but for the individual's expatriation, then any income or gain on such property (or any other property that has a basis determined in whole or in part by reference to such property) received or accrued by the corporation during the 10-year period following expatriation shall be treated as received or accrued directly by the individual and not by the corporation. If the individual disposes of any stock in the corporation (or other stock that has a basis determined in whole or part by reference to such stock) during the 10-year period referred to in section 877(a) and while the contributed property is held by the corporation, the individual is taxable on the gain that would have been recognized by the corporation had it sold a pro rata share of the property (determined by comparing the value of the stock disposed of to the value of the stock held by the individual immediately prior to the disposition) immediately before the disposition. Section 877(d)(4)(D) provides that the Secretary may prescribe such regulations as may be necessary to prevent the avoidance of the purposes of section 877(d)(4), including where the property is sold to the corporation and where the contributed property is sold by the corporation. Section 877(d)(4)(E) provides that the Secretary shall require such information reporting as is necessary to carry out the purposes of section 877(d)(4).

Anti-abuse rules and reporting requirement. Treasury and the Service intend to issue regulations under sections 877(d)(4)(D) and (E) that extend the 10-year period referred to in section 877(d)(4), set forth reporting requirements, and provide anti-abuse rules intended to prevent individuals from utilizing controlled foreign corporations to hold or dispose of property that would otherwise produce income or gain from sources within the United States. The regulations will provide that if an individual acts with a principal purpose to avoid section 877(d)(4), then the Commissioner may predetermine the U.S. tax consequences of that action as appropriate to achieve the purposes of section 877(d)(4). The regulations will apply to individuals who expatriate after February 5, 1995, and to individuals subject to section 511(g)(3)(A) of the Act (see section X of this notice).

Until regulations are issued, individuals must comply with the rules set forth below. Individuals must apply section 877(d)(4) by substituting the 15-year period beginning five years prior to expatriation for the 10-year period referred to in section 877(d)(4). However, section 877(d)(4) will not apply to any contribution during the 5-year period prior to expatriation if the contribution occurred prior to February 24, 1997.

Moreover, an individual who makes a contribution described in section 877(d)(4)(A)(i) must attach the following information to the individual's U.S. tax return for the year in which such contribution occurs (whether or not the individual is otherwise required to file a U.S. tax return):

(1) the date of the contribution;

(2) a description of the property contributed, including a good faith estimate of its fair market value (formal appraisals are not required) and a statement of its adjusted basis for U.S. tax purposes on the date of the contribution;

(3) a description of the foreign corporation to which the property is contributed, including its name, address, place of incorporation, and its U.S. employer identification number, if any; and

(4) a description of the percentage interest, by vote and by value, owned or treated as owned by the individual under section 958 (determined as if such individual were a U.S. person).

If a contribution occurs prior to expatriation, this statement must be attached to the individual's U.S. income tax return for the taxable year of the individual's expatriation. If a contribution occurred prior to 1996, the individual must attach this statement to the individual's 1996 U.S. tax return (whether or not the individual is otherwise required to file a U.S. tax return).

SECTION VII. ANNUAL INFORMATION REPORTING

Background. Section 6001 generally provides that the Secretary may require any person, by notice upon such person or by regulations, to make such returns, render such statements, or keep such records as the Secretary deems sufficient to show whether or not the person is liable for tax under the Code. Section 6011(a) generally provides that any person who is liable for tax imposed by the Code, or with respect to the collection thereof, shall make a return or statement according to forms and regulations prescribed by the Secretary. Section 6012(a)(1) generally provides that every individual whose gross income for the taxable year equals or exceeds the exemption amount must file a U.S. income tax return for such year. Section 6012(a)(1) further provides, in part, that nonresident individuals subject to tax imposed by section 871 may be exempted from making returns under section 6012 subject to conditions, limitations, and exceptions and under such regulations as may be prescribed by the Secretary. Treas. Reg. Section 1.6012-1(b)(2)(i) generally provides, in part, that a nonresident alien individual who was not engaged in a trade or business in the United States during a taxable year is not required to file a return for such year if the nonresident's tax liability for the year is fully satisfied by the withholding of tax at the source under Chapter 3 of the Code.

Section 874(a) generally provides that a nonresident alien individual will receive the benefit of deductions and credits allowed to him by Subtitle A of the Code only if such individual files a true and accurate return, including all the information that the Secretary may deem necessary for the calculation of such deductions and credits.

Annual reporting of income. Because an individual who is liable for U.S. taxes is generally required to file a return and other such statements as the Secretary may prescribe, Treasury and the Service intend to issue regulations under section 877 that will require expatriates who are liable for tax to annually report certain information for the 10-year period following expatriation. Until the issuance of such regulations, taxpayers must report information in compliance with the rules set forth below and any other information that the Secretary may require at a later date. At such time that Form 1040NR is modified to reflect the rules described below, taxpayers must report information in accordance with the instructions to Form 1040NR instead of the procedures described below. The rules below apply to expatriates who are subject to section 877 as in effect before the Act, as well as those subject to section 877 as revised by the Act.

Beginning with the 1996 taxable year, an individual who expatriated with a principal purpose to avoid U.S. taxes under section 877 as in effect before the Act must annually file a U.S. income tax return (Form 1040NR), with the information described below, for each year of the remaining 10-year period following expatriation if such individual is liable for U.S. tax under any provision of the Code (e.g. section 871(a)) for such year. An individual who expatriated with a principal purpose to avoid U.S. taxes under section 877 as amended by the Act must also annually file a U.S. income tax return (Form 1040NR), with the information described below, for each year of the 10-year period following expatriation if such individual is liable for U.S. tax under any provision of the Code (e.g. section 871(a)) for such year. [3]

The return must bear the statement "Expatriation Return" across the top of page 1 of Form 1040NR. In addition, a statement must be attached to the return that sets forth by category (e.g. dividends, interest, etc.) all items of U.S. and foreign source gross income (whether or not taxable in the United States). The statement must identify the source of such income (determined under section 877 as modified by section V of this notice) and those items of income subject to tax under section 877. In addition, any expatriate who has not previously filed an information statement under section 6039F should also attach to his or her first nonresident return a statement containing the information described in section IX of this notice.

Treasury and the Service intend to amend Treas. Reg. Section 1.6012-1(b)(2)(i) in accordance with the rules of this notice. Until the regulation is modified, an expatriate who is otherwise required to report information in accordance with this section of the notice must

---

[3] Individuals should refer to Treas. Reg. Section 1.6012.1(b)(2)(ii) for guidance on how to file a U.S. income tax return for the taxable year of the individual's expatriation.]

attach a statement to Form 1040NR, even if the individual has fully satisfied his or her tax liability through withholding of tax at source.

An expatriate who fails to furnish a complete statement in any year for which he or she is liable for any U.S. taxes will not be considered to have filed a true and accurate return. Therefore, such an individual will not be entitled to the benefit of any deductions or credits if the individual's tax liability for that year is later adjusted. *See section 874(a).*

An individual who is required to file the above statement for the taxable year that begins in 1995 will be considered to have timely filed his or her statement for that year if the individual files such statement by the due date (including extensions) for filing the individual's U.S. income tax return for the taxable year that begins in 1996.

SECTION VIII. INTERACTION WITH TAX TREATIES

Background. The legislative history of the Act indicates that Congress believed that section 877, as amended, is generally consistent with the underlying principles of U.S. income tax treaties to the extent that section 871 provides for a foreign tax credit for items taxed by another country. To the extent that there is a conflict with U.S. income tax treaties in force on August 21, 1996 (the date of enactment of section 877), Congress intended that "the purpose of section 877, as amended...[is] not to be defeated by any treaty provision." *H.R. Rep. No. 496, 104th Cong., 2d Sess. 155 (1996). See also, H.R. Conf. Rep. No. 736, 104th Cong., 2d Sess. 329 (1996).* However, any conflicting treaty provisions that remain in force 10 years after August 21, 1996, will take precedence over section 877, as revised. *Id.*

Coordination with tax treaties. In accordance with Congressional intent, Treasury and the Service will interpret section 877 as consistent with U.S. income tax treaties. To the extent that there is a conflict, however, all provisions of section 877, as amended, prevail over treaty provisions in effect on August 21, 1996. This coordination rule is effective until August 21, 2006 and applies to those provisions of section 877 that were amended by the Act as well as those that were not amended by the Act. In addition, Treasury and the Service will interpret all treaties, whether or not in force on August 21, 1996, that preserve U.S. taxing jurisdiction with respect to former U.S. citizens or former U.S. long-term residents who expatriate with a principal purpose to avoid U.S. taxes as consistent with the provisions of section 877, as amended.

SECTION IX. INITIAL INFORMATION REPORTING

Background. Section 6039F(a) requires each individual who loses U.S. citizenship to provide an information statement to the U.S. Department of State or a federal court, as applicable. The information reporting requirements of section 6039F apply to individuals who expatriate after February 5, 1995, and to individuals subject to section 511(g)(3)(A) of the Act (see section X of this notice).

Section 6039F(a)(1) requires that this information must be provided not later than the earliest date on which such individual (1) renounces the individual's U.S. nationality before a diplomatic or consular officer of the United States, (2) furnishes to the U.S. Department of State a statement of voluntary relinquishment of U.S. nationality confirming an act of expatriation, (3) is issued a certificate of loss of U.S. nationality by the U.S. Department of State, or (4) loses U.S. nationality because the individual's certificate of naturalization is cancelled by a U.S. court (collectively, the "reporting date").

Section 6039F(b) requires a former citizen to report his taxpayer identification number, mailing address of principal foreign residence, foreign country in which the individual is residing, foreign country of citizenship, information on the individual's assets and liabilities if such individual's net worth exceeds $500,000 (as adjusted by section 1(f)(3) for taxable years after 1996), and such other information as the Secretary may prescribe. Section 6039F(f) requires long-term residents who expatriate after February 5, 1995, to provide a similar statement with their U.S. tax returns for the taxable year of expatriation.

If a former citizen fails to provide the required information statement, section 6039F(d) generally provides that the individual will be subject to a penalty equal to the greater of (1) five percent of the tax required to be paid under section 877 for the taxable year ending during such year, or (2) $1,000. The penalty will be assessed for each year during which such failure continues for the 10-year period beginning on the date of loss of citizenship. The penalty will not be imposed if it is shown that such failure is due to reasonable cause and not wilful neglect. Section 6039F(f) also applies this penalty to former long-term residents.

Information Statements. Until such time that a form is issued for providing the statement required by section 6039F, individuals must file an information statement that includes the information set forth below.

(1) A former U.S. citizen whose reporting date is on or before March 10, 1997, must provide the information statement to the Internal Revenue Service, 950 L'Enfant Plaza SW, Washington, D.C. 20224, ATTN: Compliance Support & Services, by June 8, 1997. Former U.S. citizens who furnished the information enumerated in section 6039F(b) to the appropriate entity prior to February 24, 1997, are not required to provide an additional statement.

(2) A former U.S. citizen whose reporting date is after March 10, 1997, and on or before June 8, 1997, must provide the information statement to (i) the American Citizens Services Unit, Consular Section, of the nearest American Embassy or consulate, (ii) Office of Policy Review and Interagency Liaison (CA/OCS/PRI), Room 4817, Department of State, Washington D.C., 20520-4818, or (iii) a federal court (if the expatriate's certificate of nationality was cancelled by such court), on or before June 8, 1997.

(3) A former U.S. citizen whose reporting date is after June 8, 1997 must provide the information statement to the (i) American Citizens Services Unit, Consular Section, of the nearest American Embassy or consul, or (ii) a federal court (if the expatriate's certificate of nationality was cancelled by such court) on or before such reporting date.

(4) A former long-term resident who expatriated after February 5, 1995, and before January 1, 1996, must attach the information statement to either a 1996 Form 1040NR (whether or not the individual is otherwise required to file a U.S. tax return) or an amended 1995 U.S. income tax return. To comply with new section 877, an individual whose 1995 tax liability changed as a result of new section 877 must amend the individual's 1995 return accordingly and include the information statement with that amended return. A former long-term resident who expatriated in the 1995 taxable year will be deemed to have timely furnished the information statement if a statement is filed by the due date (including extensions) for filing the individual's 1996 return. A former long-term resident who expatriated after 1995 must attach an information statement to the former resident's U.S. income tax return for the year of expatriation. Former long-term residents who have already furnished the information enumerated in section 6039F(b) to the Internal Revenue Service prior to February 24, 1997, are not required to provide an additional statement.

Former citizens and former long-term residents must include the following information in their information statements:

(1) name;

(2) date of birth;

(3) taxpayer identification number;

(4) mailing address prior to expatriation;

(5) address where the individual resided prior to expatriation, if different from (4) above;

(6) mailing address of principal foreign residence, if any;

(7) address where the individual expects to reside after expatriation, if different from (6) above;

(8) all foreign countries of which the individual is a citizen and the dates and methods by which such citizenship was acquired;

(9) the number of days (including vacation and non-work days) that the individual was physically present in the United States during the year of expatriation (up to and including the date on which the information statement is filed) and each of the two preceding taxable years;

(10) in the case of an individual whose average annual net U.S. income tax (as defined in section 38(c)(1)) for the five taxable years prior to expatriation exceeded $100,000, the net

U.S. income tax for each of these years (rounded to the nearest $50,000). If the individual's average annual net U.S. income tax liability for the preceding five taxable years did not exceed $100,000, the individual must provide a representation to that effect;

(11) in the case of an individual with gross assets that have an aggregate fair market value in excess of $500,000, a balance sheet, using good faith estimates of fair market values (formal appraisals are not required), that sets forth by category (e.g. cash, marketable securities, closely-held stock, business assets, qualified and non-qualified deferred compensation arrangements, individual retirement accounts, installment obligations, U.S. real property, foreign real property, etc.) the individual's assets and liabilities immediately prior to expatriation. The balance sheet must also set forth the following:

(i) the source of income and gain, without applying the provisions of section 877, that such property would have generate during the 5-year period prior to expatriation and immediately after expatriation,

(ii) the source of income and gain, assuming that the provisions of section 877 applied (as modified by section V of this notice), that such property would have generated during the 5-year period prior to expatriation and immediately after expatriation, and

(iii) the gain or loss that would be realized if the assets were sold for their fair market values on the date of expatriation.

The individual must separately list (not by category) each partnership in which the individual holds an interest, each trust that the individual is considered to own under sections 671 through 679, each trust that the individual is considered to own under Chapter 12 of Subtitle B of the Code, and each trust in which the individual holds a beneficial interest (as determined under the procedures described in section III of this notice). The individual must also describe the types of assets held by each partnership or trust, and indicate the methodology (as described in section III of this notice) used to determine the individual's beneficial interest in each trust. In addition, the individual should indicate whether there have been significant changes in the individual's assets and liabilities for the period that began five years prior to expatriation and ends on the date that the information statement is filed. If so, the individual should attach a statement explaining the changes in the individual's assets and liabilities during such period;

(12) in the case of a former long-term U.S. resident, a representation as to whether the former resident was treated as a resident of a foreign country under a U.S. income tax treaty for any year in the preceding 15 years. If so, the individual must list the foreign countries and years when this occurred. The individual must also list any year(s) that the former resident waived the benefits of that treaty; and

(13) a representation, signed under penalties of perjury by the individual that the facts contained in the information statement are true, correct and complete to the best of the individual's knowledge and belief.

An individual who timely files a statement in accordance with the above guidelines will not be subject to the penalties described in section 6039F(d). All individuals whose reporting dates occur after such time that a form is issued for reporting information under section 6039F must complete and submit that form to comply with their reporting requirements under section 6039F.

SECTION X. TRANSITION PROVISION

Background. Sections 877 and 6039F generally apply to individuals who expatriate after February 5, 1995. However, section 511(g)(3)(A) of the Act provides a special transition provision in the case of a former citizen who performed an expatriating act specified in paragraph (1), (2), (3), or (4) of section 349(a) of the Immigration and Nationality Act (8 U.S.C. 1481(a)(1)-(4)) before February 6, 1995, but who did not on or before such date furnish to the U.S. Department of State a signed statement of voluntary relinquishment of U.S. nationality confirming the performance of such act. Such an individual would not come within the general effective date of the amendments to sections 877 and 6039F because, under the provisions for determining the date of loss of citizenship (which were not modified by the Act), the date of loss of citizenship is retroactive to the date of the expatriating act (i.e. prior to February 6, 1995). *See Treas. Reg. Section 1.1-1(c).*

The transition provision states that section 6039F and the amendments made to section 877 by the Act shall apply to such an individual, except that the 10-year period referred to in section 877(a) shall not expire before the end of the 10-year period beginning on the date the signed statement of voluntary relinquishment is furnished to the U.S. Department of State. Thus, such an individual is subject to new section 877 as of the date of loss of citizenship and the 10-year period referred to in section 877(a) shall not expire before the end of the 10-year period beginning on the date the signed statement of voluntary relinquishment is furnished to the U.S. Department of State.

Section 511(g)(3)(B) of the Act states that the transition provision of section 511(g)(3)(A) will not apply if the individual establishes to the satisfaction of the Secretary of the Treasury that the individual's loss of U.S. citizenship occurred before February 6, 1994. Accordingly, section 6039F will not apply to such an individual and he will be subject to section 877 as in effect before the amendments made by the Act.

Example. The following example illustrates the application of section 511(g)(3)(A) of the Act.

Example 10. K joined a foreign army on October 1, 1994, with the intent to relinquish his U.S. citizenship, but did not furnish a statement of voluntary relinquishment of citizenship to the U.S. Department of State until October 1, 1995. K is subject to new section 877 beginning on October 1, 1994, the date that K performed the expatriating act. However, the 10-year period referred to in section 877(a) will not expire before the end of the 10-year period beginning on the date that K furnished a statement of voluntary relinquishment of citizenship to the U.S. Department of State. K furnished this statement on October 1, 1995. Thus, K is subject to new section 877 for the period that began on October 1, 1994, and ends on September 30, 2005.

Special rule for individuals who claim to be within the exception under section 511(g)(3)(B) of the Act. An individual who (i) furnished a signed statement of voluntary relinquishment of U.S. nationality to the U.S. Department of State after February 5, 1995, and (ii) claims that new section 877 does not apply because of the exception to the transition provision in section 511(g)(3)(B) of the Act, must (whether or not the individual is otherwise required to file a U.S. tax return) attach a statement to Form 1040NR for the year in which the signed statement of voluntary relinquishment is furnished to the U.S. Department of State (or to the individual's 1996 Form 1040NR if the statement of voluntary relinquishment was furnished during 1995). The return must bear the statement "Expatriation Return" across the top of page 1 of such return. The statement attached to the return must include the nature and date of the expatriating act, the date the signed statement of voluntary relinquishment was furnished to the U.S. Department of State, and a copy of the individual's certificate of loss of nationality. An individual who does not file a statement in the manner prescribed above will not be considered to have established to the satisfaction of the Secretary of the Treasury that the individual lost U.S. citizenship before February 6, 1994.

SECTION XI. INTERACTION WITH SECTION 7701(b)(10)

Background. Section 7701(b)(10) applies to an alien individual who was treated as a resident of the United States during any period that includes at least three consecutive calendar years (the "initial residency period") and ceased to be treated as a U.S. resident, but subsequently becomes a U.S. resident before the close of the third calendar year beginning after the initial residency period. Under section 7701(b)(10), such an individual will be taxed in the manner provided by section 877(b) for the period after the close of the initial residency period and before the date on which the individual subsequently becomes a U.S. resident. This provision applies only if the tax imposed pursuant to section 877(b) exceeds the tax imposed under section 871.

Application of section 7701(b)(10). An individual described in section 7701(b)(10) will be subject to tax on U.S. source income in the manner provided by section 877(b) (as modified by section 871(d)) for the period after the close of the initial residency period and before the date on which the individual subsequently becomes a U.S. resident (the "intervening period"). Because the tax imposed by reason of section 7701(b)(10) applies regardless of whether the individual had a principal purpose to avoid U.S. taxes, sections 877(a), (c), and (f), as amended, do not apply to an individual who is subject to tax in the manner provided by section 877(b) solely by reason of section 7701(b)(10).

Section 877(e) also does not generally apply to an individual who is subject to tax in the manner provided by section 877(b) solely by reason of section 7701(b)(10). However, to treat former residents who are subject to tax by reason of section 7701(b)(10) in a similar manner as former long-term residents who are subject to section 877, all property held by an individual on the date that such individual first became a resident of the United States shall be treated solely for purposes of section 7701(b)(10) as having a basis of not less than the fair market value of the property on such date, unless the individual elects not to have this treatment apply.

Reporting requirements for individuals subject to section 7701(b)(10). An individual who is liable for U.S. tax by reason of section 7701(b)(10) during any year of the intervening period must file U.S. income tax returns (Form 1040NR) reporting such tax liability for each of those years by the due date (including extensions) for filing the individual's U.S. income tax return for the year that the individual subsequently becomes a U.S. resident. If tax returns for the years of the intervening period have already been filed, the individual must amend those returns accordingly to comply with section 7701(b)(10).

An individual described in section 7701(b)(10) who is liable for U.S. taxes under any provision of the Code during the intervening period (e.g. section 871(a)) must attach a statement to his or her U.S. tax return that sets forth, by category (e.g. dividends, interest, etc.), all items of U.S. and foreign source gross income (whether or not taxable in the United States) derived during each year of the intervening period. Such statement must identify the source of such income (determined under section 877 as modified by section V of this notice), the items of income subject to tax in the manner provided by section 877(b), and any other information that the Secretary may prescribe at a later date.

The statement must be filed even if the individual has fully satisfied his or her U.S. tax liability for a taxable year through withholding at source. As discussed in section VII of this notice, Treasury and the Service expect to modify Treas. Reg. Section 1.6012-1(b)(2)(i) in accordance with rules of this notice.

Any individual who fails to furnish a complete statement, as described above, for the years of the intervening period will not be considered to have filed a true and accurate return. Therefore, such an individual will not be entitled to the benefit of any deductions or credits if the individual's return is later adjusted. *See section 874(a).*

An individual who is required to file the above statement for the taxable year that begins in 1995 will be considered to have timely filed his or her statement for that year if the individual files such statement by the due date (including extensions) for filing the individual's U.S. income tax return for the taxable year during which the individual subsequently becomes a U.S. resident.

Exchanges under section 877(d)(2) and contributions under section 877(d)(4). An individual subject to tax by reason of section 7701(b)(10) must recognize any gain realized during the intervening period on exchanges of property described in section 877(d)(2), unless the individual enters into a gain recognition agreement in accordance with section V of this notice. The gain recognition agreement must be submitted with the individual's U.S. income tax return (Form 1040NR) for the year of the exchange. The gain recognition agreement and the return must be filed by the due date (including extensions) for filing the individual's U.S. income tax return for the year during which the individual subsequently becomes a U.S. resident. If a tax return for the year of the exchange has already been filed, the individual must amend that return and attach a gain recognition agreement to the amended return to comply with section 7701(b)(10).

The period of such a gain recognition agreement will be for the intervening period, and not the 15-year period beginning five years prior to expatriation. Moreover, annual certification is not required. Rather, the individual must submit with the gain recognition agreement a certification that the acquiror (if any) has not disposed of the transferred property, and that the individual did not dispose of the property acquired in the exchange (or any other property that has a basis determined in whole or in part by reference to such property). In addition, the certification must also state whether the individual derived any income or gain from the property acquired in the exchange during the intervening period.

If any property to which the gain recognition applies was disposed of during any year of the intervening period, the individual must recognize gain for the year of disposition. Any income or gain derived during the intervening period from a contribution described under section 877(d)(4) must also be recognized for the relevant year. However, section 7701(b)(10) will not cause an individual to recognize any income or gain with respect to any exchange under section 877(d)(2) or contribution of property under section 877(d)(4) that occurred prior to the beginning of the individual's initial residency period or after the date on which the individual subsequently becomes a U.S. resident.

Example. The following example illustrates how section 7701(b)(10) interacts with section 877 and when income that arises by reason of section 7701(b)(10) must be recognized.

> *Example 11.* L was a resident alien of the United States in 1994, 1995 and 1996 because she satisfied the substantial presence test of section 7701(b)(3) for each of those years. In 1997 and 1998, L was not a resident of the United States. In 1999, L reestablishes residency in the United States. L is subject to tax in the manner provided by section 877(b) by reason of section 7701(b)(10). On February 1, 1997, L contributed property to a "controlled foreign corporation" in a transaction described in section 877(d)(4).

Any income or gain derived from the property that L contributed to the foreign corporation during the intervening period is subject to tax in the manner provided by section 877(d)(4). Thus, L must report such income or gain by filing income tax returns for 1997 and 1998 by the due date (including extensions) for filing her 1999 U.S. income tax return. If income tax returns for 1997 and 1998 have already been filed, L must amend those returns to comply with section 7701(b)(10). Any income or gain derived after the intervening period is not taxable under section 877(d)(4).

Coordination with income tax treaties. The rules of section VIII (interaction with tax treaties) of this notice do not apply to an individual who is subject to tax in the manner provided by section 877(b) solely by reason of section 7701(b)(10). Accordingly, such an individual may claim benefits under a U.S. income tax treaty for transactions that occur during the intervening period if such individual is otherwise eligible for benefits as a foreign resident under the terms of such treaty.

Effective date. New section 877 will apply to an individual subject to tax thereunder by reason of section 7701(b)(10) if the individual's initial residency period ended after August 20, 1996.

REQUEST FOR COMMENTS

Treasury and the Service invite public comments on the guidance provided in this notice. Comments should be submitted by June 8, 1997, to:

Internal Revenue Service
P.O. Box 7604
Ben Franklin Station
Attn: CC:CORP:T:R, (Notice 97-19)
Room 5228
Washington, D.C. 20044;

or, alternatively, via the internet at:
http://www.irs.ustreas.gov/prod/tax_regs/comments.html

The comments you submit will be available for public inspection and copying.

DRAFTING INFORMATION

The principal authors of this notice are Trina L. Dang and Michael Kirsch of the Office of Associate Chief Counsel (International). For further information regarding this notice, contact Ms. Dang or Mr. Kirsch at (202) 622-3860 (not a toll-free call).

PAPERWORK REDUCTION ACT

The collections of information contained in this notice have been reviewed and approved by the Office of Management and Budget in accordance with the Paperwork Reduction Act (44 U.S.C. 3507) under control number 1545-1531.

An agency may not conduct or sponsor, and a person is not required to respond to, a collection of information unless the collection of information displays a valid control number.

The collection of information related to the submission of ruling requests is required to help the Secretary make a determination as to whether an individual expatriated with a principal purpose to avoid U.S. taxes. The collections of information related to gain recognition agreements, initial information reporting and reporting of information with respect to contributions to certain foreign controlled foreign corporations are prescribed by statute. The collection of annual reporting information is necessary to monitor compliance with the provisions of section 877, as amended. The collections of information for individuals subject to section 7701(b)(10) are necessary to administer the provisions of section 7701(b)(10) that interact with section 877. This information will be used by the Service for tax administration purposes.

The respondents will be individuals who lose U.S. citizenship, cease to be taxed as lawful permanent residents of the United States, or cease to be taxed as residents of the United States. The estimated total annual burden for all respondents is 6,300 hours. The estimated annual burden per respondent varies from 0.5 hour to 2.5 hours, depending on individual circumstances, with an estimated average of 31 minutes. The estimated number of responses is 12,300. The estimated annual frequency of responses is annually or on occasion.

Books or records relating to collections of information must be retained as long as their contents may become material in the administration of any internal revenue law. Generally, tax returns and tax return information are confidential as required by section 6103 of the Code.